T0342435

The Political Spirituality of Cesar Chavez

The Political Spirituality of Cesar Chavez

Crossing Religious Borders

Luis D. León

UNIVERSITY OF CALIFORNIA PRESS

University of California Press, one of the most
distinguished university presses in the United States,
enriches lives around the world by advancing scholarship
in the humanities, social sciences, and natural sciences. Its
activities are supported by the UC Press Foundation and
by philanthropic contributions from individuals and
institutions. For more information, visit www.ucpress.edu.

University of California Press
Oakland, California

© 2015 by The Regents of the University of California

Library of Congress Cataloging-in-Publication Data

León, Luis D., 1965– author.
    The political spirituality of Cesar Chavez : crossing
religious borders / Luis D. León.
        pages   cm
    Includes bibliographical references and index.
    ISBN 978-0-520-28368-8 (cloth : alk. paper) —
    ISBN 978-0-520-28369-5 (pbk. : alk. paper) —
    ISBN 978-0-520-95948-4 (ebook)
    1. Chavez, Cesar, 1927–1993—Religion.   2. Chavez,
Cesar, 1927–1993—Political and social views.   I. Title.
    HD6509.C48L46 2015
    331.88'13092—dc23   2014031036

Manufactured in the United States of America

24   23   22   21   20   19   18   17   16   15

10   9   8   7   6   5   4   3   2   1

In keeping with a commitment to support
environmentally responsible and sustainable printing
practices, UC Press has printed this book on Natures
Natural, a fiber that contains 30% post-consumer waste
and meets the minimum requirements of ANSI/NISO
Z39.48-1992 (R 1997) (*Permanence of Paper*).

To my grandmother, Cipriana García León,
a California farm worker

CONTENTS

List of Illustrations ix

Preface xi

(Re)Introduction. Enfleshment: Cesar's Body *1*

1. Mythology: Think Different *33*

2. Prophecy: In the Path of Gandhi and Martin Luther King *75*

3. Religion: A Revolutionary Spirit *116*

Conclusion. The Lost Gospel: "God Help Us to Be Men!" *159*

Notes *179*

Index *209*

ILLUSTRATIONS

Pilgrimage to Sacramento, 1966 *3*

Dolores Huerta, "On Strike (Huelga)," Delano, CA, 1965 *4*

Dorothy Day on the UFW picket line, Fresno, CA, 1973 *5*

President Obama at the grave of Cesar Chavez, La Paz, CA, 2012 *8*

Cesar Chavez with American flag, Salinas, CA, 1973 *20*

UFW funeral for Nagi Daifallah, Delano, CA, 1973 *51*

Cesar Chavez and his dogs, La Paz, CA, 1977 *58*

Cesar Chavez doing yoga, La Paz, CA, 1977 *60*

Coretta Scott King with Dolores Huerta, Salinas, CA, 1973 *107*

Cesar Chavez with Catholic priests, Coachella, CA, 1973 *127*

Joan Baez singing at UFW funeral for Juan de la Cruz,
    Delano, CA, 1973 *148*

Alex Donis, *Che Guevara and César Chávez* ("My Cathedral"), 1998 *167*

PREFACE

As I write this preface, laboring under a tight deadline, having worked on the manuscript for a more than a decade now, I realize that the date of its final submission to the University of California Press is March 31, 2014, which would have been Cesar Chavez's eighty-seventh birthday. Last year, 2013, when Chavez's birthday fell on Easter, the Internet giant Google honored the late leader with a doodle, a portrait of Chavez that filled the enlarged second *o* of the Google logo on the search engine's web page. In response, the right-wing media condemned the Silicon Valley–based company for slighting the Christian holiday with the drawing, declaring that users would replace Google with Bing, which adorned its home page with colorful Easter eggs.

The debate continues on how best to remember the late labor leader—or how to forget him. This book, instead of allying itself with one or the other faction claiming this discursive terrain, pursues a course that will, however unintentionally, no doubt upset some readers. Chavez sometimes gave differing accounts of his life, creating a power-ful mythological identity that was also messy and incoherent. Since his death, his legacy has become a matter of considerable deliberation.

I attended the funeral of Cesar Chavez and remember it well. A senior scholar at the University of California, Santa Barbara, rented a car and recruited a fellow doctoral student and me to make the six-hour mountainous drive to the legendary town of Delano, where the United Farm Workers established its first headquarters at the Forty Acres complex. I considered it a pilgrimage to a sacred place haunted by the ghost of Chavez; until then I had only read about it, seen images, had dreams. Even though I was not yet in preschool at the time of the "love fast" of 1968, Chavez's signature event, I felt the indelible effect of his aura as leader and national spokesman on my Chicano imagination. His death—sudden, early, tragic—shocked the Latina/o community. We drove mostly in silence, our thoughts clouded, like the highway obscured by an early morning fog that lingered low and wet on California Route 55. I tried to fathom the significance of the event, the man. Who was Cesar Chavez?

In my Chicano history courses I was taught a revised version of the standard "hero" narrative. As it turned out, in that version Chavez was primarily a labor leader—a role that placed him at once in- and outside Chicano identity, linking him more to a historically Mexican American identity.[1] Union organizer was the role assigned to him as one of the "four horsemen," a rubric delineating the leadership quartet of the Chicana/o movement.[2] I was dismayed by this limited historical representation of Chavez, but I accepted it. It was at his funeral that I came to believe there was more to his story than any single academic narrative could capture and complete.

When we arrived in Delano, I was stunned by the enormous crowd: hordes of mourners stretched as far as the eye could see across the flat, dusty picking fields. I was delighted by the collective spirit of the people; animated, exuberant, musical, insistent. It was again 1968 for this one day of the final decade of the century. The crowd surged around him as they mourned, assembled before Chavez in death as in life. He was encased in an unpainted pinewood casket made by his brother Richard Chavez. Many groups—the UFW, Catholic priests, nuns, Protestant churches, environmentalists, Chicana and Chicano activists, lesbian feminists, universities, high schools, labor unions, libraries, and more—held signs representing a multiplicity of causes, all led by a small brown cadaver in a simple splintering box.

When the body of Chavez arrived at the tent to receive its final *despedidas,* or formal goodbyes, politicians and Hollywood celebrities spoke from a makeshift pulpit. Among those paying their respects were the Reverend Jesse Jackson and members of the Kennedy Family: Ethel and her sons Joe and Robert Jr. Outside young Chicanas dressed as gang-bangers took turns performing elaborate genuflections; I was dazzled by the choreography and the poetic reinterpretations of the ancient ritual as teen after teen took her turn on the impromptu stage. Cardinal Roger Mahony of Los Angeles led the funeral Mass. In life the religious ceremonies Chavez arranged were characteristically ecumenical. But his final ceremony, his funeral, was officially and exclusively Catholic. (A seating section was reserved for clergy of other faiths.)

Later, deep in the bowels of UCSB's Chicana/o studies archives, I discovered another Chavez. His name was prominent in the movement newspapers, not only as a labor leader, not only as a Catholic leader, but also as a distinctly and broadly spiritual and moral leader. This is the Chavez I set out to learn about, describe, and interpret. This book represents my humanist genuflection: *esto es mi despedida.*[3]

ACKNOWLEDGMENTS

Research for this project began in earnest while I was in residence at the Stanford Humanities Center, which supported this work with an external faculty fellowship for the academic year 2002–3.

This research was also supported by grants from the American Academy of Religion and from the Jesuit Foundation. Denver University sponsored this project through multiple grants from the Faculty Research and Professional Development programs, as well as additional funding from the Latina/o Center for Community Engagement and Service, the Center for Inclusive Excellence, and the Interdisciplinary Research Incubator for the Study of Inequality.

Many generous colleagues remained in conversation with me about the book, helping me to navigate the complicated terrain of Cesar Chavez studies. I appreciate their attentiveness and their useful suggestions. They include: Davíd Carrasco, Theresa Delgadillo, Darrin Hicks, Jane Iwamura, Gary Laderman, Lois Lorentzen, Timothy Matovina, Lara Medina, Laura Pérez, Tink Tinker, and Miguel de la Torre. I'm also grateful for the support and friendship of my colleagues in the Religious Studies Department at the University of Denver who who listened to me and responded with valuable thoughts and recommendations: Carl Raschke, Greg Robbins, Ginni Ishimatsu, Alison Schofield, Sandra Dixon, and Andrea Stanton. Friends and colleagues across DU helped shape and inform my work in countless ways, particularly Deb Ortega, in her role as director of the Latina/o Center and as friend and mentor.

I also wish to thank Reed Malcolm, Eric Schmidt, Maeve Cornell-Taylor, and Rose Vekony at the University of California Press for the remarkable work they did with the manuscript. Stephanie Fay's extraordinary copyedit transformed it. The reviewers for UC Press did a superb job of identifying the strengths and weaknesses of the manuscript. Thank you Robert Chao Romero and the other reader who remained anonymous; your reports have produced a better book.

I also owe much gratitude to several fine librarians across the country. In Detroit, at the Cesar Chavez, Walter Reuther, and United Farm Workers of America archives, housed at the Walter P. Reuther Library, Archives of Labor and Urban Affairs, on the campus of Wayne State University, I thank especially Elizabeth Clemens, William LeFevre, and Kathy Schmeling. Additionally, Lillian Castillo-Speed, in the Ethnic Studies Library at UC Berkeley, proved invaluable at critical points during the research. I must also thank Polly Armstrong, former curator of the Fred Ross Papers and public services manager for Special Collections, Stanford University Libraries. Peggy Keeran and Michelle Kyner, at the Anderson Academic Commons at the University of Denver were indefatigable in locating rare and obscure manuscripts, magazines, and newspapers; I owe them a special debt of gratitude.

This book would not have been possible without the help of Marc Grossman, communication director at the Cesar E. Chavez Foundation, and the folks at the Cesar Chavez Center. I thank all of them for their generous embrace and support and for allowing me the pro bono use of copyrighted materials.

Finally, I wish to thank especially (one) of my remarkable and mystical grandmothers, Cipriana García León, matriarch, *curandera,* and a migrant California farmworker. I dedicate this work to her. Her spirit dwells in these pages.

Enfleshment

Cesar's Body

We need a cultural revolution among ourselves—not only in art but also in the realm of the spirit.[1]

Cesar Chavez

On Easter Sunday, 1966, Cesar Chavez and a cadre of Catholic priests, nuns, rabbis, and Protestant ministers gathered in California's capital, Sacramento, culminating a two-hundred-and-fifty-mile pilgrimage.[2] Events there included ecumenical religious services, one led by a Protestant minister, the other by a Catholic priest. Later, converging on the steps of the Capitol, they held a giant ceremony; among the ten thousand in attendance were Muslims, Hindus, Buddhists, and humanists, as well as Christians of many varieties.[3] The diversity of the congregation illustrates Chavez's ability to organize across lines of religion and culture, amalgamating many distinct communities. He recruited and "organized" even unlikely revolutionaries, including evangelicals and Pentecostals, into *La Causa,* or the Cause, which named the sum of his organizing efforts.[4] The cultural hybridity of Chavez's movement marks it as distinctly American; its membership was assembled by bricolage, from multiple faith expressions. Similarly, its purposes—its motivations and aspirations—were manifold. Overall, *La Causa* was influenced by many traditions, foremost among them the spirit of

Mexican Catholic sacrifice, Gandhian nonviolent activism, a Franciscan vow of poverty, and a Baptist optimism like that of Martin Luther King in the service of social justice. And the movement involved much more, including a commitment to Chavez and to the Cause that he came to expect and demand from his followers.

The long march to Sacramento, under the rubric "Pilgrimage, Penance, and Revolution," was a manifestation of a collective faith community organized around a gifted charismatic leader.[5] It began three weeks prior to Resurrection Sunday, in Central California. Chavez led an original group of seventy women and men who planned to walk through the heart of farm country. By the time the marchers arrived in Sacramento, their number had burgeoned to several hundred. The procession was headed from the start by pilgrims bearing a banner emblazoned with an image that fused Mexico's Virgin of Guadalupe with the totem of Chavez's crusade—a black eagle against a crimson background. For spectators, this image tore the doctrinal veil separating the sacred from the profane, by melding the primary emblem of Mexican Catholicism and the symbol of *La Causa*.

The entry of the pilgrims into California's capital city heralded Chavez's arrival on the national stage as a prophetic agent. Later that same year he declared: "If this spirit grows within the farm labor movement, one day we can use the force that we have to help correct a lot of things that are wrong in this society. But that is for the future. Before you can run, you have to learn to walk."[6]

Cesar Estrada Chavez was born to Mexican parents in Arizona on March 31, 1927; he died sixty-six years later, on April 23, also in the Grand Canyon state. He spent most of his early life as a migrant farm worker. In 1962 He founded the Farm Workers Association (FWA) with Dolores Huerta, who became its first vice president.[7] The association morphed into the United Farm Workers Organizing Committee when it joined the striking AFL-CIO–sponsored Agricultural Workers Organizing Committee, made up mostly of Filipinos, three years later. When the two unions officially merged in August 1966, members

Pilgrimage to Sacramento, 1966. Photo: Paul Richards, courtesy Harvey Richards Media Archive.

renamed themselves the United Farm Workers Organizing Committee (UFWOC) and soon thereafter, simply the UFW. But *La Causa* was much more than a labor syndicate. In 1973 Dorothy Day, a longtime UFW supporter, progressive social activist, and founder of the newspaper the *Catholic Worker,* was arrested for walking a UFW picket line. In her account, entitled "On Pilgrimage—September 1973," she confessed her belief in the leader's potential to transform society: "Cesar Chavez' union of Farm Workers has everything that belongs to a new social order."[8]

Dolores Huerta *(foreground)*, "On Strike (Huelga)," Delano, CA, 1965. Photo: Paul Richards, courtesy Harvey Richards Media Archive.

The nomenclature *La Causa* was officially adopted at the FWA's foundational convention on September 30, 1962. Although the union was founded on an avowed democratic structure, it functioned more like the papacy, with a single individual at the head, than as a government by consensus or majority rule. Chavez, who had a definite vision of the Cause, demonstrated little patience for dissent. His movement began with a compelling prophecy of liberation whose core was a spiritual mandate—that devotees, to achieve a collective greater good, make sacrifices for one another, *los sacrificios*—rather than a mandate to follow

Dorothy Day, on the UFW picket line, faces sheriff's
deputies, Fresno, CA, 1973. Bob Fitch Photo Archive,
© Stanford University Libraries.

a particular religious program or obey a singular political precept. The
leader performed acts of great sacrifice, embodying the principle for his
followers. Although he absorbed much of his political theology from
Catholicism and remained rooted in broad church ideals, particularly
an ethics of self-sacrifice and redemptive suffering, he rejected significant aspects of Catholicism's orthodoxy.

La Causa was unmistakably polysemous, lending itself to many definitions. Still, the founder's message was at once catholic, that is, universal, and Catholic, that is, defined by the rituals of the Church and

expressed in a Mexican idiom, emphasizing the rites of contrition and service to humanity. More than all other religious influences on the UFW's collective representation, Catholicism provided historically resonant symbols and morality narratives for the Cause, stressing commitment to the poor, marginalized, and disenfranchised. *La Causa* was not a Catholic movement per se; it was not limited or defined by the doctrines of the Catholic church. But Catholicism was in its DNA. *La Causa*'s leader de-territorialized the sacred, re-territorializing it in the dusty picking fields and other colonized spaces occupied by nomadic labor. Chavez was performing a discrete religious labor in part to amass devotional capital that could be spent in a national political economy in which myths and symbols were the currency traded for emotional loyalties.

Today the UFW's founder is unequivocally the most widely remembered U.S. Latino public figure across the globe. In 1972 George McGovern called him "one of the greatest living Americans."[9] In 1991 the Mexican government awarded him the Aztec Eagle, the highest state award given to a non-Mexican citizen. Since his death he has been multiply memorialized: awarded the Presidential Medal of Freedom, nominated for the Congressional Gold Medal, commemorated on a U.S. postage stamp, celebrated with an official remembrance in twelve states, and observed in eight municipalities by the closing of government schools and offices. Declaring his birthday a national holiday, if the movement to reach that goal proves successful, would be the equivalent of his reaching full American sainthood—trumping in significance even the ongoing efforts to canonize him as a Catholic saint.

In 2006 Chavez was among the first group of inductees into the California Hall of Fame, which also included the naturalist John Muir and Chavez's long-time nemesis, Ronald Reagan. Although the leader opposed Reagan both as governor of California and as president, he has a friend in President Barack Obama, who remembers him officially every year on his birthday. In 2008 Senator Obama, then a candidate for president, released his initial statement on the leader, which read in part: "We should honor him for what he's taught us about making America a stronger, more just, and more prosperous nation. That's why I support the call to make Cesar Chavez's birthday a national holiday. It's time to recognize the contributions of this American icon to the ongoing efforts to perfect our union." Perhaps Obama's admiration for the UFW founder inspired his borrowing of *La Causa*'s signature phrase for his first presidential campaign, "*Sí se puede*/yes we can," said to have been coined by Dolores Huerta as she rallied workers, encouraging them to believe that they could indeed organize for victory against the growers. President Obama's official White House press release on March 31, 2009, acknowledged his debt to the late community organizer but was tellingly silent on the question of a national holiday: "Chavez's rallying cry, 'Sí Se Puede—Yes We Can,' was more than a slogan, it was an expression of hope." In 2011 Obama's annual statement came in the form of a Presidential Proclamation declaring March 31 Cesar Chavez Day; the president stopped short, however, of ordering a closure of federal offices.

On October 8, 2012, President Obama, as a candidate for reelection, traveled to the UFW's last headquarters and Chavez's burial place, Nuestra Señora Reina de la Paz, in Keene, California, on the outskirts of Bakersfield, to dedicate a national monument to Chavez there. The president issued an executive order under the Antiquities Act, designating La Paz a national park, bypassing congressional approval. Speaking at the dedication, Obama declared that the leader of *La Causa* was one of those great Americans who believed "that out of many, we are one." He noted that national monuments tell a story of individuals "willing to devote their lives to making this country a little more just and a little more free." At Chavez's monument, he wanted visitors "to learn about a small man guided by enormous faith—in a righteous cause, a loving God, the dignity of every human being."[10] The president's deployment of Chavez's memory illustrates the way it has become a symbolic tool in political contests. Today many interests compete over Chavez's remembrance, which has enormous value as cultural

President Obama places a rose at the grave site of UFW co-founder Cesar Chavez, with Helen Chavez (*at right*), La Paz, Keene County, CA, October 8, 2012. Photo: Henry A. Barrios / *The Bakersfield Californian.*

capital. The leader arose from obscurity and poverty to achieve fame and international political influence by confronting the lingering forces of colonial racial realities and mythologies.

Joan London and Henry Anderson have written: "California is a mother to myths and social movements. Her entire recorded history is studded with legends, superlatives, tall tales—some true, some hyperbolic, some un-provable.... California's agriculture has, over the past century, created its own myths and legends, as fanciful as any woven by the most romantic '49er, or the most imaginative movie mogul.... The farm labor movement which has arisen to challenge the mythology of agribusiness nurtures some myths of its own, as movements always do."[11] Farm worker myths were crystallized in centuries of imperial

Christian discourse that dehumanized indigenous peoples to justify their colonization. Most Mexicans and Mexican Americans are of mixed race—Indian and Spanish, or *mestizo*—making them heirs to that colonial legacy. Chicana and Chicano farm workers were exploited like beasts of burden—treated as less than human. As such they were economically marginalized and forced into a struggle for survival. Chavez recounts their lives as follows: "Many [farm worker] families often lived on riverbanks or under bridges, in shacks built of linoleum scraps and cardboard cartons, or tents improvised from gunny sacks.... Though farm workers were harvesting vegetables and fruit, hunger was constant.... There was little money for food. Some families survived on nothing but beans and fried dough, or perhaps just fried oatmeal, or dandelion greens and boiled potatoes."[12]

Farm workers had no rights—they were routinely cheated out of wages, beaten, and arrested. In the face of such discrimination, Chavez's herculean task became not only to improve wages and working conditions for farm workers, but also to rehumanize them in the eyes of Euro-Americans. Central to this strategy was the narrative of the "true" man, an honorable macho. In marked contrast to revolutionary masculinities simultaneously under construction in other decolonizing contexts, *La Causa*'s new macho was nonviolent and disciplined, marked by a regulated sexuality.[13] The founder targeted men because he did not think women were the problem; it was the men who needed to change.

He spoke in theological terms. Mindful that in the United States God is the ultimate political authority and that his will is a matter of serious policy debate, Chavez recognized the urgent need for a sacred story to authorize *La Causa*'s political actions. Because Christian colonialism produced a racial ecology contingent on a religious myth of creation, dismantling it required an equally powerful and holy counterchronicle. That is, racism originated in a modern mythology of a revealed human hierarchy wherein people of color occupy the lowest rungs and are treated as wards of and servants to the master race. The leader knew that racial superiority was a fictive discursive practice that was as old as time—or at least as old as the age of European imperialism, when crown and church justified the enslavement of black and brown peoples by asserting a natural—and biblical—order of creation. He sought to upend this lie, confronting and undoing the toxic ideological mix of racism and religion. To triumph rhetorically, he needed to tell a deeply sacred cosmic story with God as protagonist—a myth.

Awed by the enormousness of his mission, he was driven to preach and implement a severe and sometimes divisive discipline within *La Causa*. Accounts of Chavez present two different visions of him as leader, some writers seeing him as narcissistic and tyrannical, others, as saintly. Chroniclers of his life agree, however, in ranking him exclusively among the devout Catholic faithful, foreclosing other religious identities and spiritual possibilities. By contrast, I approach his religious identity as a question, asked with uncertainty and phenomenological empathy, allowing its answer to emerge on its own terms. When read using this hermeneutic, some of his professions cast doubt on any single doctrinal allegiance, revealing instead a "deep conviction that we can communicate to people, either those who are for us or against us, faster and most effectively spiritually than we can in any other way."[14]

His spirituality was at least in part a political tool, suggesting that he was a make-believer rather than an outright believer—a true believer without true belief: his was not a call to Christianity or any other religion. Instead, he deployed religion as the modality of his appeal. Ultimately, the leader's praxis was a triumph of what Michel Foucault called political spirituality, whereby masses can be organized into popular rebellion. According to Foucault, "Since life and death are at stake, we can understand why revolts have easily been able to find their expression and their mode of performance in religious themes.... When the particular religion has permitted, these themes have furnished throughout the centuries not an ideological cloak but the very way to live revolts." [15]

In this book I follow Foucault's definition of *spirituality* as transformation. Personal and otherwise. He has written: "By spirituality, I understand—but I'm not sure that it is a definition which we can hold for very long—that which precisely refers to a subject acceding to a certain mode of being and to the transformations which the subject must make of himself in order to accede to this mode of being. I believe that, in ancient spirituality, there was identity or almost so between spirituality and philosophy."[16] As Jeremy Carrette has noted, Foucault's understanding of spirituality is "unsustainable," because spirituality is the condition of self-transformation whereby the subject is involved in an "ethic for the care of the self," a process that results in progress toward truth and affects the larger society.[17] Ultimately, for Foucault as for Chavez, the care of the self manifests as an implacable quest for justice. Carrette notes the ambivalence of Foucault's explanation, which represents at once a "rupture" from and reluctant continuity with theological determinations of spirituality as a means to experience God. Instead, for Foucault, spiritual engagements are part of a set of "freedom practices" that enable the subject to reach truth in an ongoing dialectic between subjectivity and veracity. This definition of political spirituality sheds fresh light on Chavez's own spiritual practices, particularly given his declaration that "truth is nonviolence. So everything really comes from truth. Truth is ultimate. Truth is God."[18]

Similarly, Theresa Delgadillo's theory of "spiritual mestizaje" complements that of Foucault and illuminates Chavez's own complex and purposeful spirituality, which was "capable of guiding the Chicana subject toward a heightened consciousness of justice that is also an embodied one." She continues: "What is this powerful and life-changing process named spiritual mestizaje? It is the transformative renewal of one's relationship to the sacred through a radical and sustained multimodal and self-reflexive critique of oppression in all its manifestations and a creative and engaged participation in shaping life that honors the sacred."[19] Like Foucault's theory, Delgadillo's delineation represents a rupture with Christianity's definition of the sacred. *Mestizo* is the Spanish word for "miscegenation," and Mexicans, as a mixed-race people, are commonly referred to as mestizos. Furthermore, idiomatically the term *mestizaje* signifies mixtures, hybridity, and a synthesis—combinations that defy singularity; spiritual mestizaje is fashioned from many different elements in the service of transforming lives and social situations. By both Foucault's and Delgadillo's definitions, however, spirituality results in transformation that leads to truth and justice.

My thesis in this work is that through myth and ritual performance, Chavez scripted a political spirituality and a spiritual mestizaje that transmuted *La Causa* into a religious movement; this is what I call religious politics. He proffered spiritual tropes as political address—a rhetorical strategy for mass conversion and social change—garnering public sympathy and support through devotional labor. By performing religion in the context of political theater, the leader won hearts and minds, eliciting the constructive response he desired, whether it was to boycott grapes or contribute time or money to the Cause. Untethered to any one institution, he invited a number of different audiences to participate in his movement, producing a religious assemblage, a kaleidoscope of faith traditions whose distinct optics each viewer could appreciate. He eschewed fundamentalism both in his words and in his quixotic practices. He told an interviewer, "See, everybody interprets our work in a different way. Some people interpret us as a union, some people interpret our work as an ethnic issue, some people interpret our work as a peace movement, some people see it as a religious movement. We can appeal to broad sectors because of these different interpretations."[20] Taking my cue from the possibilities Chavez himself suggests, I interpret his work as a broad (quasi-)religious movement. At least one history of Chavez's work has claimed: "For Chicanos, la causa was to become an almost religious mission, and Cesar its prophet."[21] In the chapters that follow I critically probe this religious mission and prophetic leadership.

My goals for this work are more modest than those of writing a definitive history or biography. Unlike the authors of other books on Chavez, I have no interest in unearthing buried secrets to expose the "true" story of the movement by interviewing those who worked with the leader; such research seems more likely to produce a story about the reminiscences of the interviewees than an account of the UFW president himself. Instead, I explore questions in both religious and ethnic studies, asking, What were the founder's goals as he constructed his public memory? What does an understanding of Chavez's myth tell us about religion? How was that myth constructed and reiterated in relation to his own self-fashioning? What is the connection between spirituality and race? How did *La Causa* mythologize, negotiate, and manage gender and sexuality? How do religion or political spirituality, myth, ritual, and symbol provide a way to "live revolutions"?

EXCAVATING CESAR CHAVEZ

This work exhumes the religious narrative of Chavez directly; I explore the myths he generated about himself, and those that continue to surround him, particularly the canonical fictions that distort his autobiography—the story of an extraordinary yet all too human life. By myth I mean narratives that make truth claims, establishing worldviews and identities not verifiable by historical, modern, or scientific methods. According to Jace Weaver, "Myth in our time has come to connote an untruth, a fairy tale. Yet, in its most precise form, a myth is simply any story that is foundational for the identity of a people."[22] Because myths are narratives that establish group and individual identities, they function like history. Nonetheless mythical narratives differ from historical stories, not in the claims they make on reality, but in the evidence they proffer to support those assertions.

Mythos defies modernity's demand for verifiability, claiming that its tellers' self-referential authority serves as an implicit evidentiary basis; this stance places mythical declarations in the hands of those without access to conventional power. The oppressed can speak and be heard in the language of myth, often challenging the status quo, whose regulatory narratives emerge as eternal truths, race and racialization among them. Bruce Lincoln argues that myth is ideology in narrative form, "wherein ideological interests escape all controls."[23]

Chavez was adept at translating myths into potent symbols that could be adopted by the Chicano movement. In the story of this movement, he was the metonymic figure for oppressed peoples, especially Mexican Americans, who were struggling for social justice in the United States. His biography provided the Chicano movement with an American tale—a sacred narrative—that was effectively situated in the hallowed discourse and sign system of the United States. Subsequently, Chavez became a larger-than-life figure on whom millions projected their own fantasies, desires, and selves. He embodied much more than his crusade: his body, his physicality—particularly his face—became emblematic of Mexican American identity.

As an American prophet, he declared the full humanity of Mexican Americans, demanding their corollary civil rights as if announcing a fresh revelation from God. He intervened concomitantly in the conversation about what it means to be an American, redefining the fluid and amalgamated national ethos to include Latinas and Latinos, who were mostly Catholic. This, then, was his crowning achievement: to reclaim for Latinas and Latinos the acknowledgment of humanity that had been lost in the ideological fog of colonialism's racializing ideology. Chavez realized that this rehumanization would be his legacy.

The posthumous literature on Chavez is also largely ideological and mythical; it is divided sharply between a subtle hagiography and an often unsubtle iconoclasm.[24] The critics, many former followers, have bitterly condemned the late leader for straying from what they insist was his true path of organizing farm workers, especially when he was well along in his career.[25] He was a highly sought after speaker and often accepted invitations to address groups, particularly at Mexican American events, and to participate in causes that distracted him from union affairs. Yet he never relinquished the UFW presidency. José Angel Gutiérrez noted: "Occasionally, he would accept appearances at other Chicano-related events.... He traveled the United States widely and often, logging more miles than any other Chicano leader of his time in the furtherance of his message."[26] He also supported myriad labor and environmental causes, peace movements, animal rights, actions on behalf of people of color, and the struggles of lesbians, gays, bisexuals, and transgender individuals (hereafter LGBT) for equality, a part of the story elided from all the historical accounts and biographies. Rather than weigh in on how the leader should be remembered, I focus on the incongruity of the representations—the competing stories.

With this focus in mind, I have organized this work according to three broad movements: Mythology, Prophecy, and Religion. Although the chapters are long, I have included subheadings in each as resting points for readers. Chavez's own self-fashioning vis-à-vis popular representations is the topic of Chapter 1. In it, I map some of the key ways the tale of Cesar Chavez is told, and I compare these tellings to his own sometimes conflicting renditions. I reexamine some of the psychic places he occupied for believers and detractors, which run the gamut from saint to sinner. Instead of taking one side or the other, I explore the conflicting realities, especially those of his spiritual commitments and identity. I argue that his religious subjectivity was not a fait accompli but a process: his public spirituality was adaptable, dynamic, and evolving, incomplete, and under construction. In his spiritual pursuits, he crossed many borders. Yet he stands in a long tradition of activists with deep roots in Catholicism who embrace aspects of the Church and value its tradition enough to identify as Catholics—while rejecting elements of the dogma.

Chapter 2 takes up the issue of prophecy and Mexican American civil rights discourse and symbols. The story of Cesar Chavez, the symbolism it yields, is foundational for the construction of Chicano identity. He became a prophet for the religion of *Chicanismo*. His role as prophetic figure enables a comparison to Gandhi and Martin Luther King—especially as each man deployed nonviolence to challenge and dismantle colonialism's mythology of a sanctified natural human hierarchy. They each gave grand homilies to rehumanize their primary racialized constituencies. Here I present a genealogy of racialization and religion, arguing that in colonial contexts, religion produces race. This argument is meant, not to negate the numerous examples of how religion has yielded social justice, but to focus on the formula whereby to justify imperialism is, in effect, to dehumanize colonized subjects, a process that occurs as Christianity carries out what Anthony M. Stevens-Arroyo has deemed a "pious colonialism."[27]

Chapter 3 is the crux of the book. In it I argue that for its adherents *La Causa* provided many of the functions of a religious movement, based on the prophetic charisma of Chavez. I demarcate the various religious elements of Chavez's work—fasting, public prayers, pilgrimages, boycotts, *los sacrificios,* and so forth. I also consider his imitation of some aspects of Synanon, a communal recovery movement that declared itself a religion in 1974, and his actual attempt to establish a religious order. Not only was *La Causa* filled with religious leaders, adorned by religious imagery, and punctuated by religious ritual, but it also had a discrete theology, sacraments, symbolism, and a soteriology, or spiritual path to salvation, manifest in its distinct aesthetics and sounds. In other words, in some key aspects it was a discrete quasi-religion.

Finally, the leader came to believe his own myth, exhibiting signs of megalomania and paranoia. Although he had built a union whose membership increased to as many as eighty-thousand, it had shrunk to five thousand by the time of his death. Some came to question his sanity. In a sense, he fit the classic definition of a tragic hero, whom Aristotle describes as someone of noble character who has reached high status, gained importance: someone who embodies virtue and greatness as inherent characteristics. Yet as a result of hamartia, or a "tragic flaw," the hero experiences failure. Although for the tragic hero the decline is self-imposed, usually a result of hubris, overall he is a sympathetic character whose "punishment" exceeds his "crime": Chavez succumbed to human flaws.

The conclusion unpacks the labor leader's religious philosophy and political theology as a discourse of Christian humanism, a relinquishing of self, of body, to a transcendent, even universal, human spirit of self-sacrifice. His soteriological teachings followed a spiritual path that led to material redemption for those who sought enough blessings for all but not too much for anyone. This lofty goal was often at odds, however, with the aims of a labor union, and many traditional unionists opposed the notion of a spiritual order rather than a traditional labor syndicate. The conclusion unpacks this humanitarianism, which involved the construction of a new, decidedly "antimacho" Mexican American man, the uplift of women, and a full embrace of the lesbian and gay community.

By the time of his death, Chavez had amassed a substantial corpus of prose, transcribed interviews, and speeches. A number of these texts are well known, even canonical. Mindful of his popular writings and of the overlooked work, I reexamine the well-known documents and introduce obscure apocryphal writings into the interpretation. My interest in public representation as opposed to hidden "reality," however, circumscribes my use of the sources. Many of Chavez's writings appeared in the UFW's newsletter, *El Malcriado: The Voice of the Farm Worker*.[28] The paper, started in the winter of 1964–65, was published until 1976. After a year's hiatus, it was reincarnated as the *President's Newsletter*, which ran from 1977 to 1979. One of the paper's founders explains the name *El Malcriado*: "The implication is a rowdy youth, 'badly raised,' who does not give due respect to his 'betters,' who does not remain silent and docile, who challenges authority."[29]

Chavez, in addition to recruiting the paper's editors, engaged the popular Los Angeles–based Chicano artist Andy Zermeno, whose satirical cartoon characters helped establish the identity of *La Causa*: "'Don Sotaco' was the short and (initially) humble and abused farm worker; 'Don Coyote' the labor contractor and field boss, skinny and devious in his service to the boss; and 'Patroncito,' the Big Boss, plump-to-fat, often with a big hat, big cigar, boots and sun glasses."[30] These characters were brought to life in El Teatro Campesino, or the Farmworkers Theater, which functioned as a cultural ministry within *La Causa*. It was founded in 1965 by the brilliant and mystical Luis Valdez, who injected Mesoamerican philosophy and art into *La Causa*, reflecting the larger Chicano movement that was permeated with Aztec aesthetics and thought. He brought to the striking farm workers plays that were often performed on the flatbed of a pickup truck, developing simple skits he called *actos,* or myths.[31] I return to El Teatro in Chapter 3.

Throughout, I reintroduce the founder by bringing a history-of-religions reading to the literature—looking especially for religious tropes. I present my exegesis of primary and secondary textual sources and quote from my conversations with key members of the Chavez tribe, Chavistas, as they are called. I have conducted research at Nuestra Señora Reina de la Paz—Chavez's last headquarters and home. (It is now on the registry of national monuments.) There he came closest to forming his beloved community.[32]

In Yuma County, Arizona, his birthplace, I visited what remains of the original Chavez ranch: a few stone walls planted deep in the sandy earth, protruding just enough for some Mexican highway workers to point them out to me across the narrow aqueducts of the leader's fond childhood recollections. From there it is a short drive to the house in which Chavez died, located in the town of San Luis. On the same street stands the dilapidated wooden one-room UFW meeting hall; it seems anachronistic, with the faded UFW logo painted on its facade. No one can tell me if it is still in use. One passerby guesses that it may be a church *de los aleluias.* The modest middle-class home where Chavez expired sits just a few steps north of the Mexican border.

Although I have pursued both field and archival research, I have not written an ethnography, or a history, or a biography. My work offers a perspective, a partial truth, suspended somewhere in the speculative ether between hagiography and other possibilities. My interpretive model for this work is structured empathy that refrains from adulation or rebuke. I have tried for a balanced approach, offering a critical mapping of the discourse about Chavez. Rather than anatomize his actual life, I write about the narrative itself. In it there is a remarkable spiritual story, foundational for the identity of millions of Mexican Americans, and for the mythology of the nation.

AMERICAN MYTHS

The late labor leader once cut to the core of his mission of social transformation as follows: "Somehow, the guys in power have to be reached by counterpower, or through a change in their hearts and minds."[33] Chavez's goal was to transform public values—thus he had to speak and be heard. He was well aware of God's influence in American governance, and the easy accessibility of divine endorsements: there is no disproving the Lord's will in ethical debates—to the extent that moral suasion can hold.

Thus, Chavez's intervention in American politics was predicated on his religious identity, comprising a broad public Christian faith, inflected by his Indian roots, enunciated in a sacred story: his own American story. In the style of the biblical prophet Jeremiah, he warned of the fall of a great civilization if it did not adhere to its vaunted principles. In his warnings to Americans about the evil effects of racism, he took his cues from Martin Luther King. As David Howard-Pitney explains: "The black Jeremiad may well reflect the influence of hegemonic ideology upon subordinate groups' public ideas and programs, but it also illustrates the shrewd and artful tendency of an oppressed group to refashion values taught by privileged classes—even as it accepts them—into ideological tools for its own ends."[34] Chavez used against those in power the very myths by which they themselves justified oppression.

He did this with the help of many important friends. On May 17, 1967, for example, Chavez sent a letter to Robert Kennedy that concluded as follows: "Farm workers have held in the highest esteem the name of Kennedy because of your brother's concern and commitment. Your own involvement on our behalf has even deepened this esteem."[35] The founder attended RFK's requiem Mass at St. Patrick's Cathedral in New York City and served on the board of the Robert Kennedy Memorial. His relationship with the Kennedys, cemented by their shared Catholic ethos, broadened his following and heightened the public

Cesar Chavez displays the American flag at a rally, Salinas, CA, 1973. Bob Fitch Photo Archive, © Stanford University Libraries.

perception of his gravitas.[36] RFK's appearance in Delano, where he literally broke bread with Chavez to end the leader's first public fast, was especially important. While working in San Jose with Saul Alinsky's Community Service Organization in 1959, Chavez had organized a campaign to register Latino voters to support John Kennedy that aided in the senator's California primary victory.[37] The Kennedys did not forget the action. In 1966 Robert Kennedy held congressional hearings in Delano on the matter of the grape strike; the UFW in turn endorsed RFK in the presidential primary campaign. Dolores Huerta shared the podium with Kennedy when he gave his victory speech and was there when he was assassinated; an urgent matter prevented Chavez's presence onstage with the senator.

Chavez's communal political theology defied a perennial American Puritanism that emphasizes the individual alone before God while simultaneously condemning material accumulation as the index and assurance of salvation. Despite its Catholic core, his message reached far beyond the pontifical share of the U.S. population. He performed a Chicano version of the American jeremiad—denouncing the sins of the people while affirming the shared religious aspirations and highest principles that constitute the national mythology.[38] As an American prophet he walked in the path of a religiously inflected political left.[39]

In the critical patriotism and hybrid religiosity of his movement, Chavez reproduced the religiosity of the nation-state, or civil religion.[40] Even while civil religion veils a cultural Protestantism, it enables minority groups in the nation to profess both belief in God and patriotism: the American masses can identify the distant civic faith as their own, despite their cultural alienation—that is, even though they hold widely different religious beliefs.[41] Civil religion has provided the idiomatic categories—empty signifiers—around which American debates unfold: freedom, liberty, justice, equality, and so forth. Chavez, like King before him, benefited from the elasticity of those categories, which accommodate a range of meanings.

A theorist comparing King's Southern Christian Leadership Conference to the UFW has written: "Both agencies attempted to convince the larger public that the symbols of their respective movements were in keeping with the values of the nation as they had been inculcated into the metaphors of earlier historical situations and became part of the accepted civil religion by the majority."[42] Chavez became a prophet of (Mexican) American values. His jeremiad collapsed religion into politics, denouncing Americans for their hypocrisy in failing to uphold their professed credo of freedom and equality. But he stopped far short of assailing America itself or its narratives of divine election and mission—its exceptionalism.

In addition, the practice of affirming the democratic ideals Americans claim for themselves was taken direct from Saul Alinsky's strategy of promoting a worker's alternative to communism, by buttressing those organizational efforts with fierce American patriotism. More like King, Chavez professed key tenets of American belief, particularly those extolling equality, and following the Baptist minister, he challenged Americans to practice what they preached. The leader capitalized on the rhetoric and affective feeling structure of what Jean-Jacques Rousseau called the "spiritual dimension of the state."[43]

Rousseau relocated sacred authority, placing it under the aegis of the state. The liberal republic, though officially secular, could retain its holiness by effecting what is perhaps modernity's greatest sleight of hand: a secular democracy whose sacred authority—divine, reflexive, and self-generating—hides while deploying its religious appeal. According to Rousseau, this civil religion should produce a citizenry that "combines divine worship with love for the laws, and, by making their country the object of the citizens' adoration, teaches them that to serve the State is to serve the guardian deity." As he saw it, a modern republic could be a kind of theocracy, "in which there ought to be no pontiff but the Prince, no other priests than the magistrates. Then to die for one's country is to suffer martyrdom, to violate the laws is to be impious, and to subject a guilty man to public execration is to devote him to the wrath of the gods: *Sacer esto.*"[44]

Robert Bellah and many others since have called attention to civil religion in the United States.[45] The religion of the democratic republic could suit modernity's demand for tangibility, efficacy, and participation while reiterating the decisive stakes of heaven and hell as a psychic technique of social regulation, underpinned by the narrative of divine election. In the words of Howard-Pitney: "No belief has been more central to American civil religion than the idea that Americans are, in some important sense, a chosen people with a historic mission to save and remake the world."[46]

Chavez, instead of denouncing civil religion, embraced it critically, becoming its prophet, speaking the idiom of public Christianity while redefining Americanism: "Everywhere we went, to school, to church, to the movies, there was an attack on our culture and language, an attempt to make us conform to the 'American way,'" he exclaimed, "What a sin!"[47] Cultural difference should be celebrated; to eschew it distorted the American way. Chavez often expressed his ideas in religious idioms, blurring the boundary between religion and politics.

CESAR'S BODY

At the core of this work is Chavez's body, especially its physical representation—its ritual construction and deconstruction through fasts and other acts of symbolic crucifixion; his symbolic resurrection occasioned a national conversation about racism and violence. By embodying multiple identities, Chavez made himself available for mass identification; people far and near related to him, bonding with him because of a quality they perceived in him. Yet these multiple identifications were also his undoing, because the core of his message was subjected to numerous and often conflicting interpretations. His was not a long life but a brief strut and fret upon the global stage, during which he produced a powerful icon, one involving a highly stylized physical undoing and remaking sometimes at odds with the myths and images that swirled around him.

Chavez, in his "spiritual corporality," spoke in a prophetic idiom, as an embodied subject, his somatic image—his unmistakably bronze skin—the synecdoche for Chicana/o identity.[18] No other Chicano *cuerpo* has been racialized, emasculated, decomposed, and reanimated like his for mainstream Americans to consume. Biographers, historians, and journalists writing of him rarely omit a detailed physical description. In 1968 Peter Matthiessen wrote:

> The man who has threatened California has an Indian's bow nose and lank black hair, with sad eyes and an open smile that is shy and friendly; at moments he is beautiful, like a dark seraph. He is five feet six inches tall, and since his twenty-five-day fast the previous winter, has weighed no more than one hundred and fifty pounds. Yet the word "slight" does not properly describe him. There is an effect of being centered in himself so that no energy is wasted, an effect of *density*; at the same time, he walks as lightly as a fox. One feels immediately that this man does not stumble, and that to get where he is going he will walk all day.[49]

To this, the biographer Jacques Levy added: "His speech was soft, sweetened by a Spanish accent, and his hands, unusually small, moved gracefully to illustrate his points. But his eyes were the focal point, dark brown and expressive, giving a sad countenance to his face until a smile flashed, transforming his features."[50] Ronald Taylor has described him as "a deceptively small, soft-spoken man with tiny hands."[51] Bill Gormley, in a newspaper article titled "Cesar Chavez: The Paradoxes of Greatness," referred to him as "the little Mexican American."[52]

José Angel Gutiérrez asserted Chavez's prototypical physicality: "He looked *mestizo*. He was dark skinned, short, with high check bones, piercing black eyes, and sparse facial hair. He was the embodiment of a Chicano. Chicanos could see themselves in Cesar: clothes, personal style, demeanor and commitment."[53] Chavez personified the motivation for colonial oppression in the Americas—the mongrel phenotype: short with dark skin. From the time of his first fast, in 1968, he complained of back problems and was often hospitalized for recuperative rest. While recovering in bed, at home or in the hospital, he would sometimes receive visitors, including photographers. His physical ailment was one that farm workers could relate to, for backbreaking field work, which often requires stooping over for long intense periods, can result in severe spinal disorders. In 1962 the life expectancy for male farm workers was only forty-nine years. Chavez's broken body exhibited the effects of its exploitation, the human cost of economic inequality. His brokenness enfleshed material injustice while it gestured in surrender or self-sacrifice. In contrast to his anticolonial contemporaries, including Che Guevara and Fidel Castro, Chavez offered his physique to the public imaginary, not as a sign of insurrection, but as a symbol of surrender—reconciliation, healing, and change—like the ravaged body of Christ. The founder enacted the sacrificed messiah, shrinking and feminine. George Mariscal has keenly described the leader's masculinity as a gender "hybrid."[54]

The features of his body have been recited publicly in standard feminine tropes: slight, small handed, dark skinned, handsome, boyish,

Indian. These terms suggest an androgyny that transgresses erotic identity—particularly that of stereotypical machismo. His was a non-threatening presence, suitable for mass American consumption. During his public fasts, impressions of him, heavily mediated, were transmitted across the globe, and his health became a national obsession. *La Causa* benefited from the public's awareness of farm workers that emerged because of the mass circulation of images at the start of the age of digital reproduction.

On November 25, 1960, the day after Thanksgiving, *CBS Reports* aired a prime-time television documentary by Edward R. Murrow called *Harvest of Shame*. Murrow's report shed light internationally on the migrant laborers, who were depicted as barefoot, filthy, and starving yet human, Christian, and American. While Americans digested an annual feast of grace, they were confronted by the horrors of the dwellings near the fields from whence their food came, conditions compared unfavorably with those of chattel slavery and sharecropping. Chavez capitalized on this pornographic imagery by exposing the farm workers' (and his own) suffering and poverty to compel the attention of the nation, and of the world; to elicit sympathy and connection; and to work his way, and that of the farm workers, into the American heart.

Today electronic signs proliferate, advancing myths and fictions through communication technology and obscuring the evidentiary distinction between history and myth. The culture industry trades on simulacra, the hyper-real, circulating information more real than reality, more true than truth.[55] God thrives in the age of digital reproduction. Certainly the liquid crystal display provides the means to reiterate the myths—resulting in domination and control, manufacturing value and desire—but it concomitantly opens a space for illustrating and circulating radical teachings about "the divine will," that is, countermyths, in ways that construct and deconstruct racial imaginaries. The leader capitalized on these nascent media wonders, which became the mode of mediation for his revolution: This revolution was indeed televised.

When Chavez began working with the Community Service Organization in the late 1950s, he sported a full, thick mustache. It was the characteristic symbol of two Mexican revolutionaries—Emiliano Zapata and Pancho Villa—both stereotypical machos, violent and libidinally unrestrained yet purposeful and heroic. Zapata, the agrarian southern-based Mexican revolutionary, was a key symbol for the UFW, owing especially to his philosophy, summed up by the phrase "land and liberty." By the time Chavez founded the union, he had rejected the sign of the *bigotes:* he shaved his mustache and remained clean-shaven for the remainder of his life.

Picture him: young, slim, dapper, sporting a shock of black hair; he was sometimes photographed with a cigarette dangling from his fingers, exhibiting great sophistication and cosmopolitanism. People wanted to be like him, a part of him. He personified the spirit of the age. He brought the world to Central California.

THE DELANO BORDERLANDS

The Chicana feminist Gloria Anzaldúa has theorized the existence of a Mexican American cultural space between nation-states: "the borderlands." Reflecting the reality of the U.S.–Mexico border, her theory builds on a metaphor: "The actual physical borderland that I'm dealing with in [her book *Borderlands/La Frontera*] is the Texas–U.S. Southwest/ Mexican border. The psychological borderlands, the sexual borderlands and the spiritual borderlands are not particular to the Southwest. In fact, the Borderlands are physically present wherever two or more cultures edge each other."[56] Chavez was a product of this reality—he thrived in the metaphorical borderlands, moving comfortably across many borders, especially those between religions. He exhibited what Anzaldúa calls mestiza consciousness: "The new *mestiza* copes by developing a tolerance for contradictions, a tolerance for ambiguity. She learns to be an Indian in Mexican culture, to be a Mexican from an Anglo point of view. She learns to juggle cultures. She has a plural personality, she operates in a pluralistic mode—nothing is thrust out, the good, the bad and the ugly, nothing rejected, nothing abandoned. Not only does she sustain contradictions, she turns the ambivalence into something else."[57]

This "faculty" or ability to negotiate disparate cultures, what Anzaldúa calls *la facultad,* is key to "mestizo consciousness," which exhibits the capacity to change forms and essences. "Rigidity means death," she warns. "*La mestiza* constantly has to shift out of habitual formations; from convergent thinking, to analytical reasoning that tends to use rationality to move toward a single goal (a Western mode), to divergent thinking, characterized by movement away from set patterns and goals toward a more whole perspective."[58] This was Chavez's work, beginning in Delano, California, which he transformed into a borderlands.

Delano is an unlikely incubator for a cultural revolution, covering an area of less than fifteen square miles. Situated on north–south Interstate 205 between Tulare and Merced, the "Crow City" in 2011 had a population of nearly fifty-four thousand, probably twice what it had been in 1962. It certainly was not San Francisco (which was 262 miles north), or Los Angeles (152 miles south). Yet somehow, making a pilgrimage to Delano to work with Cesar Chavez and Dolores Huerta was a remarkably cool thing to do; it provided spiritual satisfaction and a hip progressive credential. Perhaps it was an errand into the wilderness to live outside one's self, open to fresh experiences and to the hope of a better world. Pilgrims came from around the globe, from all walks of life. Chavez, in his 1965 "Open Letter," printed in *El Malcriado,* declared, "The name Delano is now known throughout the state, it is becoming known throughout the nation.... Delano is on the map because of a strike that will be one-hundred days old before we reach Christmas."[59] During the Great Grape Strike, or *La Huelga* (1965–70), Chavez recruited college students, activists, artists, musicians, religious laity, and clergy of all stripes to come to Delano and support the strikers. Volunteers were given room and board and paid five dollars a week. The leader was especially interested in artists and members of the clergy; he wanted them to give *La Huelga* an aesthetic, a spirituality, and a sonic identity. Delano was a laboratory for transformation; it became a node, a destination for pilgrims of sorts from around the globe, who traveled there to meet and work with Chavez and Huerta and testified to their spiritual growth as a result.[60] One pilgrim, a Protestant UFW volunteer, asked: "How did farm workers help church supporters grow in their faith? I doubt that farm workers had that intention. It happened naturally."[61] Another follower, a Franciscan, wrote of his time with *La Causa:* "It pushed me as a Friar to really think about what solidarity means.... I ask myself 'what are my vows about? How do I get myself off the hook so quickly about how I see our responsibility to be proclaimers of the Gospel, when these folks give their whole life to it?' So they were really evangelizing me."[62] That Chavez meant many different things to many different people was a triumph of his mestiza consciousness.

FROM RELIGIOUS POETICS TO RELIGIOUS POLITICS

In 1966 Eugene Nelson described Chavez as "highly intelligent, and extremely aware—in almost a *poetic* sense—of everything in life."[63] In *La Llorona's Children* I called Chavez a practitioner of religious poetics, defining that term "in the Greek, Aristotelian sense of poetry as performance, from the Greek *poesis,* doing or acting. This is true particularly ... for the religious context. Perhaps the best known of the early recorded uses of the term appears in the canonized Christian scriptures, James 1:25: 'He will be blessed in his doing.' Similarly, the Greek *poetes* signifies one who does something, or the maker of a poem."[64]

But Chavez moved beyond politically relevant mythopoesis and formulated a religious discourse to advance specific social policies. The specificity of his political goals distinguished his speech practices from those in which the exact partisan aims are left underdefined or rendered broadly in terms such as *love, justice, peace, happiness, health, prosperity,* and the like. His demands included these aims but were more fully articulated. The method of religious poetics disrupts social norms; it probes, challenges, and dismantles the oppressive structures wrought of a colonial enterprise that underpinned and still supports racial, gender, and class histories. Myths normalizing social inequality are iterated with enough frequency and plausibility to persuade any terrified, purposefully ignorant, and mystified population. The greatest triumph of state-induced mystification is achieved when a hurting and angry people directs its energies against its own interests. Conversely, a prophetic and counterhegemonic poetics of religion confronts and shakes the religious pillars of spiritual subjugation, proposing alternative forms of consciousness foregrounding social change; religious poetics is a practice of spiritual reeducation with revolutionary consequences.

Chavez went further than poesis; he announced his political agenda and mapped a direct revolutionary plan. He deployed homiletics as a rhetorical method of organizing—that is, as public political speech. The work of Chavez, then, is better understood as *religious politics*—a variation on the ways religious discourse is performed and symbols are deployed, distinguishable by an emphasis on the intersection of the sacred and the political. This junction, as a strategic formulation, is not only the goal, broadly rendered, but the focus, the target—the bull's-eye. In religious politics, discourses of the holy are recalled in service to the profane, to be reimagined, resignifying the work of the divine, the primary mover, in reordering the world—along lightly etched lines of race, class, gender, and sexuality that progress like an arc of history, under construction, bending toward justice.

The rise of twentieth-century liberation movements based in religion marks one of history's greatest ironies, because religion, particularly a distorted form of Christian mythology, provided the moral justification for colonization, dehumanization, and racial exploitation in the modern world. Chavez, like Gandhi and King before him, created a countermythology that redressed and dismantled the powerful myths supporting white Christian dominion. Mythologizing is a potent practice for the subaltern that not only gives the oppressed a grammar for reasoning and speaking but can also command mass audiences.

Chavez's goal as prophet was to amalgamate master religious narratives into a core of mutually sustaining beliefs and practices that his followers could adhere to as sacred and religious, capturing and redirecting doctrinal edicts tied to various theologies—but mostly those closely associated with the state. Because of his movement's broad and ambiguous religiosity, he was able to organize across cultural and religious boundaries, *spiritual lines,* and this crossing of borders, I propose, was the genius of his movement. He (re)constructed the sacred into a collective representation that undercut the totality of any individual dogma while reassembling key confessional artifacts under the broad canopy of similarity and kind: sacrificial love, redemptive suffering, nonviolence, and social justice. Toward this end, he combined various faiths into a discrete religious conglomeration.

Beyond his public Christianity, he was a devotee of Gandhi and St. Francis; he preached a poetic theology that traversed the borders of orthodox religion. He has proved resistant to impassioned efforts to contain him within a single master memory. Like the orisha, or demigod, Eluggua, he is a trickster, a traveler between worlds, a messenger. The play of crossings and dwellings is central to borderlands theory, which links improvisation and innovation to transgression, occupation, and justice wrought from conflict and exchange: "A borderland is a vague and undetermined place created by the emotional residue of an unnatural boundary. It is in a constant state of transition. The prohibited and forbidden are its inhabitants."[65] During the sixteenth century the Dominican ethnographer Fray Diego Durán was dismayed to learn that Indians who had submitted to Christian baptism continued their traditional native religious practices. Durán questioned an Aztec elder about this rejection of orthodoxy and recorded the following reply: "Father, do not be astonished; we are still nepantla."[66] This is the middle space, the cultural location dividing and connecting worlds, where Chavez's religious identity thrived.

The leader embodied multiple fantasies and realities, a jumbled mass of signifiers—inhabiting a place that Anzaldúa has described as *nepantla*—a locus that sits astride the borders of conflicting worldviews while paradoxically participating fully in both of them: "Bridges are thresholds to other realities, archetypal, primal symbols of shifting consciousness. They are passageways, conduits, and connectors that connote transitioning, crossing borders, and changing perspectives. Bridges span liminal (threshold) spaces between worlds, spaces I call *nepantla*, a Nahuatl word meaning *tierra entre medio*. Transformations occur in this in-between space, an unstable, unpredictable, precarious, always-in-transition space lacking clear boundaries."[67] Chavez, a nepantlero, traveled these spaces.

In this way he exhibited what Lara Medina has called "nepantla spirituality," whose defining principle is an existential equilibrium: "Bipolar duality consisting of complementary opposites or complementary parts is a constant within indigenous Mesoamerican understandings of the universe and illuminates the duality I propose with nepantla. As duality or complementary opposites exist within all things, nepantla itself is comprised of the shadow side or the bewildering state of uncertainty, and the transparent side or the state of clarity and meaning making."[68]

The record of Chavez's life on the American border illustrates the dialectic between competing forces. In addition to dwelling as a *nepantlero*, he was a transgressor of borders—crossing them and occupying terrain where his presence was prohibited. The allegory of crossing, in contrast to the imagery of dwelling, distinguishes *nepantla* from borderlands theory.

Duality and bipolarity came to describe him later in his life drama, when his shadow side was on the ascent. Perhaps this fate was an inevitable cost of genius. Nonetheless, the sum of his triumphs and tragedies was to leave the world better off than he found it.

CHAPTER ONE

Mythology

Think Different

For now we see through a glass, darkly ...

St. Paul, 1 Cornithians 13:12

There is no true version of a life, after all. There are only stories told about and around a life.[1]

Ruth Behar, *Translated Woman:*
Crossing the Border with Esperanza's Story

We can appeal to broad sectors because of these different interpretations.[2]   Cesar Chavez

In 1998 a black-and-white photo of a beleaguered Cesar Chavez graced billboards, magazines, and television screens across the United States as part of Apple Corporation's promotional campaign asking consumers to "think different." His countenance is somber. On his right shoulder he carries a shovel, a rake, and a hoe. The splintered handles of his tools and his demeanor evoke a man carrying a rugged cross. His eyes avoid the camera, as he stares down at the earth. Others memorialized in the campaign included John Lennon, Gandhi, and Martha Graham. Several variations of a poetic text were released as part of the promotion. The following is the "full version":

> Here's to the crazy ones. The misfits. The rebels. The troublemakers. The
> round pegs in the square holes. The ones who see things differently.

They're not fond of rules. And they have no respect for the status quo. You can quote them, disagree with them, glorify or vilify them. About the only thing you can't do is ignore them. Because they change things. They push the human race forward. While some may see them as the crazy ones, we see genius. Because the people who are crazy enough to think they can change the world, are the ones who do.

Of the roughly twenty-four persons celebrated in the campaign, Chavez is the only Mexican American (though the billboards also extolled Desi Arnaz, Pablo Picasso, and Joan Baez).

Cesar Chavez is without doubt the most widely remembered Chicano and perhaps U.S. Latino across the globe. Remembering him can pay dividends: they are the yield of his cultural capital. As a result, groups and individuals stake claims to Chavez's public remembrance, which also has cash value; it has been used to market everything from Indian casinos to the megacorporation Apple.

Because Chavez is always remembered in context, the memory produced is always incomplete, entailing some forgetting or amnesia. In 2001 his cartoon ghost materialized virtually in *The Simpsons,* on the Fox Network—an episode viewed by an audience of over ten million[3] —to console a hunger-striking Homer Simpson, who mistakes him for Cesar Romero (1907–1994). There is much disorder in the leader's public remembrance. He is conscripted by various interests and appropriated uncritically in discourses that are often at odds with one another. His legacy—his corporeal record and spiritual accounting—provide the raw material from which to build powerful sacred narratives for mass consumption: the memory of Cesar Chavez is a very influential myth. This chapter maps, deconstructs, and theoretically reconstructs that mythology.

First, I look to the account of his life as he told it. I then delineate and probe secondary accounts of the leader that form a canon. My thesis here is that the received and canonized story of Chavez is retold strategically, shaped and informed by a will to power. The incongruence in his iterated memory alone evinces a combination of mythos and logos, reason and psychology, especially when considered against the way he self-represented, that is, constructed his own mythology. Overall, his story emerges as a palimpsest, wherein the meaning is eked out from the layers of tellings. The question becomes, then, where to focus when telling the myth, or where to place the accent.

PLACING THE ACCENT

Chavez never used accents when spelling out his name. Yet most of those writing about him, especially those writing posthumous accounts, set accents over the letters *e* in César, and *a* in Chávez, literally correcting the record he left of his own name so that it conforms to proper Spanish spelling rules. By contrast, I am careful to note that he did not place the accents himself; I acknowledge his right to misspell his name consistently in a lifetime of signing it. I try to understand his perspective. Because my interest is more phenomenological than historical, I intend to let the phenomenon—in this case Chavez's story—emerge on its own terms. My phenomenology is also careful to distinguish between my words and his. Instead of attempting to correct the historical record, my hermeneutic probes the meaning of the incongruity.

Interpreting Chavez through his self-fashioning is usefully accomplished by identifying the tropes of the classical hero, written about by Joseph Campbell in his timeless book *The Hero with a Thousand Faces*.[4] This frame for reading, when purged of any metaphysical excess and adjusted to fit the profane and ordinary heroic narrative, enables a clearer fathoming of Chavez's story as a universal one, involving rites of passage: separation, trial, and return The plot of the leader's life lends itself well to the romance, the song of the classical hero, particularly the tragic hero, when read in tandem with Erik Erikson's psychosocial analysis of early psychic formation, distinct personality traits resulting in traumatic life-altering events—those Erikson found, for example, in the tale of Gandhi.[5] Chavez is ultimately a tragic hero in the sense that although he slayed the dragon, he succumbed to his own demons, his human flaws. Nonetheless, the myth he left remains empowering for millions of Latinos and others, who accent it in several different ways.

YOUNG MAN CESAR: THE EXPULSION

The song of Cesar Chavez as he sang it began with his family's modest but idyllic life on its simple ranch in Arizona, connected to the sandy earth, beneath the unblocked sky. When he was ten years old, racism, combined with misfortune, led to the family's expulsion from place—a physical, spiritual, and psychic displacement. During his formative years he enjoyed the warm and secure embrace of his family. But the ejection from home, the shattering of clan, prompted an emotional reaction extreme enough to shape the traits of a personality that would affect and redirect history.

Chavez tied his ethos and mission to terra firma: "I bitterly missed the ranch. Maybe that is when the rebellion started. Some had been born into the migrant stream. But we had been on the land, and I knew a different way of life. We were poor, but we had liberty. The migrant is poor, and he has no freedom."[6] If his origin story betrays an appreciation of real estate, drawing connections between property, liberty, and freedom, it also reveals a spiritual valuation of earth. He sometimes referred to farm workers as "people of the land" because they lived with their hands and feet planted in the soil. According to his own rendition the expulsion from paradise triggered his metanoia; he vowed at that moment to return and to repossess the ranch. Hence, land and its multiple sacred and profane meanings shaped Chavez's priorities from his preadolescence.

The multiple inscriptions of Chavez narrating his beginnings are key to his mythology. The first major record of the leader's life and work was Peter Matthiessen's *Sal Si Puedes: Cesar Chavez and the New American Revolution,* first published in 1969.[7] Matthiessen was a reporter working for the *New Yorker* who traveled to Delano to meet the union's founder during the summer of 1968. From those meetings he produced a pair of articles, published in the June 21 and 28, 1969, issues of the *New Yorker.* Matthiessen focused more on the formative years of *La Causa* than on Chavez's early development. He attempted to capture the revolutionary spirit of the 1960s, with *La Causa's* leader as its epitome. According to one of the book's contemporaneous reviewers, he offered "a view of a battlefield where the fight is not only for the agricultural workers but for the redemption of the [whole] country."[8]

The gospel account of Chavez according to Matthiessen records the ejection as follows: "With the loss of their land in 1937, the Chavez family began the long grim period that Manuel [Chavez's cousin] calls 'our migrating years.' Up and down the byways of California, with the armies of the dispossessed, they followed the crops. Like all the rest, the Chavezes were true paupers; their struggle was for shelter, clothing, food."[9]

The journalist Jacques Levy began interviewing the leader in 1969 and continued until Chavez's death. Levy took a leave of absence from the Santa Rosa, California, *Press Democrat* to start researching a biography of Chavez and later devoted himself full-time to the project. After publishing his book, entitled *Cesar Chavez: Autobiography of La Causa,* in 1974, Levy continued to interview the labor leader as well as family members and associates.[10] Levy's text is written in the Latin American style of the *testimonio*—an autobiography narrated by an activist and recorded by a scribe who also participates in the act of creating the narrative. Mario T. García explains: "Unlike traditional autobiography, in which there is one sole author, in *testimonios....* we find 'collaborative autobiography.'"[11]

Matthiessen's and Levy's narratives are tantamount to gospel accounts of Chavez's life, insofar as they announce the "good news" that liberation is afoot: they are also evangelistic, meant to recruit followers to *La Causa.* Nearly all the writing on Chavez from 1965 to 1970, the years of the Great Grape Strike, can be classified as proselytizing literature, meant to convert readers to the cause. For the most part, they follow the Matthiessen-Levy line in recounting details of Chavez's early life and the founding of the UFW. They tend to vary in some key places, however, especially in descriptions of Chavez's suffering while growing up on the ranch in Yuma. After the family's ejection from the farm, suffering took center stage in the stories, as the itinerant and starving Chavez family endured unfathomable miseries and deprivations, sleeping in their car and vulnerable to every exploitation devised by the growers. One chronicler opened his account as follows:

> Stooped over in the intense sun along the rows of crops, the migrants worked from early morning till nearly dark.... they harvested—men and women alongside young boys and girls, day after day, their bodies contorted in painful routine.
>
> At night, they returned to the housing camps—dirty, cramped, run-down shacks, converted chicken coops, and storage sheds, none with running water or electricity, almost all of them infested with mosquitoes. Dozens of families shared a single outhouse. Water came from nearby irrigation ditches. They never had enough food. Children went to school only when they were not needed in the fields.[12]

Richard Chavez, Cesar's younger brother, however, told a slightly different story of relatively less discomfort and instability when I interviewed him.[13]

Chavez's self-representation deviates from the notion of simple and ordinary beginnings. As one writer noted: "Life had started differently for Chavez; he and his family lived on their own small farm, not in wealth, surely, but in an independent manner only dreamed of by most farm workers. The Chavez family had a few horses, some cows, and raised grain, alfalfa, vegetables, and watermelons on their eighty acres in the Gila River Valley."[14]

The founder tells how he was nurtured by his extraordinary paternal grandparents, who were integrated into his immediate household. His father's mother, Dorotea, or Mama Tella, was raised in a Mexican convent, where she learned Latin. His grandfather, Cesario Chavez, or Papa Chayo, was a product of the Mexican revolutionary spirit, manifesting the principles of *tierra y libertad,* land and liberty. Cesar's mother, Juana Estrada, was a woman of great faith. Cesar described her as a full-blooded Yaqui Indian. Marc Grossman, the official Chavez family spokesman, insists that she was a Tarahumara Indian.[15] But Richard Chavez says that she was not Indian at all.[16]

Whether Juana Estrada Chavez was a Yaqui is less important for this project than the meaning Cesar hoped to create in disclosing that identity to foreground his own. This indigenous identification places the founder in a proud revolutionary tradition that would have appealed to his Indian followers. Take, for example, the Native American scholar Jace Weaver's response to the claim that Chavez was Yaqui: "Chavez himself was an Indian.... The Yoeme [Yaqui] differentiated themselves from Mexicans, refused to accept an inferior status, and fought fiercely to defend their sovereignty. Their resistance brought them into conflict first with the Spanish and then with the Mexican government. The dictator Porfirio Díaz brutally persecuted the Yoeme and sought to relocate them from the Sonora. Many fled to Arizona, Chavez's mother's family probably among them."[17]

Chavez further claimed that his mother was a *curandera,* a spiritual healer or medicine woman, skilled in the complicated postcolonial drama of faith healing, combining herbal remedies and ancient Meso-american ritual techniques with Catholic symbolism and prayer: "My mother had a reputation in the valley for her skill in healing, a skill she put to constant use, for she couldn't bear to see anyone in pain, and there were no doctors in the valley. She was especially knowledgeable in the use of herbs, choosing some to cool a fever, others to cure colic, and mixing brews for specific illnesses. Her faith in her skill was as strong as her belief in the saints and the Virgin of Guadalupe."[18] Her go-to remedy was the herb *manzanilla,* or chamomile, which also became Cesar's nickname. Cesar came to believe that he too possessed healing powers, and he sometimes functioned as a spiritual healer himself.

Richard Chavez disputes not only that his mother was an Indian but also that she was a *curandera.*[19] Nevertheless, Cesar repeated the claim in his eulogy for his mother: "Our mother was a folk healer. Besides delivering babies and curing common colds and headaches, she cured children of *sustos* [fright], *empacho* [indigestion], *mollera* [(problems with) the crown of an infant's head], *pujon* [constipation] *y ojo* [the evil eye]. Her favorites herbs were yerba buena [peppermint], yoposte [epazote?], yerba del pasmo [*Baccharis pteronioides*], sa[ú]co [elderflower]—and she really believed in manzanilla."[20] As he testifies, his mother was summoned by people throughout the valley for her healing services.

Juana Chavez's faith and compassion often eclipsed her economic reasoning, for she would exhaust the family's means of subsistence in helping others: her extravagant sacrifices meant that her own family lacked basic necessities. "You always have to help the needy," she reasoned, "and God will help you."[21] Cesar's description of his mother's faith resonates with what the psychosocial biographer Erickson writes of the faith of Gandhi's mother: "She was an utterly undogmatic religious person of a kind who wished to pursue only what made her feel right and clean. Indeed, she imbued her little son with a tolerance for any religion as long as it cultivated a deep sense of communion with the unseen and silent." Chavez gave a similar account of his mother, whom he had at his side during his three public fasts.

Beginning with his relationship to his mother, Cesar appears to have plotted his autobiography as an oedipal family romance in the Gandhian style. In the words of Gandhi, "Whenever she wanted me for anything, I ran to her."[22] But Cesar also channeled his mother when he practiced spiritual healing. That Richard Chavez has disputed his mother's *curanderismo* suggests that he followed an impulse to sanitize the late labor leader for popular consumption; that Cesar described his mother as a *curandera,* giving elaborate details about what appears to be her passionate devotion to her work, establishes his mystical heritage. He absorbed his mother's techniques and would later deploy them when caring for the farm workers. In addition to his knowledge of botanicals, he read books on acupuncture and taught himself chakra therapy. Chavez practiced healing with his hands, regularly treating devotees for illnesses, especially those involving headaches and chronic physical pain.[23] Richard Chavez has not contested this account but has downplayed its import by explaining that both he and Cesar once took a course on healing energy.[24] Yet according to an audio recording in an exhibit at the Cesar E. Chavez Center at La Paz, a "granddaughter" claims that the leader believed he could talk to spiders and snakes—communication with animals constituting one characteristic of the mystical *curandera* or *curandero*.

Cesar told that his mother and grandmother taught him the Catholic catechism. "As we didn't have a Church in the valley and it was very difficult to go to Yuma, it was my mother who taught us prayers," he explains. "Throughout the Southwest and Mexico where there were no priests for a long time, the amazing thing was that people kept the faith. But they were oriented more toward relics and saints." Chavez adds a disclaimer about his mother's religiosity: "My mother was very religious without being a fanatic."[25]

Cesar credits his mother with instilling in him the philosophy of nonviolence. "When I look back, I see her sermons had a tremendous impact on me. I didn't know it was nonviolence then, but after reading Gandhi, St. Francis, and other exponents of nonviolence, I began to clarify that in my mind. Now that I'm older I see she is nonviolent."[26] She dispelled for young Cesar the mystique of macho identity: "She taught her children to reject that part of a culture which too often tells its young men that you're not a man if you don't fight back."[27]

Cesar remembers his father, Librado, as a hard worker who never touched alcohol. Some anthropologists have characterized alcoholism as primary among the so-called macho vices. Librado was not a macho in the pejorative sense of the word.[28] Yet he demonstrated those qualities associated with the so-called honorable macho, animating the discourse of "honor" and "respect."[29] Cesar's father and grandfather began a homestead, clearing more than a hundred acres of dry valley floor— three years before Arizona achieved statehood. Cesar's father also taught him social justice: Librado was active in the earliest efforts to unionize farm workers.

During the Depression years the Chavez family lost its property. They fought hard to keep the family farm, but despite their best efforts they became migrant farm laborers. The leader's memories of following the crops are fraught with suffering and exploitation. As field workers in the cruel and dehumanizing megabusiness of agriculture, his family spent long hours under a blazing sun, performing monotonous and backbreaking work without rest or proper equipment. But the most difficult part of field work was performed with a tool called the short-handled hoe. Workers using it had to stoop over and contort their bodies unnaturally to execute their tasks. "That was work for an animal, not a man," Chavez remarked to Matthiessen. "Stooping and digging all day, and the beets are *heavy*—oh, that's brutal work. And then to go home to some little place, with all those kids, and hot and dirty—*that* is how a man is crucified, *Cru*-cified."[30] The founder likened working with the short-handled hoe, *el cortito,* to the passion of Christ: "There was a rhythm, it went very fast. It had to, it was all piece rate.... It was really inhuman.... And it's just like being nailed to a cross."[31] He habitually relied on religious symbolism and allegories—the vernacular of Christian America—to illustrate his experiences; he was speaking from within the master myth, deploying his jeremiad.

There is much disagreement about the quality and duration of Cesar's formal education. Nelson, in 1966, and Matthiessen, in 1968, claimed that he dropped out of the seventh grade, whereas Levy, in 1974, said that he completed eighth grade. The other writers who have discussed Chavez's education are split, some claiming he was a seventh-grade dropout, others reporting that he was an eighth-grade graduate. For the most part, however, the accounts agree on the reason he left school: to liberate his mother from backbreaking labor in the fields. His lack of formal education made him all the more exceptional—he was a self-made man.

Chavez's adolescence after graduation was marked by radical transformations of his identity. First he became a pachuco, taking up the cultural idiom of young Mexican Americans rebelling against an American society that scorned and rejected them. Pachucos were identifiable by their dramatically oversize draped jackets and pleated pants, known as zoot suits. As an adolescent Cesar began to smoke, drink beer, and dance. The erotic choreography and uninhibited parties of the pachucas and pachucos gave Chicana and Chicano youth a Dionysian ritual for expressing their alienation and rage. In 1943 zoot-suiters were savagely attacked in Los Angeles by white sailors and marines. These clashes came to be known deceptively as the Zoot Suit Riots. Chavez's pachuco period signaled a resistance to mainstream American identity.

Then, at the age of seventeen, he joined the navy, demonstrating a commitment to the very American imperialistic project he protested, albeit indirectly. He served two years in the Pacific, concluding with an assignment on Guam. In the classical mythology of the hero, pivotal life passages occur upon separation from the familiar, when the hero, in the depths of the psychic and physical unknown, experiences developmental rites occasioned by liminality; transformation occurs when he or she receives a spiritual summons. As Campbell put it: "The first stage of the mythological journey ... signifies that destiny has summoned the hero and transferred his spiritual center of gravity from within the pale of his society to a zone unknown."[32]

During his tour of naval duty Chavez confronted a local and globalized racism that led him to fresh realizations about injustice. "For him the prejudices were clear cut, brown vs. white," according to Ronald Taylor, "but in boot camp in San Diego, he discovered prejudices had other dimensions." Chavez himself recalled: "I saw this white kid fighting, because someone had called him Pollock [*sic*] and I found out he was Polish and he hated that word Pollock. He fought every time he heard it. I began to learn something, that others suffered, too."[33] As he described his naval experience, "Those two years were the worst of my life: this regimentation, this super authority that somehow somebody has the right to move you around like a piece of equipment. It's worse than being in prison. And there was lots of discrimination."[34] This episode marks a liminal period, a rite of passage, when the greatest personal evolution is possible.

While in the navy Chavez was sworn to defend God and country and indoctrinated by narratives about honor, justice, and freedom while simultaneously exposed to racism and suffering on a global scale. Perhaps it was this psychological dissonance that prompted the episode in his narrative known as his Rosa Parks moment:

> For a long time, movie theaters throughout the San Joaquin Valley were segregated. It was just accepted by the Mexicans then. In Delano, the quarter-section on the right was reserved for Mexicans, blacks, and Filipinos, while Anglos and Japanese sat elsewhere....
>
> This time something told me that I shouldn't accept such discrimination. It wasn't a question of sitting elsewhere because it was more comfortable. It was just a question that I wanted a free choice of where I wanted to be. I decided to challenge the rule, even though I was very frightened. Instead of sitting on the right, I sat down on the left....
>
> .... It was the first time I had challenged rules so brazenly.[35]

He was forced from the cinema and detained in jail. No charges were brought and he was released, but only after a police officer had threatened and degraded him. Chavez claimed that this episode was not particularly pivotal to his work; he noted that biographers have perhaps overestimated its effect on him. Nelson, for example, recorded the following account:

> It is the year 1943 in the city of Delano. A young man in his late teens is home visiting his family after working in a distant part of the state, and he decides to take in a show. He walks to a local movie house, buys his ticket, and enters the crowded theatre. As he stands at the rear of the aisle and his eyes become accustomed to the dark he observes that the people on one side of the aisle are almost all dark-skinned, Mexican-Americans like himself, while all the people on the other side of the aisle are white.... Was he not an American citizen like these Anglos? ... Was he not living in a country where all men were supposed to be equal?[36]

About this incident Chavez explains: "It was while I was in the navy that the theater incident happened in Delano, a story that's been twisted when it's been told before. I was home with a couple of navy guys from Texas on a seventy-two hour pass, and we weren't in uniform."[37]

The word *myth* has come to denote a fiction in part because the details of a story are often embellished in its recounting to serve the objective of the teller. This was Chavez's pivotal "event," according to the tropes of the myth. It awakened an already existing predilection in young Cesar, prompting a discovery, whereby "the Godly powers sought and dangerously won are revealed to have been within the heart of the hero all the time."[38] The mythology of the leader's childhood and adolescence testifies to his innate leadership potential. The tales of his youth—especially the excruciating hardship he suffered—were meant to reveal someone who overcame tremendous obstacles, a natural leader who possessed a noble spirit, a passionate heart, and a thirst for social justice—all characteristics that became key to Chavez's heroic narrative. His rites of passage culminated, of course, in his return.

RETURN

The telling and retelling of the founder's trials in the navy is comparable to the narrative of separation and return that marks the life of a hero prior to his or her homecoming to battle the perennial dragons—the ones that have tormented him since childhood. According to Campbell, "The full round, the norm of the monomyth, requires that the hero shall now begin the labor of bringing the runes of wisdom . . . back into the kingdom of humanity, where the boon may redound to the renewing of the community, the nation, the planet."[39] The truths that Chavez brought with him when he returned were not metaphysical, but they were essential to the impact he would have on humanity. He had learned that racism occurs on a global scale.

As Nelson tells it, "After he left home Cesar continued to follow the crops. He mingled with whites and learned that they had problems too, and that prejudice was not an inborn human quality but something which could be overcome; he gained a new devotion to working people of all races and beliefs. In Delano, he met and married a Mexican-American girl who shared his dedication to the cause of the farm worker, and they worked together in the fields up and down the state and began to raise a family as best they could."[40] Chavez saw with his own eyes the effects of colonialism and realized that local struggles over better wages and working conditions are inseparable from the master racializing discourse about God, creation, and the order of work, or the working order. He would have been remiss in his efforts to form a labor union had he not simultaneously waged a struggle for human equality with global reach.

In 1948 the leader returned to California. In October of that year, he married Helen Fabela, not in a Catholic church, but in a chapel in Reno, Nevada.[41] According to the official Chavez family spokesman, Marc Grossman: "Helen and Rita Chavez Medina, Cesar's older sister, together 'eloped' to Reno for a double wedding. Rita married Joe Medina, a construction worker. They picked up Cesar's dad, Librado Chavez, in San Jose who acted as witness for both services. Later, in 1949, Cesar and Helen received the sacrament of marriage at a Catholic church."[42] Cesar and Helen settled in San Jose; they eventually had eight children.

Although Chavez, according to many sources, was a lifelong reader, an "organic intellectual," his apprenticeship in the social justice teachings of the Catholic Church began in earnest upon his return.[43] In San Jose he met Father Donald McDonnell, a diocesan priest from San Francisco who, according to Chavez, mentored him in the church's teachings on redemption through helping the poor. Levy has claimed—and nearly all biographies of the leader have reiterated—that McDonnell introduced Chavez to the writings of Gandhi. In an 1988 interview, however, Chavez said that he began reading Gandhi when he was "eleven or twelve" years old and had been reading him ever since. I take up this discrepancy in the chapter that follows. The focus here is the heroic rendition of the Chavez narrative. Nelson tells the story as follows:

Cesar recalls that Father McDonnell, an expert linguist ... "sat with me [Chavez] past midnight telling me about social justice and the Church's stand on farm labor and reading from the encyclicals of Pope Leo XIII in which he upheld labor unions. I would do anything to get the Father to tell me more about labor history. I began going to the bracero camps with him to help with Mass, to the city jail with him to talk to the prisoners, anything to be with him so that he could tell me more about the farm labor movement.[44]

McDonnell studied at St. Patrick's Seminary in Menlo Park, California, where he was schooled in the Church's teachings on labor, particularly *Rerum novarum,* by Pope Leo XIII (1891), and *Quadragesimo anno,* by Pope Pius XI (1931). There he also learned the tradition of activist priests who advocated for organized labor: "For most of the seminarians, it was a revelation to learn that 'workingmen's associations' were held by the most authoritative teachings of the Church to be consonant with Natural Law; hence, workers had not only a right to join unions but a moral duty."[45]

In 1952 Chavez met Fred Ross (1910–1992), who became his most formidable mentor, wielding the most influence over him. Ross worked on organizing Chicano communities for civic action in Los Angeles and was expanding to San Jose; he was with the Community Service Organization (CSO), directed by Saul Alinsky (1909–1972). Alinsky was a Chicago-born Jew who has been called the founder of modern community organizing.[46] Cesar soon became Ross's disciple, and Ross secured a full-time position for his young apprentice as a community organizer. Chavez claimed that Ross changed his life.[47] Though he was a successful community organizer, he became frustrated by the lack of support for his efforts to organize a labor union for farm workers. He gave the CSO an ultimatum: either they let him devote his time to labor organizing, or he would quit. When his threat proved unavailing, he quit the CSO dramatically in 1961, on his birthday, to dedicate his time to building a union for farm workers. The date marked a new birth for Chavez, a fresh beginning.

From early on Chavez was adept at capitalizing on the free and accessible symbolism of time to establish a cosmic meaning for his story. In 1977, when Chavez moved to establish a union holiday, Founder's Day, he chose to memorialize his own birthday, March 31, rather than the date of the first Farm Workers Association (FWA) convention (September 30, 1962). At the foundational convention, the union unveiled its totemic emblem—a black silhouette set against a crimson background. Matthiessen has noted that "some people like to think that the eagle appeared to Cesar Chavez in a dream."[48] According to Victor Villaseñor, the symbolic scheme was Mexican: "Red for blood, black for death, and of course the bird for hope. It was the same way in Mexico ... these colors were universal."[49]

Chavez's story of leaving the CSO and founding the union has a mystical resonance: it is perhaps the most hagiographic of the UFW origin myths. Motivated only by gallantry and altruism, Chavez abnegated what amounted to salvation in a capitalist system—a well-paid career that he enjoyed. He also rejected a lucrative offer to head the Central American branch of the Peace Corps. His sacrifice is all the more significant in light of what he renounced. The Chavezes made a faith journey. They packed up their belongings and, with $1,200 in savings, headed for Delano, where Helen's family and Richard Chavez lived. Like Jesus of the Christian Gospels, the leader began to call on his disciples—in Chavez's case Dolores Huerta, the first UFW vice president, and his cousin Manuel Chavez, both of whom had comfortable and steady jobs—to leave their professions and follow him into the desert. They did so, going into the wilderness with Chavez to do God's work.

The simple question for the founders became, then, "How do we eat?" Cesar recounted how he responded: "I didn't know. But as we later found out, somebody in the Cause would never starve. The people would never let you." This revelation became a foundational doctrine for *La Causa*. "We found out many useful things after we began to not be so concerned with ourselves, and how we looked, what we ate, and what we said. And we began to find out a lot of beautiful things, how people really are, how the poorer they are, the more open they are, and the more beautiful they are."[50]

Their task became signing up members for what Cesar called the Farm Workers Association, preferring *association* to the more grandiose and potentially intimidating *labor union.* This language additionally recalls Pope Leo XIII's 1891 encyclical on the rights of labor, *Rerum novarum.* In its earliest incarnation the FWA developed a distinct Catholic identity; its foundational Statement of Purpose begins as follows:

> As Christians and workers we wish to realize the ideals of the Church in our lives and in the world in which we live. We see in the twentieth century a sincere and agonizing attempt on the part of the Church to apply ancient truths and teachings to new and terrible problems, and we are hopeful that her efforts will contribute to a truly human community where each man works for the common good, where each enjoys abundant fruit from his labor, and each has the opportunity to develop to the fullest his human potentialities.
>
> In the teachings of the Popes, and especially in the encyclicals of the late Pope John XXIII, we find expressed the sentiments and convictions which we share: the "overwhelming sadness" at "the sorry spectacle of millions of workers in many lands and entire continents condemned through the inadequacy of their wages to live with their families in utterly subhuman conditions."

The document goes on to cite the pope's explicit affirmation of the "dignity" of agricultural work, his encouragement of workers to form "associations." It ends by entreating "all Christians" to work for social justice: "Our desire is to work together with all Christians, under the guidance of conscience and right reason, to create a high degree [of a] just economic order which we believe that all Christians desire."[51] Members of the fledgling FWA were making converts and saving souls.

While they pursued their mission in the field, their story assumed even greater religious significance because their survival depended on miracles, including the kindness of strangers. As they traveled the length of California's Central Valley attempting to organize workers, they would spend days on the road without eating. Finally, over Cesar's objections, Manuel said he was going to knock on a door to ask for food. "'This is the place that's going to give us food,' Manuel said as we knocked on the door." By the time the organizers "left that house, they [those who had given them food] were convinced. They began to work with us full time the next day." Chavez said that "from then on, asking for food or for help became another tool in organizing."[52] In another miracle story, Helen Chavez won a hundred dollars at a grocery store. "I told the checker, 'This is going to be my winner,' and he laughed."[53] The prize money was enough to pay Cesar's gasoline bill and keep the fledgling FWA from folding.

Those who joined the FWA were required to pay $3.50 a month, for which they received membership in an organization that was working for their human dignity and also for practical matters such as a death benefit. Average life expectancy at that time was forty-nine years for a male farm worker and seventy-eight years for all American males. Farm workers lived under the constant threat of death, and Chavez himself exhibited a fixation on mortality that led him, like Gandhi, to teach the sacrifice of one's own body and life for the greater good. Chavez accepted no money from other organizations (until the FWA merged in 1965 with the AFL-CIO); he wanted farm workers to undergo the sacrifice required to build their own association.

DELANO REVISITED

The majority of migrant farm workers lived on the west side of Delano; the leader and his family lived on the east side, though he did not own their home. The west side of town was inhabited by Mexican Americans, along with Filipinos, a small number of Puerto Ricans, and African Americans. During the 1970s Muslims of Arab descent began populating Delano's west side. In fact, the UFW's first official "martyr" was an immigrant from Yemen, Nagi Daifallah (1949–1973); the UFW gave him a traditional Muslim funeral.[54] Whites had also lived in

UFW funeral for Nagi Daifallah, displaying the flag of the Yemen Arab
Republic (1962–1990), Delano, CA, 1973. Bob Fitch Photo Archive, © Stanford
University Libraries.

Delano, migrating from the dust bowl during the Great Depression. All
were exploited: The 1935 National Labor Relations Act, which allowed
American employees to unionize, denied farm workers that right. But
when the farm workers called their first strike, in 1965, white farm workers constituted a separate and more privileged class of agricultural
labor.

Eventually the UFW purchased a plot of land, the Forty Acres, in
Delano to establish a headquarters, building structures there with
adobe walls and red tile roofs. Chavez explained to Matthiessen: "The
people wanted something more modern—you know, kind of flashy—to
show that they had a terrific union going here, but I wanted something
that would not go out of fashion, something that would last." He planned
to transform Forty Acres into a sacred center: "'There will be little hol-
lows in the walls—you know, niches—where people can put little stat-
ues if they want, or birds and things. We'll have frescoes. [The Mexican

painter David Alfaro] Siqueiros [1896–1974] is interested in doing that, I think. This place is for the people, it has to grow naturally out of their needs.' He smiled. 'It will be kind of a religious place.'"⁵⁵

Though initially Catholic, the movement forged a distinct religious identity for itself during the great strike—including signature rituals such as pray-ins, fasting, boycotting, and marches. By the time of the *huelga,* or strike, Chavez had fully returned and was prepared to do battle. The Great Grape Strike was precipitated by the lapse of the Mexican guest worker, or *bracero,* program. Mexican *braceros*—literally "arms"—arrived in the United States as temporary workers for agribusiness beginning in 1942. When the *bracero* program was terminated, Chavez's FWA joined with the Filipinos to create the Agricultural Workers Organizing Committee (AWOC). The group called a strike against grape growers in the Coachella Valley, in California, that continued for more than five years.

Ten years later, in 1975, Governor Jerry Brown signed into law the California Agricultural Labor Relations Act; this changed the entire game for the UFW. The law largely obviated the need for a strike, and the struggle became a matter of a vote by the workers for or against a union; the UFW lost some of these votes to the Teamsters, who asked far less of their members than did *La Causa*. Confrontations between the UFW and growers generally moved from the fields into the boardrooms where contracts and elections were negotiated. Chavez had anticipated the need to change his strategy. By the mid-1970s he shifted himself, his family, and the majority of the UFW's operations to his remote retreat in the Tehachapi Mountains, thirty-five miles southeast of Bakersfield and about a two-hour drive northeast from Los Angeles. At this retreat, a former tuberculosis asylum purchased and donated to *La Causa* by a wealthy Los Angeles–based supporter, Chavez intended to found his community. He named the site Nuestra Señora Reina de la Paz (Our Lady Queen of Peace), but it was called simply La Paz. It was there that the founder grew increasingly isolated and paranoid, exhibiting signs of megalomania. There he became distracted from the prob-

lems of farm workers, focusing instead on the movement for social justice more broadly.

When the leader began moving the main operations of *La Causa* to
his Gandhi-style ashram in the remote town of Tehachapi in the mid-
1970s, he knew that the move marked a personal transformation. In 1978
he announced: "I think my role has changed from one of an organizer to
possibly one of a teacher.... Mostly I want to teach people to initiate
and accept change within the movement because we can't live in the
late '70s with the concepts we had in the mid '60s. The things we did in
1965 are no longer necessary, valid, or even important."[56]

In 1983 Chavez told the UFW annual convention that he had formed
a "Chicano lobby" to support Democratic candidates.[57] I take up the La
Paz years in Chapter 3. Here, it is enough to say that Chavez exhibited
mestiza consciousness: he was many things to many people, and because
he continued to evolve throughout his life, attempts to capture him in a
single master narrative will inevitably fall short.

THE MISEDUCATION

Despite Chavez's multivalent, fluid, and evolving identity, writers have
not shied away from claiming that they have uncovered the authentic
Chavez, the one whom everyone must know. Speaking for him requires
that he be declared illiterate and incapable of speaking for himself. As
early as 1967 the illiteracy myth was beginning to unfold: "It is in no
way extraordinary that the Valley was unable to understand Cesar
Chavez. He belongs to that inarticulate subculture of farm workers
upon whom the Valley depends but whose existence does not impinge
heavily on the Valley consciousness.... This was the birthright of Cesar
Chavez. He went on the road at the age of ten, eking out a seventh-
grade education in some three dozen farm community schools."[58] Even
Levy describes him as "small of stature, quiet, self-effacing, soft-spoken, poorly educated."[59] From very early on in his work, Chavez suffered from unfavorable comparisons: "Whether or not Chávez will

become the next Martin Luther King remains to be seen. To date, he has not penned any great essays."[60]

Ilan Stavans, also comparing Chavez to King, advances the notion of an idiot savant: "Chavez wasn't a rhetorician," he asserts, "unlike Martin Luther King Jr.... Chavez had little talent for highbrow oratory." Stavans continues: "His discourses were neither preconceived nor sophisticated. Yet he was eloquent, precisely because his improvisational, pragmatic mind always found what it needed." Stavans explains away his eloquence as "improvisational" and "pragmatic." He literally speaks for Chavez, putting words into his mouth by citing the comment of "a black migrant worker," attributing them to the leader: "'But you know what I—what I really think? You know what I really think? I really believe the world gonna [*sic*] be great one day.' This was Chavez's view as well."[61] Chavez never spoke of a future so utterly utopian, nor is it possible for anyone to uncover what he actually believed. Stavans renders judgment as if it were empirical fact when he implies the limitations of Chavez's intellect: "He humbly exhibited his philosophy at every turn, proving that poor people might lack the sophistication to build fanciful sentences but not conviction and clarity of mind."[62] Stavans conscripts Chavez into the ranks of the folksy but noble, the (un)remarkable everyday Chicano.

In 1972 Matt S. Meier and Feliciano Rivera published a foundational text in Chicano history, entitled *The Chicanos: A History of Mexican Americans,*[63] which counted Chavez as one of the Four Horsemen who together delineated and led the Chicano power movement. The others were Reies López Tijerina (b. 1926), Rodolfo "Corky" Gonzáles (1928–2005), and José Angel Gutiérrez (b. 1944). Meier and Rivera place Chavez first among them, describing him as "a gentle apostle of a nonviolent approach to reform, [who] quickly became recognized as a spiritual leader of Chicanos."[64] Describing his background, they add, "Chavez came out of the largely inarticulate subculture of the migrant farm worker, characterized by extreme poverty, lack of organization, and paucity of leadership."[65] Assigning him those origins was necessary to mark him as unexceptional, to make him more accessible, and to romanticize the poor and oppressed.

Presenting Chavez as an everyday Mexican American becomes the trope for his appropriation as a Chicano hero. Perhaps Luis Valdez put it best when he said of Chavez that "the essence of his greatness [was] his simple humanity. All who had the opportunity to know and work with him in his day to day struggle know this to be true: he was not a saint; he was not a miracle worker; he was just a man. That's why his impact on history is so remarkable. This is the common man, inspiring leader and unforgettable brother that lives."[66] Valdez's key words—"simple," "common," "inspiring," "brother"—clarify his interests. Chavez embodied the populist revolutionary ideal, a Chicano prototype, inasmuch as he rejected extravagant book learning for more authentic epistemes. José Angel Gutiérrez has accepted this canonical memory but has added a macho element: "He was tireless in all his roles[:] as father, husband, Catholic, leader, Chicano, organizer, staff manager, and man. In his personal simplicity he was poignant."[67]

Yet even as this Chicano everyman discourse was developing, other authors recognized a different leader. In 1975 Sam Kushner wrote: "Despite Chavez's limited formal education, he was an avid reader, who had literally devoured all that had been previously written about farm-labor strikes."[68] Kushner's description of Chavez portrays an organic intellectual as defined by Antonio Gramsci, an intellectual born of the needs of a particular social movement: the founder employed his reading and experience to bind his union together and maximize its impact with the greatest possible efficacy. There was an urgency about his learning—for him, reading was purposeful rather than recreational— inspired by the political movement that nurtured him. He studied texts that would enable him to theorize and enact social change. And he studied religions.

Although some have recognized Chavez's intellect, they diminish his status as an intellectual with a modifier that creates a new category for him. José-Antonio Orosco, for example, wrote in 2008: "I maintain that he was a sophisticated thinker who, through the course of his activism, reflected carefully on the nature of nonviolence and American society and sought to understand the conditions for bringing about social change in the United States. Chavez is more akin to what Mario T. Garcia calls a "community intellectual."[69] There is no need to invent an entirely new category of intellectual for Chavez; he fits the description of the classical "organic intellectual": someone who is not tied to a university appointment but instead is concerned with the life of the mind and intends to have an impact on the social body. He is one who reads and develops ideas purposefully, for social change. For the organic intellectual the flourishing life of the mind is incubated in a political movement.

The discursive maneuver of recognizing Chavez's intellectualism but qualifying and thus diminishing it is nonetheless instructive: in such a practice his orthodoxy depends on either an erasure or a dilution of his capacity for original ideas. Matthiessen, though he recognizes Chavez's extensive reading, declares that he was "a realist, not an intellectual, and his realism has been fortified by extensive acquaintance with political treatises, from St. Paul to Churchill, and from Jefferson to all the dictators; his self education in the CSO years included reading in Goebbels and Machiavelli and Lord Acton."[70]

The leader also encouraged his followers to study: "Maybe we'll have to learn all over again how to organize. You could learn a lot from Goebbels; that's why I wanted some of you to read him.... That's one thing Goebbels really understood—how to bring people together."[71] Terzian and Cramer reported as early as 1972 that Chavez credited book learning for his transformation and leadership: When "someone else ... asked how come Cesar knew so much now when in the old days he knew so little.... [he responded,] 'There are always books, Julio. Maybe if you spend a little less time in the poolroom and a little more in the library, you won't need me to tell you what it's all about.'"[72] Since his youth, the founder had studied photography. Helen Chavez revealed

Cesar's scholarly and creative passions when she mentioned her worry about passing book stores with him, when she would say to herself, "I hope it isn't open. Books and camera stores—he'll be in there all night."[73]

In 1972 one observer wrote: "Despite his limited formal education, Chavez had done a great deal of reading, particularly the biographies and prose of men whose political and social philosophies he particularly admired. His office was decorated with pictures of two of these American heroes, the late President John F. Kennedy and the Negro leader Martin Luther King, Jr. But his particular hero was Mahatma Gandhi."[74] Others continue to devalue the depth of his intellect even as they attribute to him a complex worldview. Consider the following passage from a history of Chavez published in 1995, *A Triumph of Spirit*, by the Chicano historians Richard Griswold del Castillo and Richard A. Garcia: "Throughout this book we will examine a man who came to believe that there was a basic, reciprocal relationship between God, man/woman, truth, justice, and nature.... Ultimately, he was a man who lived a simple life and preached a simple guiding dictum: *Sí Se Puede* (Yes, it can be done). Faith in humanity, a belief in action, and a need for courage, as well as an unadulterated belief in God, shaped his personal, intellectual, and spiritual self."[75]

Although many remember Chavez as a simple man of faith, Dolores Huerta thought of him differently, confessing in the early 1970s: "I find him a very complicated person."[76] Frank Bardacke has described Chavez as follows:

> A classic autodidact, throughout his life he would suck up one subject after another, move from one enthusiasm to the next: the art of shooting pool, Catholic Social Action, the theory and practice of Saul Alinsky, the life of Gandhi, the history of unionism in the fields, the varieties of religious experience, the intricacies of labor law, printing, faith healing, the Synanon Game, theories of scientific management. His biographer Jacques Levy, who was also a dog trainer and helped Chavez train his two dogs, told me that Cesar was the most absorbed, committed student of dog training he had ever met.[77]

Cesar Chavez and his two dogs, Boycott and Huelga, La Paz, Keene County, CA, 1977. © Cathy Murphy Photographer (www.cathymurphyphotography. com)

The communication studies scholars Richard Jensen and John Hammerback were careful to follow orthodoxy. They noted his lack of formal education: "The education of this leader would be from informal sources.... his literary tour provided him with insights as well as tactics for ideas and topics that would surface in his discourse throughout his career."[78] Yet they distort his political spirituality:

> Chavez's public address reflected his interrelated perceptions of God, reform, and rhetoric. A devout Roman Catholic, he described the church as a "powerful moral and spiritual force" in the world; God controls the earth's events and people, seeing to it that good causes triumph. As a labor leader Chavez developed an optimistic interpretation of history and the future based on his beliefs in God, the injustices suffered by the poor, the need to organize workers, and the power of public address to achieve that end.... Chavez identified himself and other farm-worker orators as essential agents in God's design to eliminate injustice toward the poor and minorities.[79]

In fact, although Chavez himself spoke often of social change as a function of human action, in the text to which Jensen and Hammerback
refer, the leader actually admonished Chicanos to use the power of "the
whole Church," defining it

> as an ecumenical body spread around the world, and not just its particular
> form in a parish in a local community.
>
> The Church we are talking about is a tremendously powerful institu-
> tion in our society, and in the world. That Church is one form of the Pres-
> ence of God on Earth, and so naturally it is powerful. It is powerful by
> definition. It is a powerful moral and spiritual force which cannot be
> ignored by any movement. Furthermore, it is an organization with tremen-
> dous wealth. Since the Church is to be servant to the poor, it is our fault if
> that wealth is not channeled to help the poor in our world.[80]

The leader here attributed worldly power to the Church—an institution whose tremendous wealth and cultural capital give it political and
moral influence. He recognized that its powers are this-worldly. His
own concerns, moreover, were material and practical.

Still, Hammerback purported to know what was in his heart of
hearts: "Chavez believed in God, and believed that God had a plan for
the world."[81] Chavez's own profession on theism is far less clear: "Truth
is God."[82] I propose a heresy, based on the founder's statements, that
disrupts the fictions created about his faith. The declaration that "Truth
is God" is not a confession of theism, but something else. Moreover,
although Chavez often attended Mass, he also attended synagogue and
Pentecostal services, and he meditated and practiced yoga. He crossed
religious borders. I agree with Jennifer Reed-Bouley's assertion that
"Catholic social teaching did not form, but authoritatively confirmed,
the rightness of the United Farm Worker's moral actions."[83]

A Christian identity, moreover, obviated a commitment to communism: "Everywhere I went to organize they would bluntly ask, 'Are you
a Communist?' ... Later I found out that when they learned I was close
to the church, they wouldn't question me so much. So I'd get the priests
to come out and give me their blessing."[84] Ultimately, the sincerity of

Cesar Chavez doing yoga, La Paz, Keene County, CA, 1977. Photo: Cathy Murphy. © Cathy Murphy Photographer (www.cathymurphyphotography.com)

his faith is irretrievable, a gnosis he took to his grave. All that remains is the record, the memory, and the myth.

THE SAINT

In 1997 the American painter Robert Lentz, a Franciscan brother, painted a now famous portrait, *César Chávez de California,* in which *La Causa's* leader is depicted as a Byzantine icon (see the cover of this book). In his right hand he holds a scroll on which the U.S Constitution is printed. He faces the viewer directly, looking her in the eye while pointing at her as if calling her into a relationship with the image, with its signification. The pink sweatshirt seems like a deliberate choice; its color dominates the painting's color scheme, signifying femininity and love. Lentz has deployed this genre to depict saintly figures, including Gandhi and Martin Luther King. His artistic statement for the Chavez work reads in part: "He remains in our midst ... as a patron of all the poor, but especially of immigrant minorities who suffer solely because they will not watch their families starve. In this icon he carries the Constitution of the United States, for whose guarantees he fought, on behalf of all the oppressed."[85]

Similarly, Victor Salandini, who ministered to the UFW congregation and was known affectionately as the "Tortilla Priest" for his culturally relevant choice of communion wafer, hints that Chavez is a candidate for sainthood. In his book *Confessions of the Tortilla Priest,* Salandini includes a hagiographic account of Chavez's life. In it he compares Chavez to Jesus: "Countless people who have been associated with Cesar over the years especially admire one outstanding quality about Cesar Chavez: that he is truly a servant to other people—just as Christ our Savior was." Salandini closes the section on Chavez with a general call for canonization, that of Martin Luther King in particular: "The purpose of every man in every walk of life should be to become a saint," he writes. "The world needs saints today as much as it did in the days of Diocletian. ... I am convinced that there are many good people in the world today, people who have the qualities of which saints are made. ... How great it would be if the Catholic Church would canonize Dr. King!"[86]

Several authors writing about Chavez, including Matthiessen, have claimed that his Catholicism pitted him against abortion.[87] Ken Irrgang, a Catholic priest who worked with Chavez at La Paz from 1977 to 1989, however, tells a different story: "Cesar never spoke out against birth control or abortion, but he never was judgmental about people's religious attitudes."[88]

Framing Chavez's spirituality exclusively within Catholicism denominationalizes him and does not fully serve his complex spiritual pursuits. The leader belonged to a tradition of radical Catholicism that valued many things about the Church but was not limited by its creed. Instead, he had greater ambitions: his political spirituality was meant to transform all people of faith as well as those who espoused no faith at all. He thrived in a state of religious liminality: "Father, do not be astonished; we are still nepantla."[89] Yet others see it differently.

Consider the following claim made by John Dalton: "While César respected other religious and moral traditions, actively promoted an ecumenical spirit within the union, and incorporated meditation and yoga into his own spirituality, he was quite open about his commitment to the [Catholic] Church. Chavez *always* identified himself as a member of the *Catholic* faith community."[90] Dalton's claim relies for evidence on the following passage from a book by Friar Mark Day, published in 1971:

> I asked Cesar about his feelings toward the church one evening when he and his wife, Helen, had supper at Guadalupe church rectory with me and some visiting priests. "Most farm workers are Chicanos," Cesar said, "And most Chicanos are Catholics. The church is the only institution which our people are closely associated with. When the church does not respond to us, we get offended, and we are tempted to lash out against it.
>
> "You know," he continued, "there are many changes in the church today. But many of these changes, like the new ritual of the mass, are merely external. What I like to see is a priest get up and speak about things like racism and poverty. But, even when you hear about these things from the pulpit, you get the feeling that they aren't doing anything significant to alleviate these evils. They are just talking about them.
>
> "Here in Delano, the church has been such a stranger to us, that our own people tend to put it together with all the powers and institutions that oppose them."[91]

This supper in the rectory provided the occasion for Chavez to make— indeed, it prompted him to make—a faith and commitment statement. But as usual, Chavez was unable to offer a confession of faith to oblige those who insisted he express allegiance to the Catholic church; instead, he offered a distancing criticism.

In the same vein, Mario T. García professed Chavez's piety in claiming that "in his praxis and reflections [Chavez] displayed a profound spirituality based on his deep Catholic faith."[92] García references the following statement recorded in Levy: "While most people drawn toward liberalism or radicalism leave the church, I went the other way. I drew closer to the church the more I learned and understood."[93]

Chavez's own definition of "the church" bears clarification. He prepared an address entitled "The Mexican American and the Church" during his twenty-five-day "spiritual fast," beginning February 14, 1968. The address was later published. In it he wrote: "Of course, when we refer to the Church we should define the word a little. We mean the whole Church, the Church as an *ecumenical body* spread around the world, and not just its particular form in a parish in a local community."[94] The *New Oxford American Dictionary* defines the word *ecumenical* as "representing a number of Christian churches." Chavez knew the definition and knew also that his reference to the generic church could be read as referring to the Catholic Church or to the Christian church in general. But according to the definition he gave, he was speaking of the ecumenical Christian church.

As Chavez acknowledged, he had faith in the power of truth and human action, though others often cast and authorized that faith according to specific religious categories. Again, ponder his own words—in his eulogy for René López, who, shot by a goon presumably hired by a grower, was deemed a UFW martyr. Chavez asked, "How many more Farm Workers must fall? How many more martyrs must there be before we can be free? When will the day come when the joy becomes great and the grief becomes small? The answer, my brothers and sisters, is in our hands. The answer is in *our* hands."[95] This statement is a call to action far removed from the declarations made for him about his reliance on God.

The leader's actual self-professed religious identity can be discovered only in the texts he himself authored, and even such texts do not fully disclose the depth of any author's sincerity. His religious convictions are ultimately irretrievable—as is universally true. Authentic faith exists in the realm of interiority; despite individuals' religious practices, the authenticity of their belief remains inaccessible. No one can *truly* know the heart of another. Chavez's own words betray nuance, complexity, ambiguity, and transgression. Take into account what he told Levy:

> It's not necessary to have a religion to act selflessly. I know many agnostics who are more religious in their own way than most people who claim to be believers. While most people drawn toward liberalism or radicalism leave the church, I went the other way. I drew closer to the church the more I learned and understood.
>
> To me, religion is a most beautiful thing. And over the years, I have come to realize that all religions are beautiful. Your religion just happens to depend a lot on your upbringing and your culture.
>
> For me, Christianity happens to be *a* natural *source* of *faith*. I have read what Christ said when he was here. He was very clear in what he meant and knew exactly what he sought after. He was extremely radical, and he was for social change.[96]

Chavez relativized religion, attaching it to cultural identity, suggesting that all religions are equally good. Instead of identifying himself specifically as a Catholic, he claimed "Christianity" as "a source of faith," though in other places he identifies as Catholic. The passage above mentions and affirms the practice of agnostics, evidently because Chavez thought them more admirable in their lives than many who claim to be religious Christians; he criticized and dismissed some "believers" for their hypocrisy. But he continued to preach the relativity of religion. His description of "all religions" as "beautiful" echoes Gandhi, who also famously said that all religions are true, and that all contain error. Religion for Chavez was not dogmatic truth but an accident of birth.

There was at least one occasion, however, when Chavez clearly identified himself as specifically and emotionally Catholic: his audience with Pope Paul VI, on September 25, 1974. Chavez had not requested it; U.S. bishops initiated it as part of their new campaign to officially support the UFW. It was a twenty-minute meeting arranged by the Apostolic Delegate in Washington DC. The leader had been planning a trip to Europe that fall to urge labor activists there to support the lettuce boycott. The flight was paid for by the National Council of Churches.

During the visit, the leader followed protocol and kissed the pope's ring. He then dramatically unfurled a UFW flag and presented it to the pontiff while photographers shot pictures. Of this meeting Chavez remarked: "I have difficulty expressing its meaning, except that being a Catholic, having a chance to see the Holy Father in person, to have a special audience, is like a small miracle." The Vatican later made a statement supporting the farm workers—for Chavez, the most important result of the meeting: "What was *really* significant was the statement that [the pope] made about the farm workers and the Mexican-Americans in the United States."[97] In his undated "Report on European Tour," the founder recounted a conversation he had with an American, Monsignor Regazzi, prior to meeting the Bishop of Rome. When Chavez expressed trepidation about the audience, Regazzi said: "Cesar, don't worry. These days if you are black, brown or Protestant you can come in.... To see the Pope is a big thing in Europe, not just religiously, but politically too."[98]

After the meeting, Chavez responded with an enthusiasm that was at once sentimental and pragmatic: he made clear his emotional identification with the church and his feelings of awe, but he stopped far short of claiming that his was a Catholic movement or that he himself was committed solely to the church. The Vicar of Christ took care of that. The Vatican released the following statement the day after Chavez's private audience.

> Our welcome goes this morning to Cesar Chavez whom we are happy to receive as a loyal son of the Catholic Church and as a distinguished leader and representative of the Mexican-American community in the United States.

We wish to tell you of the real joy that is ours to be informed of the fidelity of the people of your culture and origin, our beloved sons and daughters, to the Church of Christ and to know of their generous endeavor to foster adherence to their glorious Catholic spirit. We know, in particular, of your sustained effort to apply the principles of Christian social teaching, and that in striving to do so you have faithfully worked together with the Bishops of your country and with the support of their authoritative representatives, the members of the United States Catholic Bishops' Ad Hoc Committee on Farm Labor.

We pray that this laudable spirit of cooperation will continue and that, through the all-powerful assistance of the Lord, harmony and understanding will be promoted with liberty and justice for all.

In the spirit of our own predecessors in the See of Peter we renew the full measure of our solicitude for the human and Christian condition of labor and for the genuine good of all those who lend support to this lofty vocation.

Our special affectionate greetings go to the Mexican-American community in the United States, which, in harmony with other esteemed ethnic groups, makes up the fabric of the nation, while furnishing its particular and important contribution rooted in Christian principles.

We willingly invoke the blessings of authentic Christian living in justice, peace and love upon our sons and daughters whom we see represented here, and upon all the members of the larger communities in which they live and work.[99]

In 1975 Chavez explained his faith to the *National Catholic Reporter* as follows: "I think there are three elements to my faith. It's God, myself and my brother. I'm traditional. I'm Catholic traditional. I go to Church regularly and faithfully.... But besides that, I also have what I consider is a renewal religion. I go out and do things. That's what I think is a real faith, and that's what I think Christ really taught us: to go do something."[100] Chavez deploys a Catholic identity in context, at least in part as a rhetorical device in the service of advancing his own new or "renewal" religion, a triumph of his political spirituality.

To confess belief for another person, to assert for that person a sacred truth, is blasphemous. Chavez is more comprehensible and perhaps inspirational when released from the grip of a narrow institutional subjectivity.

THE SINNER

Since Chavez's death, several authors have weighed in on his legacy. Some criticisms seem apt; others seem exaggerated and sensationalistic. Few have become part of the canonical account of Chavez's life. In academic writing, critical assessments of important figures whose lives have ended are encouraged and expected; affirming biographies are suspect and may be dismissed as biased or as the work of an activist supporter. But the severity of criticism is not necessarily a measure of its true judgment of an individual.

Among the recent assessments of the leader is Richard Rodriguez's essay "Saint Cesar of Delano." Rodriguez, who thrives on controversy, wrote: "When Cesar Chavez died in his sleep in 1993, not yet a very old man at 66, he died—as he had so often portrayed himself in life—as a loser. The ... union he had cofounded was in decline; the union had 5,000 members, equivalent to the population of one very small Central Valley town."[101] Rodriguez insisted that Chavez became a "Mexican saint and an American hero" who embodied what Rodriguez understood as a distinct Mesoamerican ethic of ritual suffering. Rodriguez challenged the canonical narratives about the leader and reframed him bombastically, capitulating to an ancient tradition: that Chavez was cut from the same cloth as St. Francis of Assisi—another of Chavez's expressed muses. As Rodriguez figured it, if the leader was a loser, he suffered his losses in service to the redemptive discipline of St. Francis and the crucifixion of Christ.

Rodriguez's figuration of Chavez as loser and saint appears in his review of the journalist Miriam Pawel's unauthorized biography, *The Union of Their Dreams: Power, Hope, and Struggle in Cesar Chavez's Farm Worker Movement*, published in 2009. From January 9 to January 11, 2006, as a prelude to the publication of that book, Pawel published a series of shrill articles in the *Los Angeles Times* that accused the UFW of neglecting its members and engaging in financial improprieties and condemned the late leader and his family. On December 18 of that same year, the California attorney general released the findings of his investigation of Pawel's allegations, which he found to be "without merit."[102]

Although Pawel's book and Rodriguez's review are unbalanced, both are essential contributions to a greater appreciation of one of history's flawed and tragic architects. Pawel's narrative is organized around many in-depth interviews, anchored by eight profiles. The profiles are rendered in prose fraught with sentimentality and pathos, making saints of the interviewees while concomitantly demonizing Chavez. Unfortunately, the text contains no thoughtful critical consideration of historiography and memory. Pawel accepted each account uncritically, even though she avers in the introduction to her book that she attempted to confirm an interviewee's recollections with a second source, not as a rule but "whenever possible."

In her epilogue Pawel unwittingly condemns her own interviews. Stepping out of her long-failed role as objective reporter, she wags her finger righteously at Chavez and complains that at his funeral one of his "most famous quotes" had been altered to include women in its construction of humanity. Chavez's prayer, "God help us to be men," was printed and recited as "God help us to be human." In response, Pawel writes: "Political correctness trumped truth.... [Devotees] had learned from Chavez how to rewrite history to suit their needs."[103] Ironically, her book represents a prime example of the impulse of devotees to rewrite history to suit their own needs, in this case psychological catharsis. They produce what I call "revisionist memory," whereby history is "corrected" to favor the narrator, the person who is telling the history.[104]

Chief among those staking a claim to Chavez's remembrance are folks who worked with him. Those who knew and worked with the leader may in fact be in a privileged position to recount events as eyewitnesses; they may not be accurate, however, given the volatility of personal memory and the myopia factor. Marshall Ganz, formerly a high priest in the UFW, now an iconoclast, has criticized Chavez in his own book and as a key source for Pawel and others. His *Why David*

Sometimes Wins: Leadership, Organization, and Strategy in the California Farm Worker Movement, was published in 2009. The author worked closely with Chavez until he was "purged" for fomenting dissent in the late 1970s. His book is a political and legal history from the earliest efforts to organize farm workers, during the 1920s, to the end of the 1960s. Ganz amassed an impressive amount of information, which he used to illustrate his argument and defend his thesis: that the UFW was "successful" when it deployed the greatest "strategic capacity" to organize. In his epilogue Ganz reveals Chavez's sins: "Others argue that social movement organizations like the UFW are inherently unstable. Led by zealots who are poor administrators, they pursue ideological goals, interpret dissent as disloyalty, and splinter or collapse like religious sects. They may influence thousands of individuals and create a cultural legacy, but rarely do they institutionalize firmly enough to survive the death of the charismatic founder."[105]

Ganz forgets, or fails to remember, the creation of a cultural legacy that empowered millions (not thousands) of Chicana/os and Latina/os to command the respect and dignity they had regularly been denied. The psychosocial empowerment of Latinos, their entrance into the mainstream of the American religio-ethnic hybrid, was perhaps Chavez's crowning achievement.

Another former Chavista, Frank Bardacke has written an eight-hundred-page tome criticizing the leader. For Bardacke, who called Chavez a "lay Catholic activist," the leader was at once saint and sinner. In tortured prose he writes of the UFW president: "If there is a geometry of the soul ... we would see two strong parallel lines, one marked 'Catholic faith,' and the other 'anger at injustice.'"[106] Bardacke ties Chavez to the regime of Spain's General Francisco Franco (1892–1975) through the *Cursillo* movement, named for the three-day retreats that were offered to Latino men on Catholicism, *Cursillos de la Cristiandad,* or "little courses on Christianity." The *Cursillos* were intended to introduce men to Catholic doctrine. Bardacke charges that Chavez, as *Cursillista,* evinced his Catholic fascism: "Cesar Chavez did his *Cursillo* in the late

1950s or early 1960s, according to his brother Richard. Richard's uncertainty about the date comes from the air of secrecy that surrounded the early *Cursillos,* and from Chavez's own subsequent reluctance to talk about his commitment to the movement."[107] Chavez was a *Cursillista* in July 1962. The notebook he kept during this time is available in the archives at Wayne State University in the UFW Office of the President files.[108] According to Chavez's notes, discussion focused on how to become a better Christian man, husband, father, brother, and so forth. There was no secrecy or political conspiracy surrounding the *Cursillos,* which were openly advertised.[109]

Yet, as Bardacke tells it, Chavez's Catholicism trumps all other concerns. "His deepest origins were not in Alinsky's radical Community Service Organization but in the *Cursillos de Cristiandad* movement ... first developed by the clergy in Franco's Spain and transplanted to the New World in the 1950s. The song they brought with them was 'De Colores,' and their ideology was a combination of anticommunism and personal commitment of ordinary lay people to the Gospel's version of social justice. Chavez, throughout his public life, remained true to that commitment."[110] Had Chavez been committed to the version of social justice recorded in the Catholic catechism and expressed in the fascism of Spain's Franco, the labor leader's ministry would have looked very different indeed. Yet for better or worse, myths are unconstrained by the rules of historical inquiry; they are fluid, accessible products of a will to power, political context, and the ability to speak and to be heard.

While I welcome historical accounts of Chavez's complex character, such work is accountable to the regulatory mechanisms of scholarship. In addition to (and in some cases instead of) deepening a historical understanding of the UFW and its founder, the iconoclastic works I have discussed above deepen our understanding of a group of disillusioned former Chavez devotees; although these narratives constitute a valuable discourse, complicating Cesar Chavez studies, they should be considered works in a discrete literary genre, that of "revisionist memory." Such stories need to be heard because of what they say about the leader's complex mythology, to which they have added the trope of monster and madman. But they need to be regarded as products of human memory, with all its imperfections, rather than as accounts of absolute truth.

My focus throughout is not to resolve historical disputes but to interpret the meaning of the incongruent readings. I do not deny that Chavez acted like an enfant terrible. I question, however, the extent to which that behavior invalidates his prophetic work. The Gospel of Matthew records an admonition given by Jesus to his disciples: "A prophet is not without honor except in his own town and in his own home" (Matthew 13:57). Few teachings disclose the humanity of the Christian Savior as much as this passage.

CONCLUSION: THINK DIFFERENT

Apple Corporation released several different versions of the narrative for its "Think Different" campaign. The "original" version is shorter than the "full version" cited near the beginning of this chapter):

> You can quote them, disagree with them, glorify or vilify them.
>
> About the only thing you can't do is ignore them. Because they change things. They invent. They imagine. They heal. They explore. They create. They inspire. They push the human race forward.
>
> Maybe they have to be crazy.

This text might just as well have been talking about Chavez alone, but the distinguished company in which he was placed goes far to explain and, yes, perhaps defend what seem to be tragic flaws in his humanity.

Chavez defies conventional and singular classification: he had multiple personalities, some of which inhabited that shadow side of his *nepantla* soul. I celebrate the impulse to surrender to one's humanity; if we celebrated only heroes without flaws, our heroic pantheon would be very small indeed. Victor Villaseñor notes that the leader "was not well thought of in many parts of Mexico. No, he was ridiculed, despised, and pushed into that realm of other great men who'd been despised and ridiculed—Lincoln, Juárez, Kennedy, King. And, of course, your own true self, if you've been good enough to have developed enemies. Especially spiritual ones. For no man or woman is worth their salt here on earth unless they have people who despise them and, hence, have proven to the world that he or she, indeed, stands for something. Down deep inside and real."

That he slowly descended into paranoia, increasingly given to fits of rage, does not invalidate his prophetic work but makes his legacy more complex. Accounts of Chavez's life need to be similarly complex and multilayered. Attempts to either canonize or vilify him inevitably fail, because they level a narrative better served by including all the rough topography of his multifaceted life.

Chavez's multivalent mythology is limited by his presumed identity, his "authorship"; it is more concerned with who he was then what he said and did. In "The Death of the Author" Roland Barthes argues that "authorship" issues from "positivism, resume and the result of capitalist ideology, which has accorded the greatest importance to the author's 'person.' The author still rules in manuals of literary history, in biographies of writers, in magazine interviews, and even in the awareness of literary men, anxious to unite, by their private journals, their person and their work; the image of literature to be found in contemporary culture is tyrannically centered on the author, his person, his history, his tastes, his passions."[111]

Cesar Chavez studies have come to be dominated by immodest attempts to unmask the "True Chavez," the essential author, that either negate the virtue in his authorship or conscript him into the service of diverse projects, some of which he opposed. My agreement with Barthes explains my interpretation of Chavez as someone who, "by refusing to assign to the text (and to the world as text) a 'secret': that is, an ultimate meaning, liberates an activity which we might call counter-theological, properly revolutionary, for to refuse to arrest meaning is finally to refuse God and his hypostases, reason, science, the law." Killing the Creator empowers the interpreter: "We know that to restore to writing its future, we must reverse its myth: the birth of the reader must be ransomed by the death of the Author."[112]

I do not propose that interpreters of Chavez ignore his life, but rather that they refuse to let it distort his work and his message—his text. When discussing identity more specifically, I follow Michel Foucault, who proposes that subjectivity "should be reconsidered, not to restore the theme of an originating subject, but to seize its function, its intervention in discourse, and its system of dependencies." Understanding and appreciating *La Causa*'s founder requires focusing on the intersection of race, religion, class, gender, sexuality, and other categories. Following Foucault, my work asks: "Under what conditions and through what forms can an entity like the subject appear in the order of discourse; what position does it occupy; what functions does it exhibit; and what rules does it follow in each type of discourse. In short, the subject (and its substitutes) must be stripped of its creative role and analyzed as a complex and variable function of discourse."[113] Chavez's myth emerges provisionally, produced by signifying practices as a response to and function of capitalist marginalization in a postcolonial context.

Chavez was the subject of myths, and he made myths, many of them incommensurate with conventional historical methods of interpretation: indeed, there is no "true" Chavez, saint or sinner, but only the multiple stories he told of himself and others tell about him.

Mythology is perhaps the most powerful form of discourse available to the subaltern, for it allows him or her to speak and to be heard. Mythos is the language of the oppressed. Campbell elaborates: "When scrutinized in terms not of what it is but of how it functions, of how it has served mankind in the past, of how it may serve today, mythology shows itself to be as amenable as life itself to the obsessions and requirements of the individual, the race, the age."[114] Myth, a symbolic and authoritative discourse, is not only the modality for articulating hegemony but also the vehicle for its destabilization: by means of myth the colonized confront and dismantle the master narratives of the colonizers. Chavez recognized this fact, taking his cues from Gandhi and Martin Luther King. The discussion now turns to them.

CHAPTER TWO

Prophecy

In the Path of Gandhi and Martin Luther King

And though I have the gift of prophecy, and understand all
mysteries, and all knowledge; and though I have all faith, so
that I could remove mountains, and have not love, I am
nothing.   St. Paul, 1 Corinthians 13:2

Those who say that religion has nothing to do with politics
do not know what religion means.   Gandhi[1]

But there must be a better distribution of wealth within this
country for all God's children.
                          Rev. Dr. Martin Luther King Jr.[2]

It was all done by Christ and Gandhi and St. Francis of Assisi
and Dr. King. They did it all. We don't have to think about
new ideas; we just have to implement what they said, just get
the work done. Gandhi offered everything there is in his
message.[3]

   Just as Dr. King was a disciple of Gandhi and Christ, we
must now be Dr. King's disciples.[4]   Cesar Chavez

I told him "I feel so bad when I fight with you." He said,
"Don't ever stop. Don't ever stop fighting with me. You're the
one that really helps me think." You know, he was just a
person, not a saint. He was a great person, but he was a
human being, and he would make mistakes like other people.
                                          Dolores Huerta[5]

On August 8, 1994, President Bill Clinton, awarding the Presidential Medal of Freedom posthumously to the UFW's founder, eulogized him: "Cesar Chavez ... had become a champion of working people everywhere.... He was, for his own people, a Moses figure. The farm workers who labored in the fields and yearned for respect and self-sufficiency pinned their hopes on this remarkable man, who with faith and discipline, with soft-spoken humility and amazing inner strength led a very courageous life and in so doing brought dignity to the lives of so many others and provided for us inspiration for the rest of our Nation's history."

Clinton was not alone in recognizing Chavez's prophetic role in America. The leader's death prompted eulogies from across the globe. Archbishop Roger Mahony of Los Angeles called him prophetic. Art Torres, the California state senator, spoke for millions of Latinos when he declared Cesar Chavez "our Gandhi, our Martin Luther King."[6]

The Mexican *norteño* band Los Tigres del Norte has recorded a song whose chorus melodically "compares" Cesar Chavez to Gandhi and Martin Luther King Jr., claiming that Chavez now owns "a separate place in the Heavens."[7] Even though Chavez is less well known than Gandhi and King, the comparison rings true, and the similarities of the three leaders illuminate a broad and perhaps ironic strategy of leadership in the modern age that deploys religious elements as tools in political struggles.

Chavez and King were both followers of Gandhi, working at the intersection of religion and politics: they were satyagrahis, committed to the core values of satyagraha (truth force), ahimsa (nonviolence), and *sarvodaya*, or self-sacrificial love and devotion to others.[8] They also each rejected fundamentalist doctrines in favor of a fluid religious ethos sometimes wrought by first dismantling existing traditions. In what follows I map the connections of the three leaders, focusing on their shared zeitgeist, their commitment to a strategy of nonviolent direct action, and their articulation of a theological response to racism and the colonial condition. One origin of race and the racializing process, or racialization, was colonialism, which occasioned theologies that delineated hierarchies of humanity, placing people of color, the colonized, at the lowest stages. In short, through the technologies of colonialism, religion produces race.[9]

These leaders confronted the discourse and realities of racialization by deploying religious strategies that challenged and dismantled the perennial effects of Christian imperialism: each argued that all people are created equal. Hence, in addition to the monotonous details of confronting baleful racism on a daily basis, they engaged in a spiritual discourse, a national and global conversation about what it means to be human: they were doing religious work—in a prophetic mode. This chapter argues that Chavez emulated the modern prophet King, following in the line of Gandhi, but that he transformed the identity of prophet to address his particular sociological context.

The struggles of Gandhi, King, and Chavez resonate, especially because each man waged a religious crusade exposing what had been obfuscated by a modern racial discourse: all people are equivalently human despite race—since all are children of God. Therefore, racism offends God: racism is evil and sinful. Ironically, religion, modernity's foil, became the effective mechanism by which to transform modern times. Gandhi, King, and Chavez understood the civic religious code that transmuted the authority of the church into the realm of the state, where republican governments scramble existing religious grammars to invent their own language of the sacred, what Nietzsche's prophet Zarathustra called "tongues of good and evil."

These three leaders have been tied together philosophically by their allegiance to nonviolence.[10] Each, moreover, was caught up in the broader movement of their time: a rapidly decolonizing world, an anticolonial spirit of the age, in which men of color were encouraged to seek spiritual rejuvenation through revolutionary violence. Malcolm X, Fidel Castro, Che Guevara, and Frantz Fanon were Chavez's contemporaries who exhorted colonized men to free themselves by revolutionary struggle for personal sovereignty and social equality. Chavez responded to the crisis of "internal colonization" in the United States by preaching love and sacrifice, modeling a new revolutionary man as militantly nonviolent, producing a fresh masculinity that embraced traditionally feminine characteristics. (I elaborate on this "hybrid" masculinity in the concluding chapter of this book.) His lofty rhetoric in this work of human liberation was gendered, conceived and expressed in male terms. He performed models of masculinity intended especially for male audiences, identifying violence among men as the problem; he intended to disrupt stereotypical male behaviors in favor of peace and fraternity.[11]

The life of each leader was marked by, and is therefore traceable through, the rites of life passage: Gandhi, King, and Chavez replicated and revised the life of the mythological hero, according to a pattern involving liminality and transformation by separation, trial, and return.[12] The heroic narrative imputes neither freedom from human error nor saintliness to any of these men; Chavez complained when outsiders thought of him and his followers as "saints." That each of the men was flawed bears repeating as much as does their common humanity. That they rose despite their flaws makes their legacy remarkable; each achieved for his constituency the prodigious goal of unshackling it from colonized thought processes and attaining for it a collective rehumanization.

In the section that follows I describe the common historical beast each leader sought to slay: colonialism, dehumanization, and racialization. I then reflect on the prophetic vocation that became the modality in which each enunciated new revelations about humanity and citizenship and in which King and Chavez discoursed on what it means to be an American. My focus in the end is the differing construction of time that distinguishes Chavez from King. Chavez, I suggest, was attuned to Catholic rhythms, meting out salvation as an angler metes out fishing line. He sometimes quoted a Mexican maxim, or *dicho:* "There is more time than life." By contrast, King, a Baptist minister, preached the "urgency of now," reflecting a Protestant soteriological model, wherein salvation is near and immediate, always accessible, and contingent on the will of the believer alone. Each man reflected the exigencies of his historical situation in his prophetic politics, but each man marked that politics in a different sacred meter.

Prophetic voices arise out of oppressive contexts.

THE BEAST: TOWARD A GENEALOGY OF RACIAL MEMORY

The scientific community has vacated, for the most part, the notion of an evidentiary basis for racial inequalities. According to Howard Winant: "Race was once thought to be a natural phenomenon, not a social one.... Today the race concept is more problematic than ever before. Racially-based social structures—of inequality and exclusion, and of resistance and autonomy as well—persist, but their legitimacy is questioned far more strongly than it was in the past.... While racial identity remains a major component of individuality and group recognition, it partakes of a certain flexibility and fungibility that was formerly rare."[13]

The "naturalization" of race was a triumph of colonialism. For centuries Europe legitimated its expansionist policies with narratives of religious and cultural superiority—preaching myths of a human hierarchy designed by God. In the eighteenth century, Deists and philosophers gave the notion of natural racial superiority a rationalist basis. Cornel West has written: "The category of race—denoting primarily skin color—was first employed as a means of classifying human bodies by François Bernier, a French physician, in 1684. He divided humankind into basically four races: Europeans, Africans, Orientals and Laaps. The first authoritative racial division of humankind is found in the influential *Natural System* (1735) of the most preeminent naturalist of the eighteenth century, Carolus Linnaeus."[14] Racialization discourse has undergone major shifts since its first iteration in Christian propositions on humanity that connected skin color to the predicament of the soul, bifurcating humans into categories marked by race: savage and civilized.

Charles Long rightly notes that racial narrative was appended to colonial policies: "The notion of race became the theater of the entire European myth of conquest, while the color of the Indian assured his admission to the theater on the basis of race. The myth of the Indian and the African as inferior human beings, lazy, savage, heathen, wild, noble and ignoble—the crass and vulgar side of the dramatic myths of the Elizabethans—took on popular expression only after the real issue of domination had been decided, at a time when the native peoples of the Americas could no longer hamper European exploration and exploitation."[15]

Colonialism preceded the category of race as defined by color and other characteristics. According to the racial theorist Robert Bernasconi, "The invention of the concept of race ... took place some time after the introduction of the broad division of peoples on the basis of color, nationality, and other inherited characteristics that could not be overcome subsequently, as religious differences could be overcome by conversion."[16] Hence religion precedes race in a chain of colonizing events.

The biblical scholar Musa Dube delineates the relationship between Scripture and colonization, repeating a traditional African story: "When the white man came to our country he had the Bible and we had the land. The white man said to us, 'let us pray.' After the prayer, the white man had the land and we had the Bible."[17] As she explains it, the Bible "facilitated" European Christian violence and imperialism. Armed with readings of their sacred text, Christian missionaries believed they had been "divinely commissioned" to dispossess and colonize natives, convinced that in doing so, they lived out Christ's commandment as recorded in Matthew 28:18–20: "Go ... and make disciples of all nations," teaching them to "obey everything" that he has commanded them. Dube's exegetical reading of Scripture uncovers the colonial plan: "Outsiders must not only be characterized as evil and dangerous, womenlike, and worthless dogs but also be seen as those who beg for salvation from a very reluctant and nationalistic Jesus."[18] These discourses of religious and national otherness yielded colonialist narratives fixated on race.

Racializing discourses emerged from a rhizomatous structure with a vast and complex network of sites for the reiteration of racial propositions; it is possible to trace and chart connections between them, producing a genealogy of racial appearance. In his *Pagans in the Promised Land*, Steven T. Newcomb has mapped the points of articulation between the Doctrine of Christian Discovery, dispossession, colonization, and U.S. federal Indian law. The crux of their relationship for Newcomb was in the papal bull *Inter Caetera* of May 4, 1493, where "Pope Alexander [VI] declared it his desire that 'barbarous nations' be overthrown or subjugated and brought to the Catholic faith and Christian religion 'for the honor of God himself and for the spread of the Christian Empire.'"[19] The bull began by appealing to the authority of "Almighty God, Peter, and the Vicarship of Jesus Christ." Once a Christian monarch had vested that power in explorers, it gave them the right to claim all lands "discovered," so that they would be inhabited by Christians.

Non-Christian lands were thereby deemed uninhabited and consequently available to be "discovered," claimed, and exploited, with the proviso that if the "pagan" occupants could be converted, they might be spared. If not, they could be enslaved or killed. In 1823 the landmark Supreme Court decision in *Johnson v. McIntosh* affirmed the tragic Doctrine of Christian Discovery, deciding that Indians were not living in conditions that qualified as proper occupation or possession of lands occupied by Christian crowns. Chief Justice John Marshall, in his written opinion, cited the fifteenth-century papal bull and established religion as a legal foundation for racial superiority and colonization. The opening passage of the ruling proclaims that "the vast extent" of the American continent "offered an ample field to the ambition and enterprise of all; and the character and religion of its inhabitants afforded an apology for considering them as people over whom the superior genius of Europe might claim ascendancy."[20] As Newcomb demonstrates, *Johnson* became the basis for several court decisions dispossessing Indians because of their perceived natural inferiority, registered by their "heathenism." In the *Johnson* ruling, religion produces race.

Racialization is a myth told about God in the sense that race has been thought to be embedded in the very fabric of divine creation. Race is also a colonial story. Colonizing necessitated a distinct Christian theology, articulated in the fifteenth-century Doctrine of Discovery, according to which non-Christians constitute a discrete caste based on a spiritual condition expressed in what the historian of religions Charles Long has called "the absurd meanings" of their obscure bodies, from which fresh religious meanings arose. According to Long: "These opaque ones were centers from which gods were made. They were the concrete embodiments of matter made significant in the modern world. They formed new rhythms in time and space; these bodies of opacity were facts of history and symbols of a new religious depth."[21]

In other words, racism originated in a modern mythology of human hierarchy wherein people of color occupied the lowest stages, their physical and (presumed) spiritual conditions marking them as savage—a trope that justified their subjugation. The bodies of the colonized became the focus of an emergent discourse and its attendant human constructions. Long argued, "The self-conscious realization of the Western European rise to the level of civilization must be seen simultaneously in its relationship to the discovery of a new world which must necessarily be perceived as inhabited by savages and primitives who constitute the lowest rung on the ladder of cultural reality."[22] Hence dismantling colonization and its child, race, requires telling grand counternarratives—myths—about the cosmos that challenge racializing narratives rooted in Christian mythology. Decolonization is religious work.

Like Gandhi and King, Chavez knew that race was a human invention, a lie at least as old as the beginnings of European imperialism, when crown and church justified the enslavement of black and brown peoples by asserting a natural—and biblical—order of being. In his prophetic labors, each of the three leaders sought to unravel the mythology of race and sever racism from religion. Rhetorical suasion required them to speak prophetically, telling a deeply holy cosmic story with God as protagonist—a countermythology that worked in the American master myth: both men announced fresh prophesies, performing versions of an American jeremiad.

In the United States, Christian racializing discourses colluded with those emanating from Enlightenment Deist thought. Beginning in the eighteenth century, imperial racialized narratives of humanity were enunciated as scientific truth and attributed to the Creator Deity. Following on the heels of Immanuel Kant's essay "Of the Different Human Races," first published in English in 1777, Deist thinkers in America stratified humanity. Perhaps Thomas Jefferson put it best in his essay entitled "Race," published in 1781: "The first difference which strikes us is that of color.... [The] difference is fixed in nature, and is as real as if its seat and cause were better known to us. And is this difference of no importance?"[23] Reflecting at once Enlightenment, Deist, and Christian reasoning, he considered racial differences to be prelinguistic, "fixed in nature," with "nature" signifying a Creator (God for some) who had designed the world to follow a distinct set of laws—especially racial mandates. For him racial mapping, as a religious exercise, depended on narratives of creation that reveal the order of the world existing in an idealized space well outside the capacity of language to represent.

Deist and Christian mission projects producing racializing discourses required the existence of God, idiosyncratically construed, if they were to tell stories that allowed them to fulfill their colonial destinies. European colonizing occasioned the production of an episteme that delimited humanity to justify the internecine horrors of imperialism, especially Native American dispossession, genocide, and African enslavement. Corporeality yielded cosmic meanings, answering metaphysical questions: Who is favored by God? Who should rule? Who should perform various types of labor? In the United States, Protestant-ism came to mark civilization. In the Puritan model, the unrepentant "savages" were subhuman, incidental, often an obstacle to God's heavenly plan.

Jefferson concluded his meditations on race with a chilling proposition: "I advance it therefore as a suspicion only, that the blacks, whether originally a distinct race [owing to polygenesis] or made distinct by time and circumstances, are inferior to the whites in the endowments both of body and mind. It is not against experience to suppose, that different species of the same genus, or varieties of the same species, may possess different qualifications."[24] Article 1, section 2, of the U.S. Constitution reflected this suspicion in apportioning representation in the House of Representatives among the states according to a formula that counted each slave in the state's population as three-fifths of a free person; Indians were explicitly not counted at all.

Mexico and Native Mexicans were likewise subjected to dehumanizing racial discursive practices. Spanish invaders justified the atrocities of colonial conquest with elaborate constructions of human hierarchies said to be formed by God; European Christian men stood at the top, and indigenous women were at the bottom.[25] Catholic thinkers were in a bind: missionizing the Indians was the core rationale for colonization, but if Native Americans were deemed inhuman, bereft of souls, then they were incapable of receiving Christian salvation—the mission of the Christian churches. This quandary was articulated and recorded in debates waged in Spain, resonating in arguments justifying war against Islamic "infidels." The realization that Indians were not Muslims prompted new imperial questions. The historian of religions Davíd Carrasco explains: "Treatment of native peoples became so brutal and dehumanizing, justified in part by racial stereotypes, that in 1550 Charles V of Spain suspended all expeditions to America and summoned into session a *junta* of foremost theologians. This Council of the Fourteen, in Valladolid, Spain, was called to consider a debate on the question of whether it is 'lawful for the King to wage war on the Indians before preaching the faith to them in order to subject them to his rule, so that afterwards, they may more easily be instructed in the faith.'"[26]

Central to this debate were the competing monologues of Juan Ginés de Sepúlveda (1489–1573), a champion of Indian enslavement, and the Indian advocate bishop of Chiapas, Mexico, the Dominican Bartolomé de las Casas (1484–1566). Ginés de Sepúlveda argued that the natives were less than human and were therefore "natural slaves." His analogy became foundational for racial construction in the Americas:

> And all of this is by natural decree and law, which commands that the most perfect and powerful should rule over the imperfect and unequal.... By this law, man rules over woman, the adult over the child, the father over his children, that is to say, the most powerful and most perfect over the weakest and most imperfect.
>
> The same thing is seen among men, with some being masters by nature, and others being slaves. Those who exceed others in prudence and intelligence, if not in physical strength, are by nature masters; those, on the other hand, who are mentally slow and lazy, though they have the physical strength to fulfill all their necessary obligations, are by nature slaves, and it is useful that they be, and we even see this sanctioned by divine law itself.[27]

Las Casas opposed the enslavement of Indians by means of the *encomienda* or *repartimiento* systems, wherein natives were regarded as beasts and allotted to Spanish conquistadores as property. He insisted that Indians constituted a civil society by Aristotelian categories—in short, that they were humans—and therefore their souls should be cared for so they could achieve Christian salvation. Las Casas stands as first in a long line of dissenters in the Church who have worked for social justice for Indians under colonial and postcolonial rule. But in a sense both sides in the debate won, for the Spanish Crown proceeded with its evangelizing mission but also treated the colonized Indians as if they were less human than Christian Spaniards. Although they were capable of receiving salvation, they constituted a degraded form of humanity that needed to be civilized, their capacity for reason more akin to that of children than that of adults.

By the eighteenth century, dehumanization was charted in colonial Spain by elaborate categories of racial miscegenation, each with its attendant social location, illustrated literally in the lucrative art of "caste" paintings. In these paintings caste mixings ranged from the simple Indian combined with Spaniard, to produce a mestizo, to elaborate fantasies of reemergent whiteness, known as a "torno atrás" (literally, "a turn back").[28] These categories, which tied race to God, caste, and labor, produced at least sixteen distinct registers. The most prominent of them were the mestizos (half Amerindian and half Spanish), castizos (three-fourths Spanish and one-fourth Amerindian), cholos (three-fourths Amerindian and one-fourth Spanish), and zambos (half Amerindian and half African). The level of Spanish Christian blood became the measure of humanity. Any Spaniard tainted by Indian plasma was assigned a lower step on the staircase of human progress. In 1822 Mexico officially banned the practice of racial designation; but it continued in church baptismal records.

Meanwhile, across the northern border, nineteenth-century American thinkers elaborated myths of America and Americans as chosen by God, most favored among global peoples and granted a destiny that wedded imperialism to notions of nature, civilization, and human progress. President Andrew Jackson's Indian Removal Act of 1830 described even the so-called civilized Indian tribes as "children in need of guidance." He argued that removing natives "will separate the Indians from immediate contact with settlements of whites ... enable them to pursue happiness in their own way and under their own rude institutions ... and perhaps cause them gradually, under the protection of the Government and through the influences of good counsels, to cast off their savage habits and become an interesting, civilized, and Christian community."

In 1839 John O'Sullivan published "The Great Nation of Futurity," an essay that enunciated the myths propelling manifest destiny. In it he refashioned old discourses into newly (narrowly) refined deployments.

All this will be our future history, to establish on earth the moral dignity and salvation of man—the immutable truth and beneficence of God. For this blessed mission to the nations of the world, which are shut out from the life-giving light of truth, has America been chosen; and her high example shall smite unto death the tyranny of kings, hierarchs, and oligarchs, and carry the glad tidings of peace and good will where myriads now endure an existence scarcely more enviable than that of beasts of the field. Who, then, can doubt that our country is destined to be *the great nation* of futurity?[29]

Manifest destiny collapsed narratives of skin color, religion, and spirituality or personality, implying God's preference for European races, while concomitantly dehumanizing Mexicans.

Similarly, Richard Henry Dana's *Two Years before the Mast,* published in 1840, noted the spectrum of skin colors of the Californians, correlating darker pigmentation with declinations of industry and the increase of idleness and superstition, leading him to declare, "In the hands of an enterprising people, what a country this might be!"[30] His rhetorical proposition echoed O'Sullivan's and informed James Polk's discourses on war with Mexico, a country Polk referred to as "uncivilized, untrustworthy, and menacing." Often overlooked in discussions of manifest destiny are the idea's long history and subtle mutations.

Americans have believed and invested in their glorious calling since the earliest Christian invasion of Indian territories, inspired by delusional sermonizing, ratifying a contract with God that sanctioned conquest, occupation, and genocide. John Winthrop, in his sermon of 1630 "A Model of Christian Charity," sought to quiet rational misgivings about the Puritans' imperial enterprise by proposing a calculation of God's grace. Should his sectarians run afoul of their part of the bargain with the Divine, they would perish. Should their revelation prove true, however, their hard work would earn history's blessings and God Himself would see to it that they flourished and bore fruit. Accumulation and prosperity, then, became the metric of salvation.

The "savages" played minor roles in a divine tragedy whose plot, which entailed decimating or enslaving Indigenous populations while snaring Americans in a psychic iron cage of their own design, culminated in a Protestant sect (Capitalism) whose never-ending process of material acquisition itself represents at once spiritual redemption and subjugation.[31] Central to this divine world order was the human binary: civilized and savage, a couplet pivoting on the dogma of the human soul and its materialization in the human body. The colonists, in perpetuating violence against Indians, not only discharged personal anxieties, but also received the psychic bonus of displacing religious doubt. God's grace was confirmed in, and measured by, Indian corpses littering the promised land, opening spaces for Christians to bear fruit.[32]

Even after the Mexican war, the sense of white Christian civilization in opposition to dark savagery and the convergence of ideas about religion and race suffused the discourse of manifest destiny. In John Gast's 1872 painting *American Progress,* a young woman, wearing a chiton, flies gracefully westward. Her name is America. On her forehead she sports the "Star of Empire"; in her right hand she has a schoolbook; in her left is a line of cable that she dispenses. Indians, fleeing her approach, disappear into the fury of storm waves in the Pacific Ocean. According to George A. Crofutt, who reproduced Gast's painting as a chromolithograph for subscribers in 1872, the "Star" was "too much for them."[33]

In 1885 Josiah Strong, a Presbyterian minister and champion of the social gospel, made the following prediction: "The time is coming when the pressure of population on the means of subsistence will be felt here as it is now felt in Europe and Asia. Then will the world enter upon a new stage of its history—the final competition of races, for which the Anglo-Saxon is being schooled.... If I read not amiss, this powerful race will move down upon Mexico.... And can anyone doubt that the result of this competition of races will be the 'survival of the fittest'?"[34] A few years later, the historian of the American West Hubert Howe Bancroft, in his revisionist and apologetic history, obscured the porous border between race and religion, describing Mexicans in California as "the largest order of animals then known, as well as the dirtiest; a people wholly lying in wickedness and lacking soap. They were supercilious, yet ignorant and superstitious, and full of beastly habits."[35] These accounts were the antecedents of the narratives Chavez confronted in which religion, race, and political power coalesced.

John Gregory Dunne, in his book *Delano*, of 1967, recounts the details of a University of California study of farm workers, prepared in 1920, that ascribed behavioral characteristics to race and nature: "Mexicans were 'childish, lazy, unambitious'; ... Hindus were 'lean, lanky and enervated'; and Negroes were 'notorious prevaricators.'" Dunne lamented this racism, describing this report as "the dogma of ethnically sensitive California."[36] These dehumanizing constructions were used in justifying the exploitation of Mexican farm labor. One Delano grower declared: "We protect our farmers here in Kern County. They are our best people. They are always with us. They keep the country going.... But the Mexicans are trash. They have no standard of living. We herd them like pigs."[37] Racial subjugation in the United States and elsewhere is a product of a discourse that fantasizes levels of humanity; the narrative of that subjugation is associated with nature, theism, and Christendom.

REHUMANIZATION

Chavez was a product of "internal colonization,"[38] which begins with a forced entry into territories claimed by an imperial regime. Colonial subjects, marked by their questionable humanity, are concentrated in peripheral spaces and forced into the secondary labor market. Chavez, mindful of the root of the problem, struggled for the rehumanization of farm workers. In 1965 he criticized Mexico's attitude toward agricultural laborers: "The Mexican consulate seems to think, or they act, at least, as if they own the man's body and soul."[39] In 1966, at congressional hearings on farm workers held in Delano, the leader articulated the prevailing racial ideology that kept Chicanos subjugated. Nothing had changed, he bemoaned: "The same exploitation of child labor, the same idea that farm workers are a different breed of people—humble, happy, built close to the ground—prevails."[40]

Chavez identified his movement as, at its core, a struggle for the rehumanization of people who were once colonized, or decolonial rehumanization:

> No issue can get people excited and interested in doing something about a problem as much as when personal dignity is involved. No injury is greater than not being looked upon as a human being. The deepest kind of hurt is when you find you're not welcome, when even by the tone of voice you are addressed, you know that you are not considered to be anyone. The working conditions and the wages, the lack of drinking water, the lack of education, the lack of housing, all hurt but not so deeply as personal injury. Wages are not our main issue in the strike. If this was our main issue, it would disappear after you got the union in to get an increase in the pay.... We cannot help people or even help ourselves unless we understand first of all that they are human beings.[41]

The problem of dehumanization straddled the U.S.–Mexican border.

According to Dunne, "Whatever one felt about the movement itself, few would deny that a vast body of the American public were second-class citizens, none more so than the Mexican-American farm workers." Chavez evoked the issue of rehumanization again in January 1974, after nineteen Mexican farm workers, who had crossed the border to tend crops in California, were killed in a bus accident. In his eulogy, he unearthed the cause of the accident as racism's persistent dehumanizing of the farm workers: "There have been too many accidents in the fields ... so many accidents involving farm workers. People ask if they are deliberate. They are deliberate in the sense that they are the direct result of a farm labor system that treats workers like agricultural implements and not human beings."[42]

Similarly, Martin Luther King recognized the master colonial discourse that dehumanizes populations and thereby legitimates their domination, remarking while in India: "I am absolutely convinced that there is no basic difference between colonialism and segregation. They are both based on a contempt for life, and a tragic doctrine of white supremacy. So our struggles are not only similar; they are in a real sense one."[43]

Gandhi, King, and Chavez confronted the same beast. Modern colonial governments encoded racial prejudice into godly idioms of statecraft, particularly the governance of colonized peoples. A totalizing racial hierarchy, according to which so-called inferior peoples benefited from the tutelage of the advanced and civilized, became essential to the global development of modern industrial markets and labor systems. Initially, this ideal hierarchical order was thought natural, something that came from God. The enslavement of Africans, the genocide perpetrated against Native Americans, the conquest of Mexico and the exploitation of Mexican Americans, and the conquest of India were all driven by the modern racial assumptions that delimit the humanity of the vanquished.

For Gandhi the connection between religion and race was clear, woven into the Hindu caste system and reified in the colonial mechanism of regulation by the British. The term *caste* derives from the Portuguese word for "color," and, as we have seen, color, as the condition of one's birth, determined human status and its attendant social value in the colonized Americas. *Varna*, a Sanskrit term that also means "color" or caste, has four categories: Brahmans (priests), Kshatriyas (kings and nobles), Vaisyas (merchants), and Sudras (servants and workers). Under these broad divisions exist the *Jati*, a pan-Indian term denoting the thousands of different birth groups. The *varna* and *Jati* system functioned regionally, organized according to local agricultural labor relationships. Endogamy characterized the caste system, as well as the rules governing social intercourse and labor. Those who fell outside the caste system, that is, those thought to be without an inherited caste, were known as untouchables, and these outcastes bore the stigma of pollution.

When the British colonized India in 1858, they instituted a national census that reified and cemented the caste system, conceiving and redesigning it as a racial hierarchy that corresponded to occupation and socioeconomic status. According to Diane Mines, "Because the population was enumerated by caste in the census, and because British officials recognized caste as an authentic category of public interest at a national level, Indian subjects responded by participating in the creation of caste as a route to self-understanding as well as political organization."[44]

Gandhi's views on caste evolved over his life. He was from the Vaisya, or merchant caste, and his name translates as "grocer." He defied expectations for his own caste by traveling to England to study law. When he began establishing his South African ashrams in 1904, he eschewed class boundaries, requiring that residents perform all types of work without distinction, including cleaning toilets—a task reserved for the outcastes in traditional Indian society. Beginning in 1916, he consistently opposed dividing humanity into higher and lower castes. Until 1926, however, he upheld the four major caste distinctions, believing that they provided needed discipline and organization. Nonetheless, he was a longtime opponent of the outcaste designation and advocated its eradication. He sought to rename the untouchables Harijan, or "Children of God," a name that was ultimately rejected, considered patronizing and condescending, in favor of Dalit, or "Scheduled Classes."

During the 1920s Gandhi became embroiled in a debate with the Indian congressional leader B.R. Ambedkar (1891–1956), who was himself from the outcastes. Gandhi sought to work within Hinduism to reform the caste system and to redefine the untouchables, giving them greater rights of citizenship and equality. Ambedkar disagreed, however, arguing, according to Mines, that "caste had its origins in religion and Brahmanical Hinduism in particular. Religion, therefore, could not be the course for real change. Ambedkar called for the legal abolition of caste." Yet that extreme proposition, because it alienated the religious population, was unsuccessful. In 1932 Gandhi and Ambedkar reached a compromise, which "resolved to end discrimination against Untouchables in the use of public wells, schools, and roads and also advanced the cause of temple entry."[45]

Ultimately the mahatma advocated the abandonment of prohibitions separating the classes, including that of intermarriage. In 1935 his "denunciation of the entire caste system was complete; he authored an article entitled 'Caste Has to Go' and declared that 'untouchability' is a crime against humanity."[46] Gandhi wavered on this question, however. He once said: "My aim is not to be consistent with my earlier statements on a given question, but to be consistent with the truth as it presents itself to me at a given moment."[47]

King's battle for rehumanization reached fruition in 1968 during his campaign to support striking sanitation workers in Memphis. There, over two hundred striking workers marched, wearing sandwich boards declaring: "I Am a Man," addressing centuries-old myths that assign people of color a less-than-human status. The fact that rehumanization struggles have been waged in male terms has not escaped the critical purview of feminists of color. Cherríe Moraga has written: "Men have to give up their subscription to male superiority. I remember during the Civil Rights Movement seeing newsreel footage of young Black men carrying protest signs reading 'I AM A MAN.' It was a powerful statement, publicly declaring their humanness in a society that daily told them otherwise. But they didn't write 'I AM HUMAN,' they wrote 'MAN.' Conceiving of their liberation in male terms, they were unwittingly demanding the right to share the whiteman's position of male dominance."[48] Moraga evokes Sojourner Truth's "Ain't I a Woman?" speech, in which her call for "a free Black womanhood in a Black- and woman-hating society required the freedom of all enslaved and disenfranchised peoples."[49]

Early on in his work, Chavez spoke to men, especially in his most formidable statement, when he terminated his 1968 fast for nonviolence: "God help us to be men." At that time he identified men as the problem; he was unable, on several levels, to critique womanhood. His movement was principally humanistic, struggling for full rehumanization. In 1969 he summarized this mandate as follows: "As human beings we have a very special mission in this life, and that is service to humanity."[50]

PROPHECY

Chavez's campaign for rehumanization was a moral crusade in which he deployed religious elements—myths, rituals, and symbols from different traditions. His religious identification, complex and fluctuating, erudite and innovative, was central to establishing his "prophetic" vocation.[51] Thus, Richard Rodriguez is only partially correct when he asserts: "Chavez wielded a spiritual authority … [;] if it was political at all, it was not mundane and had to be exerted in large, priestly ways or it was squandered."[52] Chavez says he did in fact consider the Catholic priesthood. "I guess one time I thought about becoming a priest," he told Matthiessen, "but I did this instead and I'm happy to be a part of it."[53]

The sociology of religion makes a categorical distinction between a prophet and a priest. According to Max Weber, a prophet is "a purely individual bearer of charisma, who by virtue of his mission proclaims a religious doctrine or divine commandment." For Weber, to have charisma meant to be endowed with "extraordinary powers," a magnetic attraction. Chavez's followers claimed to believe that he was endowed with those extraordinary powers Weber called charisma.[54] Eugene Nelson wrote admiringly of the leader as follows: "He undoubtedly has a great deal of personal magnetism which is probably the single greatest key to his success, as well as an undeniably keen intelligence and exceedingly pleasant if not handsome appearance. There is something arrestingly candid about him when one first meets him."[55]

Weber drew "no radical distinction" between "a 'renewer of religion' who preaches an older revelation, actual or supposititious, and a 'founder of religion' who claims to bring completely new deliverances. The two types merge into one another."[56] Chavez fits this description insofar as his mission blurred the border between renewing Christianity; emphasizing its capacity for ecumenicalism and its core teachings on service to others, especially the poor; and efforts to establish what appears in many respects to be a new religious movement—*La Causa*.

For Weber, the distinction between priest and prophet turns on the matter of the "personal call." A priest is a keeper of tradition who emanates authority by virtue of his office, whereas a prophet lays claim to spiritual authority based on a divine revelation. The key is charisma and how it obtains. The vocation of prophet affords a more powerful and accessible charismatic potency; the priesthood has staying power. Prophetic charisma is subject to decline, routinization, and demise; charismatic fire burns hot and fast, as it did for Chavez in *La Causa*.

Weber's figuration of the prophet is either *ethical*, text based, or *exemplary*, based in image and symbol. Chavez was both an ethical and an exemplary prophet—deploying both word and sign, bridging the idioms of Protestantism (text) and Catholicism (ritual). As such, he spoke on behalf of the poor and of the oppressed without respect to denomination, claiming his message a fresh revelation received directly from God. Perhaps most important in relation to Chavez is that the prophetic hero *seizes* rather than *submits* to power. The prophet may act like an outlaw if his or her truth requires civil disobedience, a teaching the leader embraced at least partly as a result of his reading of Henry David Thoreau.

His mythology did not emerge out of nowhere. Like the sociologist's prophet, Chavez stressed parts of extant religious teachings that had been underemphasized; in addition, he reinterpreted doctrines. His mythos is unique for the way it was assembled, not necessarily for the individual pieces themselves. A religious *bricoleur*, he picked and chose elements for a new assemblage: his was a borderlands tradition, unpure and heterodox, occupying a *nepantla* space between a living religion and an emerging religious formation. For Weber the priest and the prophet are at once purveyors of salvation, but the mode of their enunciation and its limit distinguish them. The prophet emphasizes the message, aims for the target by speaking a religious politics that includes a specific critique, a set of denunciations, a warning, and a program for change and justice—a jeremiad. A priest, in contrast, speaks to those already congregated. Organizing is not his main task. He or she speaks orthodoxy intended for a predetermined audience and for others who may be interested in the canonical discourse. The prophet, who speaks to all those concerned with a (re)new(ed) idea, can thereby unite disparate populations, a strategy used by King and Gandhi. But

Chavez too united people, particularly Mexicans and Filipinos, who had historically been at odds in Delano, and also people of various religions. According to Griswold del Castillo and Garcia, "Protestant ministers were drawn to *La Causa,* indicating another important Chavez strength: his ability to bridge the traditional mistrust and hostility between Roman Catholic and Protestant."[57]

Even as the leader spoke a prophetic message that would be described by Cornel West as "race transcending," he became absorbed into and synonymous with Chicano identity, and more than any other single leader, he moved *Chicanismo* from the margins to the center, spinning it into the American mix of culture. That is, he took the "natural symbols and paradigms within the minority tradition which can be recognized by the [dominant] group itself as characterizing its traditions. These must be vital symbols which pervade daily life and secular as well as sacred existence and are political as well as religious."[58] Chicanos needed to make an impact on the soul of America; toward this end the founder (re)defined the myths and symbols of *Chicanismo* for mass consumption.

THE CHICANO JEREMIAD

On July 4, 1969, Chavez was featured on the cover of *Time* magazine. The accompanying article dubbed him the "mystical" and "earthy" leader of the Mexican American civil rights movement, and the Chicano Martin Luther King Jr. The symbolism of the date, American Independence Day, bespeaks Chavez's status: he had become a prophet of America's political church, or its civil religion. Rather than think of America as a singular formation, however, it is perhaps better to think of multiple churches or congregations, organized around an imaginary union of like-minded believers, whose principal tenets are freedom and democracy and whose collective representation, the United States, is endowed with an aura of holiness that mixes the Constitution with the Bible. In the words of Gary Laderman, the nation has "multiple civil religions."[59] Freedom and liberty are empty signifiers, philosophical tropes void of meaning until they are given a context and attached to an event. Each discursive community understands and relates to these broad ideals through its own cultural, class, and racial filters, uploading group experience as the content of the form.

Middle-class and otherwise privileged white Protestants recognize their reflection in the national religious discourse and sign system. Those beliefs outside the mainstream require translation; they must be interpreted. Chavez translated *Chicanismo* for a national congregation, prophetically critiquing and reshaping the larger conversation on what it means to be an American—a mystical identity willed into being through the incantation *e pluribus unum*. Even while that declaration, "from the many one," was adopted as one of three official U.S. mottoes in 1781, few have understood it better than Chavez. *Chicanismo,* as construed by the leader and as lived by Mexican Americans, was a spiritual movement, a franchise of civil religion, a local instance of religious and political commitment, at first separate from but increasingly incorporated into a national commitment. This was the purpose and effect of Chavez's prophetic spiritual leadership.

The Chicano movement's foundational document, "El Plan Espiritual de Aztlán," introduced in 1969, established *Chicanismo* as a spiritual formation that provided its adherents with a statement of their primary and ultimate concerns—sovereignty and a return to the land. Mario T. García described his own conversion by saying that "*Chicanismo* replaced Catholicism as my faith."[60] Histories of the United States record a conflicted relationship between Chicana/os and the Catholic Church, characterized by a dual impulse toward resistance and affirmation, whereby, ironically, even the discourse of opposition is indelibly stamped by a Catholic moral imagination and a worldview broader than that of the catechism alone. The leader deployed Christian—especially Catholic—narratives and symbols as a (sometimes ironic) strategy to claim moral terrain, begging the question of the extent to which *Chicanismo* was then and is now a religious movement itself.

As catechistic excess spilled over boundaries—creating secular schisms, especially in the Mexican American civil rights struggles— the borders between sacred and profane were blurred, and contests over material matters assumed spiritual import, while the spiritual was materialized.

Chicana/o identity is not only conferred; one must also accept it; it needs to be affirmed by a speaking subject who has embraced its core principles and beliefs. In short, Chicana/o identity is performed, and the first ritual act is a confession of belief in Cesar Chavez. Consider the profession of the Chavista Gary Soto: "Cesar inspired us all through his will for justice, a will that was nonviolent, single-minded, and, dare I say, saintly.... Who could argue that his efforts were not pious? ... In the course of this movement, Cesar became—whether he accepted this status or not—a spiritual leader for all Chicanos. He had no choice; we needed him to remind us of our social responsibilities; today we need him more than ever."[61]

In May 1969 Chavez met with a group of Chicano leaders in El Paso, Texas. According to their description, "They were constructing a new spiritual reality around a man who, for the most part, just listened. Nobody said so, but many perceived Chavez as a spiritual rather than a political leader—a savior in their midst."[62] In 1972 Luis A. Solis-Garza published an essay in which he asked, rhetorically: "Cesar Chavez: The Chicano Messiah?" He concluded: "To be sure, he has a certain messianic quality about him which draws people to him, and yet Chavez firmly denies being a great leader. Still, his following grows larger, and Cesar Chavez's denial grows almost futile. In an age where the world offers little hope to people of all races, Chavez and his movement stand out."[63] That same year, Meier and Rivera ranked Chavez first among the "Four Horseman," the Chicano leadership, describing him as "a gentle apostle of a non-violent approach to reform, [who] quickly became recognized as a spiritual leader of Chicanos."[64] The entry on Cesar Chavez in the *Dictionary of Chicano Folklore,* published in 2000, described him as a "spiritual savior," who "became almost a divine leader," who had a "spiritual aura about him" that lifted his "presence" above the "temporal" to the "mythical."[65]

Oscar Zeta Acosta, in his historical novel *The Revolt of the Cockroach People,* published in 1973, described Chavez as a "guru" for Chicanos, confessing: "All through law school, my secret dream had been to work for Chavez and the *campesinos.*" Acosta told of his pilgrimage to see the leader on the last day of his twenty-five-day fast in 1968, painting the scene as follows: "We are inside the chapel. Everything, including the altar, is homemade.... An oil painting of *La Virgen de Guadalupe,* the patron saint of the *campesino,* hangs above the flowers.... There is no Christ in the homey green temple." As Acosta approached the fasting leader, he heard: "Is that you, Buffalo?" Much later, after the two men had spoken and sat in silence, Acosta wrote of his wonder that "The Father of Chicanos, Cesar Chavez, has *heard* of me." He narrated the conclusion of this emotional meeting:

> Again he falls back. I hold my breath until I can hear his own breathing. Now it is my turn to sigh deeply as I wipe tears from my squinting eyes. The door opens behind me. The woman puts her finger to her mouth to indicate my time is up. I arise to leave.
> "Buffalo?"
> "Yeah, Cesar."
> "You go back to LA and take care of business, OK, *viejo?*"[66]

According to Acosta (and others), this meeting inspired Chicano activists in East Los Angeles to form a political group that they called Católicos por la Raza (CPLR). CPLR gained fame for holding a disruptive protest at the newly erected St. Basil's Cathedral on fashionable Wilshire Boulevard on Christmas Eve 1969. Ricardo Cruz, the founder of CPLR, traveled to Salinas to organize workers; there he met the leader and, before leaving, "Cruz promised Chavez he would see what he could do to get Church support."[67]

Chavez defined and embodied *Chicanismo,* prophetically translating his enigmatic identity construct(s) into the American vernacular for a society with evolving attitudes about race, labor, and humanity.

A SINGLE GARMENT OF DESTINY: IN LIGHT OF
MARTIN LUTHER KING AND GANDHI

The lives of Gandhi, King, and Chavez shared key themes, and the work of the three men has also shared a critical reception marked by intellectual devaluation. A writer analyzing King's life and work considered the minister "neither a systematic theologian nor a great religious thinker. His ideas always arose not from theoretical reflection but from the specific demands of a concrete historical situation that required an active response."[68] Another writer has made a similar claim about the mahatma: "Gandhi was neither a theorist nor philosopher."[69] In one sense these claims contribute to the mythology of the unexceptional and thus accessible common man. Yet King, unlike Chavez, had advanced degrees in theology and wrote philosophical treatises on love and nonviolence. Gandhi was a barrister; he coined the term *satyagraha*. His quest was for truth, a master pursuit he shared with philosophers.

Like Chavez, King and Gandhi countermythologized, creating philosophical, religious, and political myths that confronted and dismantled racial memory. That each man articulated a religious response to dehumanization binds together the movements of all three leaders. Each emphasized that the racialized are equally children of God, and that to regard them as less offends the Creator. Each arrived at this realization after a rite of passage; their myths are psychosocial dramas of separation, trial, and return. Although Gandhi is said to have been quiet and shy, he shunned caste expectations and abandoned his native India to become a barrister, first in England and then in South Africa, before returning home to work for Indian independence from Britain. King, after graduating from Morehouse College, left his childhood home and his father's church in Atlanta, Georgia, to study in the North and then to take a congregation in Birmingham, Alabama, before returning to his hometown, where he founded the Southern Christian Leadership Conference (SCLC) in 1957. All three men were more or less working class, but only Chavez's story tells of extreme deprivation.

Gandhi died in 1948; King and Chavez knew him only through his writings and his followers. King claimed that Gandhi had been the inspiration for his movement since the beginning of the Montgomery bus boycott. In 1959 King made a "pilgrimage" to India, where he met with Gandhi's disciples, including Prime Minister Jawaharlal Nehru (1889–1964). This visit enabled King to draw connections between the struggles of the internally colonized minorities in the United States and global anticolonial struggles. The Indians regarded King as a brother because of his skin color. "But the strongest bond of fraternity," he said, "was the common cause of minority and colonial peoples in America, Africa, and Asia struggling to throw off racism and imperialism."[70] King and Chavez agreed that the conditions of racialized minorities in the United States replicated those of the colonized around the world, beginning with the discourses on the meaning of being human. Along these lines, Chavez compared his struggles to those of Gandhi: "Oh, there are a lot of similarities. Gandhi was dealing with the powerless and the poor and the ones who were discriminated against, and we have that now—the poor, and the people who are discriminated against. We have classism, racism. Gandhi was also working against foreign domination, and this is similar to our situation in that agribusiness is really like a foreign domination. They don't live here."[71]

Chavez came increasingly to imbricate his own mythology with that of Gandhi. In 1968 he told Matthiessen: "I read everything I could get my hands on, Gandhi, and I read some of the things that he had read, and I read Thoreau, which I liked very much. But I couldn't really understand Gandhi until I was actually in the fast; then the book became much more clear. Things I understood but didn't feel—well, in the fast I *felt* them, and there were some real insights. There wasn't a day or a night that I lost. I slept in the day when I could, and at night, and I read."[72] Yet a standard trope in the literature, beginning very early, was to diminish Chavez in relation to Gandhi and King. In 1966 Nelson wrote: "Whether Cesar Chavez will become the Martin Luther King of the Mexican-Americans remains to be seen. While he has penned no brilliant essays like King's, he has demonstrated remarkable leadership qualities, and there is no one else of his stature in sight in the Mexican-American community."[73]

In 1974 Jacques Levy claimed that Chavez "knew very little about Gandhi except for what he read in papers and saw in newsreels."[74] By contrast, in 1988 Chavez claimed that he had spent his life studying Gandhi:

> I was eleven or twelve years old, and I went to a movie. In those days, in between movies they had newsreels, and in one of the newsreels there was a report on Gandhi. It said that this half-naked man without a gun had con-quered the might of the British empire.... It really impressed me because I couldn't conceive of how that had happened without guns. Even though I had never heard the name Gandhi before, the next day I went to my teacher and asked her if she knew anything about him. She said, "No, but I have a friend who knows quite a bit about him." Then she gave me the name of her friend, a construction worker who was studying Gandhi. He gave me a little book on Gandhi. As I grew up, I started learning more, and ever since then, I have made a life project of reading about Gandhi and his message.[75]

Chavez's story rings true for the level of detail it offers. In 1974, how-ever, Levy reported a different story that is repeated in virtually all the secondary literature. In it the leader was tutored by Father Donald McDonnell, a missionary priest who in 1952 began ministering to Sal Si Puedes, a Chicano barrio in San Jose, California.

> That's when I started reading the Encyclicals, St. Francis, and Gandhi....
>
> In the St. Francis biography, there was a reference to Gandhi and others who practiced nonviolence. That was a theme that struck a very responsive chord, probably because of the foundation laid by my mother. So the next thing I read after St. Francis was the Louis Fischer biography of Gandhi.
>
> Since then I've been greatly influenced by Gandhi's philosophy and have read a great deal about what he said and did. But in those days I knew very little about him except what I read in the papers and saw in news-reels.... Gandhi was going to a meeting with a high British official in India. There were throngs of people as he walked all but naked out of his little hut....

Not too long ago I was speaking to a group of Indians including three who had worked with Gandhi. When I said I thought Gandhi was the most perfect man, not including Christ, they all laughed.[76]

It is possible, however unlikely, that both stories are true even though they offer conflicting accounts of when Chavez began reading Gandhi. Another possibility is that he came to believe that a stronger association with Gandhi better served his mythology.

A QUESTION OF (NON)VIOLENCE

By the 1950s colonized peoples began organizing en masse to resist their exploitation, many formulating military responses to it. The question for the colonized was no longer whether to revolt, but whether to revolt by violent means. Gandhi, King, and Chavez agreed: nonviolence was the way. In this agreement the synergism of the leaders reached a culmination. King and Chavez looked to Gandhi's twin principles of ahimsa, or the Vedic principle of nonviolence, and satyagraha, or "truth force"—a term Gandhi coined to describe the principle of his movement: the striving toward truth and a self-sacrificial love.[77] Gandhi's master text was the Bhagavad Gita; Gandhi called it a "spiritual reference book." But he also read Thoreau and was a disciple of Leo Tolstoy, the Russian guru of nonviolence and revolutionary communal living.

Gandhi espoused principles he found in the Gita, particularly *sarvodaya*—a principle of service to others that especially resonated with Chavez—and ahimsa; *himsa* is the Sanskrit word for "violence," and *ahimsa* means "against violence or refraining from violence." "No one has been able to describe God fully," Gandhi claimed, and "the same can be said for ahimsa."[78] Gandhi's original philosophical contribution, however, is the teaching of satyagraha, which he developed in 1906. According to one translator, "*Satya* means 'truth' in Sanskrit, and comes from *sat*, which means simply 'that which is.' The idea behind *satya* is that truth alone exists.... Evil, injustice, hatred, Gandhi argued, exist only insofar as we support them; they have no existence of their own.

Without our cooperation, unintentional or intentional, injustice cannot continue. This is the great spiritual teaching behind nonviolent noncooperation."[79]

Gandhi claimed that he developed the concept—prompted by the Zulu "rebellion," which took place when he was in South Africa—even before coining the term. He wrote in *My Experiments with Truth:* "When . . . I found that the term 'passive resistance' was too narrowly construed, that it was supposed to be a weapon of the weak, that it could be characterized by hatred, and that it could finally manifest itself as violence, I had to demur to all these statements and explain the real nature of the Indian movement. It was clear that a new word must be coined by the Indians to designate their struggle."[80] He announced a public competition to create the new term. It ultimately produced the word *satyagraha.*

Satyagraha is to be used with someone, not against someone. Meant to convert an opponent into a friend, it emphasizes the importance of the interrelationship between "faith in the goodness of [people], truth, non-violence, self-suffering, the relationship of the means to the end, a rejection of coercion, and fearlessness."[81] When Gandhi and Chavez fasted publicly, however, that act was largely misinterpreted as a response to and protest against a particular opponent. In 1932 Gandhi staged a fast after the Indian National Congress passed a law that granted a separate vote to the Dalit population. Because of the fast, the Indian Congress relented and repealed the law. In 1947 the mahatma fasted to oppose the partition of India. Similarly, Chavez, in May 1972, began a twenty-four-day fast in Phoenix to protest a set of Arizona laws that prohibited UFW strike and boycott activities. He denied that his action was a hunger strike meant to pressure the legislature. In a statement issued June 4, ending the fast, he described his purpose as follows: "The Fast was meant as a call to sacrifice for justice and a reminder of how much suffering there is among farm workers." He made no mention of the Arizona statutes.

Gandhi elaborated *satyagraha* as "pure soul-force. Truth is the very substance of the soul. That is why this force is called satyagraha. The soul is informed with knowledge. In it burns the flame of love. If someone gives us pain through ignorance, we shall win him through love."[82] He deified truth: "My prayerful search gave me the revealing maxim 'Truth is God' instead of the usual one, 'God is Truth.' That maxim enables me to see God face to face as it were. I feel Him pervade every fiber of my being."[83] Even though Gandhi referred to God using the male pronoun, it is clear in his equation that God is a metaphor, a way of righteous being in the world. Chavez proclaimed similarly, "Truth is nonviolence. So everything really comes from truth. Truth is the ultimate. Truth is God.... Truth is on our side, even more than justice, because truth can't be changed. It has a way of manifesting itself. It has to come out, so sooner or later we'll win."[84] His acceptance of eventuality, of what would happen "sooner or later," and his orientation to time set him apart from King; I develop that difference below.

For Chavez, satyagraha involved temporality, numbers, and sacrifice—sacrifice in the form of what Gandhi called *tapasya,* which means "heat" and has emerged from the Vedas to refer to purposeful ritual suffering, self-mortification, and austerity. Gandhi explained: "The suffering that has to be undergone in satyagraha is *tapasya* in its purest form."[85] For Chavez, *tapasya* coalesced with the Catholic teaching on redemptive suffering; he insisted on sacrifice from his followers: "Once people are willing to make these sacrifices, you develop a power of the spirit which can affect your adversaries in ways you can hardly imagine. Gandhi called this power 'moral jujitsu.'"[86] Unlike violent action, satyagraha requires circumspection: "Nonviolence also has one big demand—the need to be creative, to develop strategy," Chavez explained, again citing Gandhi's characterizing phrase: "Gandhi described it as 'moral jujitsu.' Always hit the opposition off balance, but keep your principles."[87]

Remarkably, however, Gandhi and Chavez agreed that violence is preferable to fear. In the words of Gandhi: "It is a thousand times better that we die trying to acquire the strength of the arm. Using physical force with courage is far superior to cowardice. At least we would have attempted to act like men."[88] On this teaching Chavez concurred:

"Gandhi once said he'd rather have a man be violent than be a coward. I agree. If he's a coward, then what good is he for anyone? But it is our job to see he's not a coward. That's really the beginning point of our training."[89] The leader elaborated: "Nonviolence is not cowardice. A nonviolent person cannot be fearful. He must be on his toes at all times. He must be a strategist. He must know how to deal with people, above all. You see, nonviolence means that you involve people in creative ways. The real force of nonviolence is in the numbers."[90] Gandhi once said that his commitment was to truth, not consistency in his statements; truth is a function of understanding, which evolves. Still, for both Chavez and Gandhi, the greatest act of courage and "manliness" was sacrificing one's life for the greater good. This extreme principle was central to Gandhi's philosophy: "To lay down one's life for what one considers to be right is the very core of satyagraha."[91]

Chavez had been accused of tolerating violence within his movement, especially during the Great Grape Strike. Growers charged that the leader was at least complicit in the violence against them if he did not actually incite it. To this charge, the leader responded with his "Good Friday Letter," which appeared in both the *National Catholic Reporter* and the *Christian Century* on April 23, 1969. Modeled after King's 1963 "Letter from Birmingham Jail," it addressed grape growers:

> I am sad to hear about your accusations in the press that our union movement and table grape boycott have been successful because we have used violence and terror tactics. If what you say is true, I have been a failure and should withdraw from the struggle....
>
> Today on Good Friday 1969 we remember the life and the sacrifice of Martin Luther King, Jr., who gave himself totally to the nonviolent struggle for peace and justice....
>
> You must understand—I must make you understand—that our membership and the hopes and aspirations of the hundreds of thousands of the poor and dispossessed that have been raised on our account are, above all, human beings, no better and no worse than any other cross-section of human society; we are not saints because we are poor, but by the same measure neither are we immoral.[92]

Coretta Scott King with Dolores Huerta, United Farmworkers Union vice president, when Cesar Chavez was jailed in Salinas, CA, 1973. Bob Fitch Photo Archive, © Stanford University Libraries.

TO REDEEM THE SOUL OF AMERICA: CORETTA SCOTT KING IN SALINAS

On December 4, 1970, Cesar Chavez was jailed in Salinas, California, for violating a recently enacted law that criminalized strike activities. He was charged with violating an injunction, issued by the Salinas Superior Court, that called for an end to the UFW's boycott of a farming operation that had a contract with the Teamsters Union, and was sentenced to two consecutive five-day jail sentences. While in jail he received several high-profile visitors, including Ethel Kennedy and Coretta Scott King. Scott King recounted the conversation in an interview conducted after the meeting: "I said to him that my husband had great admiration for him. And he said to me that my husband had been an example to him and to all of his people. That their struggle began halfway between the time the Civil Rights Movement began and now, and his great belief that non-violence is the method to bring about social change, peacefully.... I brought the support of the Civil Rights Movement which I'm a part of, the Southern Christian Leadership Conference has [long] supported the efforts of the Farm Workers."[93]

During the same interview session the Reverend Andrew Young was asked if he linked the boycotts of the UFW and the SCLC. Young responded, "The two causes are really one." To this statement Scott King responded, "Amen." She noted in an essay honoring the late leader, "Cesar considered himself a disciple of Martin, just as my husband was a disciple of Gandhi. Cesar told me that the United Farm Workers modeled many of their campaigns on the nonviolent principles and strategies we employed in the Civil Rights Movement."[94]

In the wake of the Montgomery bus boycott in 1955, King founded the Southern Christian Leadership Conference; its expressed goal was to "redeem the soul of America." Chavez recalled his debt to King:

> I had followed King's actions from the beginning of the bus boycott in Montgomery, when I was organizing the Community Service Organization, and he gave me hope and ideas. When the bus boycott was victorious, I thought then of applying boycotts to organizing the Union. Then every time something came out in the newspapers, his civil rights struggle would just jump out of the pages at me.
>
> Although I met some of the people that were working with King and saw him on television, I never talked with him except on the phone. But Martin Luther King definitely influenced me, and much more after his death. The spirit doesn't die, the ideas remain. I read them, and they're alive.[95]

In 1968, following Chavez's first public fast, the "love fast," King was in Los Angeles and had hoped to travel north to visit Chavez, but as one chronicler reports: "He said his schedule did not then permit a trip to Delano to see Chavez, but that he planned to do so in the very near future. Plans were announced for a national unity meeting in Washington on April 22, where Blacks, Chicanos and the poor whites from Appalachia would assemble."[96]

On March 5, 1968, during Chavez's love fast, King sent him a telegram from Atlanta commending his efforts:

> I am deeply moved by your courage in fasting as your personal sacrifice for justice through nonviolence. Your past and present commitment is eloquent testimony to the constructive power of nonviolent action and the destructive impotence of violent reprisal. You stand today as a living example of the Gandhian tradition with its great force for social progress and its healing spiritual powers. My colleagues and I commend you for your bravery, salute you for your indefatigable work against poverty and injustice, and pray for your health and your continuing service as one of the outstanding men of America. The plight of your people and ours is so grave that we all desperately need the inspiring example and effective leadership you have given.[97]

At the conclusion of Chavez's fast, he received another telegram from King:

> As brothers in the fight for equality, I extend the hand of fellowship and good will and wish continuing success to you and your members. The fight for equality must be fought on many fronts—in the urban slums, in the sweat shops of the factories and fields. Our separate struggles are really one—a struggle for freedom, for dignity, and for humanity. You and your valiant fellow workers have demonstrated your commitment to righting grievous wrongs forced upon exploited people. We are together with you in spirit and in determination that our dreams for a better tomorrow will be realized.[98]

King understood that he and Chavez were kindred spirits whose simultaneous struggles were suspended in a postcolonial web of racial exploitation—King declared: "We are caught in an inescapable network of mutuality, tied in a single garment of destiny."[99] Ultimately, their histories and destinies were linked by their racialization and exploitation, engineered through a discourse that dehumanized them and thereby justified their subjugation. The question for anticolonial revolutionaries was the mode of revolt, the method of struggle; it became, more specifically, a question about violence. King and Chavez modeled a militant nonviolent uprising; in this regard, Chavez acknowledged his debt to both Gandhi and King. Upon Dr. King's assassination, Chavez sent a telegram to Coretta Scott King, dated April, 6 1968:

> We are deeply saddened to learn of the death of your husband.
> Our prayers are for you and your children in your sorrow.
> It is my belief that much of the courage which we have found in our struggle for justice in the fields has had its roots in the example set by your husband and by those multitudes who followed his non violent leadership. We owe so much to Dr Martin Luther King that words alone can not express our gratitude. Despite the tragic violence which took your husband there is much that is good about our nation. It was to that goodness that your husband appealed. It was that compassion in all of us that he reached out to touch.
> His non violence was that of action not that of one contemplating action. Because of that he will always be to us more than a philosopher of non violence. Rather he will be remembered by us as a man of peace.[100]

Chavez continued to work with Scott King, the Reverend Ralph Abernathy, and Jesse Jackson. On April 7, 1968, Chavez spoke at a public memorial for King at the Los Angeles Coliseum, organized by the Urban League. Additionally, the UFW was a "sponsoring organization" for the Poor People's Campaign, started by King, but Chavez did not attend the event because of his health. Yet as relations between the conference organizers and the Chicanos in attendance began to deteriorate, the Reverend Abernathy addressed a telegram to Chavez's office, on June 4, 1968, urging, "Please tell Chavez to come to Washington immediately. The Poor People's March needs him now."[101] Chavez responded to Abernathy's request with regrets.

Chavez was invited, in a letter dated July 18, 1969, to serve on the Advisory Board of the Poor People's Campaign, declining the next day, as follows: "I am writing in response to your letter of July 18, regarding your plans to enlarge the Advisory Board of the Poor People's Development Foundation. I would like very much to be of service, but my health forbids such a commitment on my part at this time. I am now confined to bed under doctor's orders, and my activities are severely restricted."[102]

When the leader was jailed in 1970 for breaking a newly established law against boycotting, he received a telegram, dated December 8, from Ralph Abernathy: "The SCLC wants you to know that we support you fully in your efforts to better the lives of poor working Americans. These are extremely difficult days in which we live and those who intend to continue the struggle for justice and equality will find it very difficult. The Conference stands ready to join you in your fight."[103]

A few days later, on December 11, Chavez received a telegram from Coretta Scott King, who visited him soon thereafter in jail. "I want you to know how much I appreciated your firm commitment to non violence and your willingness to pay the high price that such a commitment exacts. Despite the seemingly overwhelming odds against your current efforts you will ultimately win for the workers the rights by which they were endowed by the creator. Let me know what I can do that might be helpful to you."[104]

Scott King subsequently wrote a poetic epistle to Chavez, connecting his cause to the American foundational deity, our creator. She came out to Delano to meet with Chavez and to deliver a speech, wherein she says, "As your Union in this day fights to live, those who control the billion dollar economy have said that blacks and Chicanos do not have the right to decent lives or to human dignity. They must live on the crumbs from the table, drowning with food. Cesar Chavez is in jail because he believes that you should have the same rights and privileges that all Americans should enjoy.... But as my husband often said, you cannot keep truth in jail, truth and justice leap barriers."[105]

In January 1974 Chavez traveled to Atlanta to attend the forty-fourth birthday celebration of Martin Luther King. While there he received the second annual Martin Luther King Peace Award. (Andrew Young had received the first.) The following month, Coretta Scott King wrote to Chavez: "'Keeping the Dream Alive' requires dedication and hard work, but if we are able to reach the minds and hearts of more and more people, it is all worth the effort. I look forward to our continued relationship between the United Farm Workers and the Martin Luther

King Center for Social Change, and pray God's blessings upon your efforts."[106]

In April 1978, on the tenth anniversary of Martin Luther King's assassination, Chavez published a tribute to King, entitled "Martin Luther King Jr.: He Showed Us the Way," in which he wrote:

> In honoring Martin Luther King, Jr's memory we also acknowledge non-violence as a truly powerful weapon to achieve equality and liberation—in fact, the only weapon that Christians who struggle for social change can claim as their own.
>
> Dr. King's entire life was an example of [the] power that nonviolence brings to bear in the real world. It is an example that inspired much of the philosophy and strategy of the farm worker's movement. . . .
>
> Our conviction is that human life is a very special possession given by God to man and that no one has the right to take it for any reason or for any cause, however just it may be.
>
> We are also convinced that nonviolence is more powerful than violence. Nonviolence supports you if you have a just and moral cause. Nonviolence provides the opportunity to stay on the offensive, and that is of crucial importance to win any contest.[107]

But he cautioned that nonviolent struggle must be focused and informed. For if it "fails our only alternative is to turn to violence. So we must balance the strategy with a clear understanding of what we are doing."[108]

On January 12, 1990, Chavez gave a lecture entitled "Lessons of Dr. Martin Luther King, Jr." At twenty thousand words, it is one of his longest essays (though not all of it was new material). He began by explaining his affection for the late civil rights leader: "What makes him special to me, the truth many people don't want you to remember, is that Dr. King was a great activist, fighting for radical social change with radical methods." Chavez's social critique, written just three years prior to his own death, was even more urgent:

> Our nation continues to wage war upon its neighbors, and upon itself.
>
> The powers that be rule over a racist society, filled with hatred and ignorance.

Our nation continues to be segregated along racial and economic lines.

The powers that be make themselves richer by exploiting the poor. Our nation continues to allow children to go hungry, and will not even house its own people. The time is now for people, of all races and backgrounds, to sound the trumpets of change. As Dr. King proclaimed "There comes a time when people get tired of being trampled over by the iron feet of oppression."

The leader goes on to clarify his appreciation of King and once again credits the leader as his muse:

The enemies of justice want you to think of Dr. King as only a civil rights leader, but he had a much broader agenda. He was a tireless crusader for the rights of the poor, for an end to the war in Vietnam long before it was popular to take that stand, and for the rights of workers everywhere.

Many people find it convenient to forget that Martin was murdered while supporting a desperate strike on that tragic day in Memphis, Tennessee. He died while fighting for the rights of sanitation workers.

Dr. King's dedication to the rights of the workers who are so often exploited by the forces of greed has profoundly touched my life and guided my struggle.[109]

MORE TIME THAN LIFE

As Chavez saw it, there were two essential ingredients for a successful movement, time and money: "An individual who is willing to give his time is more important than an individual who is willing to give his money. I think money would be number two."[110] In this he took cues from Gandhi: "It's amazing how people lose track of basics. Gandhi was one of the best fund-raisers the world has ever seen! (Laughter.) But people don't look at it that way! They don't!"[111]

I agree with José-Antonio Orosco's argument that the leader's thought and practice departed from King's in relation to his philosophy of time; but later in his life King became more attuned to the rhythms of Chavez's movement. As Orosco has noted, "Although Chavez and King shared a commitment to nonviolence as a way of life and as a strategy for social change, it is clear that they understood nonviolence to be making very different claims on people's time."[112] He distinguished Chavez as an original thinker who influenced King, concluding: "King came more and more to embrace forms of political organizing that were at the center of Chavez's efforts with the United Farm Workers, namely a devotion to the empowerment of marginalized people as autonomous, democratic agents and the building of alternative institutions within civil society as sites of resistance to corporate capitalism and violent militarism."[113]

In 1964 King published a book entitled *Why We Can't Wait,* in which he elaborated many of the themes articulated in his 1963 "Letter From a Birmingham Jail," where he used the phrase "justice too long delayed is justice denied." In that letter and in the book he expressed his theology of time, dispelling what he called "the strangely irrational notion that there is something in the very flow of time that will inevitably cure all ills. Actually time is neutral.... We must use time creatively, and forever realize that the time is always ripe to do right." Yet in the book he also declared: "A methodology and philosophy of revolution is neither born nor accepted overnight."[114] He recognized that social change on a large scale requires time. He wrote, in a borrowed aphorism that he made his own, "The arc of the moral universe is long, but it bends toward justice."

Similarly, Chavez acknowledged time as essential to social transformation, explaining, "Truth needs another element, and that is time. If you have those two elements, truth and time ... sooner or later the truth is going to be exposed.... It cannot be hidden.... Mankind has never been able to deal with the suppression of truth."[115] Elsewhere, he clarified: "'*Hay más tiempo que vida*'—that's one of our dichos. 'There is more time than life.' We don't worry about time, because time and history are on our side."[116]

Perhaps this distinction in emphasis is best understood in relation to differing tempi of soteriology. Chavez, baptized a Catholic, trusted in a salvation marked by passages, transitions, faithful repetitions, and returns. King, a Baptist minister, was accustomed to instant transformation wrought by the Holy Spirit; his movement, animated by immediacy, sought a state of rapture, a condition of free and radical grace, occasioned by the eternal fall and volatile redemption. Both, however, worked to achieve a vision of the "beloved community." King did so by "the way of non-violence [that] leads to redemption."[117] Chavez worked toward a similar vision of peace and justice, moving beyond race, gender, religion, sexuality, and other classifications that create divisions and violence. Both men's peaceful visions followed those of Gandhi.

Each waged a prophetic movement, responding to a mandate for rehumanization—against centuries of Christian myths legitimating well-heeled interests. Of course each of their movements addressed local and culturally specific urgencies and was therefore distinct from the others; but each, I argue, was spiritual if not religious in its nature. The chapter that follows focuses on *La Causa* as a religious movement, established by the prophetic (though all too human) agency of Chavez.

CHAPTER THREE

Religion

A Revolutionary Spirit

Love does not delight in evil but rejoices with the truth. It
always protects, always trusts, always hopes, always perse-
veres. Love never fails. But where there are prophecies, they
will cease; where there are tongues, they will be stilled; where
there is knowledge, it will pass away.

> St. Paul, 1 Corinthians 13:6–9

Hence, I have made sedition my dharma ... to be loyal is a
sin.... I regard this as a religious movement.[1]

> Gandhi

It wasn't that saving my soul was more important than the
strike. On the contrary, I said to myself, if I'm going to save
my soul, it's going to be through the struggle for social
justice.[2]

> Cesar Chavez

On Valentine's Day, 1968, Cesar Chavez announced that he was willing
to die for the farm workers, risking his life by abstaining from food for
as long as it took to recommit the movement to its nonviolent foundational principles. This was the Fast for Nonviolence, or the love fast.
According to Matthiessen, Chavez made the dramatic announcement
before the union's leadership: "Throughout the speech Chavez quoted
Gandhi and the Epistles of St. Paul. 'His act was intensely personal,'
LeRoy Chatfield recalled, 'and the whole theme of his speech was love.

In fact, his last words to us ... were something like 'I am doing this because I love you.'"[3] Nothing did more to assure the leader's messianic identity than his public fasts, especially the love fast. There, at the Forty Acres in Delano, he set up a monastic "cell," which he occupied for the next twenty-five days, instructing devotees to paint the windows in multiple colors replicating the stained glass windows of a chapel. From Wednesday, February 14, until Sunday, March 10, he lived on water and the body of Christ: an ecumenical Mass was said each night.

He fasted in direct response to some acts of violence committed by men of the UFW as an act of contrition and a "penance." His "cell" quickly became a pilgrimage destination, as hundreds of tents sprang up around him. Pilgrims waited in line for a chance to speak with Chavez, who occupied his time reading, meditating, and praying. Followers urged him to eat; at least one tried to force-feed him. Ultimately the leader broke bread with Senator Robert Kennedy, who had traveled to Central California for the occasion. In fall 1968, largely as a result of the fast, a *New York Times* reporter declared that the Great Grape Strike had become *La Causa,* a social justice crusade encompassing, but not limited to, organizing farm workers.[4] That same year, Saul Alinsky quipped reproachfully: "This isn't a union, this is a civil rights movement."[5] But as early as 1964 the leader had told a reporter that his goals for the movement were sui generis: "A union is building a group with a spirit and existence all its own."[6]

On several occasions Chavez disclosed the larger religious objectives of his struggle. In 1975 he waxed prophetic to a reporter: "Scripture ... is so clear on the question of social justice. I guess there came at some point a realization that I couldn't practice my faith unless I was doing something about it.... One gets rather impatient ... with just preaching and not doing something about Christ's clear message. It has to be more than economic struggle. If that was all there was to it, I don't think our cause could survive."[7]

In February 1977 Chavez sought approval from the Vatican to start a new "religious order" to be called Los Menos, or "the least." It would consist of Catholics and Protestants, women and men, single and married.[8] Later that year, he was interviewed by a journalist from *Sojourners* for an article whose epigraph was "The more trouble we get, the more religious we get." In it he speaks explicitly about his religious intentions: "If we choose this community style we will have some kind of religion—either we invent one or we keep what we have, but we cannot be without one. It is very meaningful and important."[9] In the end he *reinvented* religion, acting as both a "renewer" and "founder," extending his spiritual reach outside institutional borders, into the revolutionary picking fields, streets, and base communities.

A religious identity would serve Chavez's movement in many registers. Followers needed to be convinced that the struggle, *La Causa,* involved their individual beliefs and concerns, indeed embodied them but also superseded them, taking priority over them—because the collective need outweighed that of the individual. His devotees were to be converted to his mode of thought—"organized." My thesis in this chapter is that *La Causa* was a gestalt; it functioned as both a spiritual community and a religious system—with its own (albeit sometimes derivative) myths, rituals, and symbols—which yielded a distinct moral economy. According to the historians Griswold del Castillo and Garcia, "La Causa was each Mexicano's need for redemption from modernity."[10]

The purpose of *La Causa* was not some divine reward, however, but political transformation—*La Causa* engaged in religious politics rather than religion per se. It had a political spirituality involving soteriology (redemption), eschatology (utopian promise), Christology, and Mariology—a revision of the Holy Mother and Son—all bound to the body of Chavez, its public signification, its Chicana/o identification, its feminine element, and its propensity for dying and rising, eliciting an emotional response from the public. With this in mind, I explore *La Causa* as a religious movement—what Emile Durkheim called a totemic collective representation—established by the charisma of Chavez and eventuating in demystification, or routinization, and decline.

Chavez's union was a triumph of Durkheim's theory of social organization, the totality of a group's identities and values, writ large—the collective representation—projected onto the cosmos and reflected back to distinguish those things that are sacred from those that are profane. Durkheim demonstrated the universality of religious group formation in human societies, wherein face-to-face communities replicate the pattern of explicitly religious congregations that are shaped and reshaped in the struggle for political power.[11] For Durkheim, "It is not in human nature in general that we must seek the determining causes of religious phenomena; it is in the nature of the societies to which [those causes] relate."[12] Religion is best understood, not as something reified, standing alone, but as something that influences or changes other social fields and discourses.

In what follows I look first to Chavez's spiritual development in the *Cursillo* movement and then to the religious production emergent during the Great Grape Strike, from 1965 to 1970. The chapter focuses subsequently on the pilgrimage to Sacramento that arrived there on Easter Sunday 1966 and on the leader's three public fasts, paying special attention to the Fast for Nonviolence in 1968. The remaining section puts the spotlight on La Paz before offering concluding thoughts.

EL CURSILLISTA

Central to Chavez's adult spiritual formation was a Catholic retreat for Latino men, the *Cursillos de la Cristindad,* or "little courses" in Christianity. The *Cursillos* began in the 1940s as a movement intended to prepare Spanish adolescents in Mallorca for pilgrimage to Santiago de Compostela. The goal was to renew and enliven young men's Christian faith over a three-day weekend.[13] Eventually the program began targeting adult men: *Cursillos* were intended to place them more firmly in the Catholic communion, transforming typical male attitudes of disrespect toward or indifference to the Church, which many viewed as little more than a pastime for older women.

Beginning in the 1960s, *Cursillos* came to the United States, targeting Latino men. Hispanic *Cursillistas* were taken on a retreat, during which they were expected to have a personal encounter with Christ and an emotional experience with other Latino Catholic men, thereby making Catholicism personally meaningful to them. Eventually, *Cursillos* were organized for Latinas as well as Latinos. Overall, however, *Cursillos* were designed to occasion and shape Latino masculine fellowship, which involved community service. According to one historian, "Though the *Cursillo* was presented as a religious rather than a social action movement, it nevertheless motivated many Mexican Americans to become actively involved in the pursuit of social justice. Thus it functioned as a leadership school."[14] Although the *Cursillo* grew from local movements, one analyst notes, "Yet, we are all linked to, not separated from, people who join movements, be it the *cursillo*, the *jamaa*, the *vailala* madness, or *pentecostalism*."[15]

As I have already noted, Frank Bardacke accused Chavez of concealing his "commitment" to the *Cursillo*: "Cesar Chavez did his *Cursillo* in the late 1950s or early 1960s, according to his brother Richard. Richard's uncertainty about the date comes from the air of secrecy that surrounded the early *Cursillos*, and from Chavez's own subsequent reluctance to talk about his commitment to the movement."[16] The leader participated in the *Cursillo* organized by the Archdiocese of San Francisco on July 20 and July 21, 1962, just a few months after founding the FWA. According to one account, *Cursillistas* were among Chavez's first recruits to the new association.[17] The notebook he kept from the *Cursillo* is available in the UFW collection at the Walter P. Reuther Library at Wayne State University.[18] Bardacke has implied that Chavez was silent about the *Cursillos*, fearing a betrayal of their ties to the fascism of Franco's Spain.[19]

The *Cursillo* consisted of a series of workshops, or "*rollos*," which were led by Latino priests and conducted in both English and Spanish. In Chavez's experience, the *Cursillos* offered several workshops on topics germane to men, especially the essential elements of Christian masculinity. As Adrian Bautista has observed, these retreats often involved uninhibited ceremonies where men wept openly while embracing and comforting one another. "This sort of religiosity included new levels of intimacy with men, particularly at the Cursillo retreat, as well as encounters with sacrality based on mutuality, deep friendship, and love."[20]

Chavez took copious notes during the *rollos,* in English and in Spanish.[21] Sections were divided by the order of the *rollo* and the topics it would cover. Those included a discussion of penance, "grace," the sacraments, and marriage. Although *Cursillos* are three days long, Chavez's notebook records only two days, a Friday and a Saturday. In addition to enumerating each *rollo,* Chavez recorded the name of the workshop leader; the most abundant aggregation of notes occurs under the workshop led by someone named "Flores." This was most likely Patrick Flores, ordained to the Catholic priesthood in 1956 and appointed bishop of San Antonio in 1979. (Chavez read from the writings of St. Paul at the diocesan ceremony where Flores was ordained a bishop.)

The notes adumbrate some of the key concepts that would come to define the leader's political theology, especially the meaning of manhood, focusing on penance. Of special import in this regard is a lecture offered by Padre Flores. Chavez's notes on the talk, which he organized as bulleted points, include the following:

- The body is the temple of the Holy Spirit
- Our Lord desires to live within us
- He makes of us a temple of faith
- We are members of Christ—the mystical body of Our Lord
- all strength comes from God
- brotherhood is divine.

In a note on a section titled *beatos,* or "blessings," Chavez listed penance and confession as challenges to machismo. Other bulleted points include the following:

- The grace of God costs—penance
- The Grace of God costs—penance and a spirit of charity
- Repentance, humility, charity, compassion are acts of actual grace

Included among the teachings on manhood are the following:

- Man is: body—soul and grace
- Repentance, humility, charity, and compassion are acts of actual grace
- Man is called to live super naturally
- Discourse on marriage—to make one flesh
- Companionship
- Your spouse is your companion [*compañera*]

Beside this last notation in the list is scribbled a reference to Ephesians 5:22, where St. Paul entreats, "Wives submit yourselves to your own husbands as you do to the Lord."

Chavez recorded in the notebook concepts, such as the sacredness of the human body when it bends to submission, sacrifice, and penance, that are reflected in his later work. The notebook also emphasized the holiness of community and the profanity of individualism and solitary existence. The *Cursillo* seems to have affected him particularly during the early years of *La Causa* when the movement exhibited a pronounced Catholic identity. Later, especially at La Paz, the movement developed a more hybrid and idiosyncratic religious character. According to one description of the FWA's founding, "Appeals were not based on the dogma of organized labor, which was considered foreign and suspect in the field. They relied, rather, on the Roman Catholic Church. It was the one institution that was known and supported by virtually all of the workers and by many of their employers."[22]

The FWA's "Statement of Purpose" suggests a Christian, if not altogether Catholic, organization, yet among Chavez's early recruits were members of tiny Pentecostal congregations that celebrated *cultos,* or services, in their homes. *La Causa* lost Protestant support, however, when the association decided, in 1966, to carry a banner with the image of Our Lady of Guadalupe during its Lenten pilgrimage to Sacramento. Of this event Huerta quipped: "We put the Virgin to a motion, and virginity won."[23] Chavez abstained from the vote.

In addition to the Pentecostals who remained in the union despite its Catholic ethos, the Presbyterian minister Chris Hartmire, who directed the Migrant Ministry for the National Council of Churches, made his organization's considerable resources available to the leader. Deftly negotiating the tension in the association between Catholics and Protestants, Chavez referred to himself often as a generic Christian and much less frequently as a Catholic. He cited Scripture and spoke of reading the Bible—most likely as a nod to his Protestant followers.[24]

¡HUELGA!

The origin legend of the strike, which itself constitutes a chapter of *La Causa's* mythology, traces its beginnings to Mexican Independence Day, September 16, 1965, when the FWA is said to have voted, at the Guadalupe church in Delano, to join the striking Filipino workers of the Agricultural Workers Organizing Committee (AWOC), targeting the Central Valley's grape producers.

The assembly space was auspicious: Guadalupe church in Delano was adorned with Mexican flags and images of Latino revolutionary icons. A painting of the Virgin of Guadalupe herself presided over the event, blessing the meeting from her altar. From the pulpit, Chavez read a prepared statement: "155 years ago, in the state of Guanajuato in Mexico, a padre [Hidalgo] proclaimed the struggle for liberty. He was killed, but ten years later Mexico won its independence.... We are engaged in another struggle for the freedom and dignity which poverty denies us. But it must not be a violent struggle, even if violence is used against us. Violence can only hurt us and our cause.... We are all humans. This is a just cause. Let's go on strike!"[25] There in the church, amid the energetic crowd, the leader is said to have put the strike to a vote and, receiving a positive result, to have called the strike on.[26]

The mythology of September 16 has been repeated in many accounts, including one in A. V. Krebs's hagiographic book *La Causa: The Word Was Made Flesh*. According to Krebs, in the days following the declaration, "Each morning before dawn, small bands of roving pickets began to appear at the edge of the Delano vineyards on the county roads criss-crossing the land, shouting to workers in the fields, 'Huelga! Huelga!' Large, round, orange and black signs with the Aztec eagle were held aloft by the strikers beckoning to the workers who remained in the fields harvesting grapes to join them picketing the fields."[27]

El Malcriado delineated the myth of origins for the Great Grape Strike, first in Spanish in the fall 1965 edition, and again in English in March 1966. The newsletter often reproduced religious images and made reference to God, the Church, Pope John, and Catholicism. The cover of *El Malcriado* on March 15, 1967, featured a drawing of Pope John XXIII with a tear falling from his eye. The image is captioned, " ... Because this is simple justice, and justice comes before charity..." (ellipses in original). Images of the Madonna and Child, frequently used on the paper's cover, are identifiable as every mother. For the farm workers the Christian iconography was more than a reference to the Holy Family; strikers embodied, performed, and resignified the icons.

According to Father Ken Irrgang, a UFW volunteer, "It was a good time for labor unions in the church."[28] One issue of *El Malcriado* announcing the strike featured a quotation from the 1891 encyclical *Rerum Novarum,* under the heading VIVA LA CAUSA! It began with Pope Leo XIII's admonition to men who are rich and able to treat the poor justly, lest they incur the wrath of heaven. An editorial entitled "Christ Loves Us" that follows the quotation reads: "In Christ God reconciled the world to him. This sounds pretty but it is rare for a man to say this at the hour of his crucifixion.... We say that we are very weak for this struggle. But through his love and justice God gives us strength for this task. He is not a distant God who doesn't care. He has become united to us in this life of difficulties. He goes before us in suffering and death."[29]

In addition to impressing potential converts with the godliness of the FWA, the religious imagery and text were intended to nullify the force of the incessant red-baiting of *La Causa*. After all, as one writer noted, "It was difficult to charge Chavez with being a communist, when he was surrounded by prominent Protestant and Catholic leaders."[30]

It may have been "difficult" to accuse Chavez of being a communist, but the accusers, undeterred, simply made the same accusation against the clergy. In the month after the strike was called, one grower leveled the following charge in a Delano paper: "How naïve can this clergy be, dependent on the largesse of its members ... ? They march in picket lines with avowed communists whose ultimate goal is the destruction of all religious faith." On December 13, 1965, a group of eleven "religious leaders" visited Delano as part of a twenty-four-hour fact-finding tour. The group included both Catholic and Protestant clergy, a rabbi, and the theologian Robert McAfee Brown. While the group was there, a grower confronted Father James Vizzard, who had publicly endorsed the strikers. "You're no Jesuit priest," charged the grower, "you're a God-damn Communist!"[31] On December 14, the delegation released a statement, signed by each member:

> The right of churches and synagogues to engage in such action is absolutely clear to us. We reject the heresy that churches and synagogues are to be concerned only with "spiritual matters." We believe that this is God's world.... [W]hatever goes on in this world must be our concern, particularly when his will for the well-being of any of his children is being violated. We believe furthermore in the unity of the human person, made in God's image, and are persuaded that any indignity to any human person, whether to his soul or his body, must be our immediate concern.[32]

The religious alliances created by the strike echoed Chavez's appeals to civil religious values and his insistence that farm workers be treated humanely.

In fact, Americans (as well as Canadians and Europeans), exhorted to enlist in the Cause, did so by boycotting grapes. Although exact numbers are unavailable, the boycott had a negative impact on the grape industry, resulting in a significant loss of revenue for growers, who resorted to trickery rather than negotiate. The leader maximized the effects of the boycott by sending teams to cities across the country to establish "boycott houses"—places where participants in the boycott could live in monastic conditions on a diet consisting largely of bologna sandwiches. Those who inhabited these houses picketed supermarkets, convincing many of their managers to stop carrying grapes. Boycott teams also entreated churches and synagogues for donations and often lodging. Living in the boycott houses required great sacrifices—a religious commitment. Farm workers who had never left Kern County suddenly found themselves in cities far removed from their homes, cohabitating with privileged white college kids who enjoyed vastly different life experiences. Tensions were high and the distribution of resources caused conflict between the strikers and the boycotters. Synagogues and churches, both Catholic and Protestant, were crucial in keeping the boycott alive.

The Catholic church's position on the strike and boycott was complicated, however, by the growers, many of whom were also Catholic and contributed to the valley churches in amounts impossible for subsistence farm workers to match. Many of the growers came from Italy and Yugoslavia and brought with them to California the strong identity markers connecting their church and their ethnicity.[33] Even though *La Causa* received pivotal support from the Catholic clergy, some of its members opposed the strike and boycott. According to one observer, "In the 1960s and '70s virtually every major religious body in the United States and many in Europe and Canada gave attention to U.S. farm workers, took positions on what the workers were doing, and were a significant force in rallying 17 million Americans to participate in the common act of not buying grapes."[34] Still, the Catholic Church withheld its formal endorsement, maintaining an official position of neutrality and acting as mediator between growers and strikers.

Chavez formally petitioned the United States Conference of Catholic Bishops for its official support in 1968, and again in 1969; on both occasions his request was denied. In 1969 the church assembled an ad hoc committee to study the farm workers' strike, but it remained publicly neutral until the lettuce boycott in 1973, when it endorsed *La Causa*.[35] During the Great Grape Strike, however, the UFW benefited

Cesar Chavez with Catholic priests, Coachella, CA, 1973. Bob Fitch Photo Archive, © Stanford University Libraries.

tremendously from the support of Catholic clergy, including California bishops who pressured growers to negotiate with the strikers. On December 10, 1965, *Time* magazine ran a story on clerical support for the strike. It began by tracking the activities of two priests, Arnold Meagher and Keith Kenny, who was also a pilot; the two men flew a small plane over a struck vineyard in Delano, shouting "Huelga!" at "Mexican grape pickers" through a bull horn. "Landing a bit later in Delano, they were met by two priests representing the local bishop, Aloysius Willinger of Monterey-Fresno. They told the flying fathers to stop inciting the strike: 'The bishop feels that this is none of your business and asks that you go back to your own diocese.' Protested Kenny, later on: 'Where the poor are, Christ should be.'"[36]

Central to the religious support for Chavez was the National Council of Churches and its California affiliate—especially its California Migrant Ministry (CMM), started during the depression years and headed since 1961 by the Presbyterian minister Chris Hartmire and his assistant Reverend Jim Drake of the United Church of Christ; both were graduates of Union Theological Seminary. With deep pockets, Hartmire and Drake were able to underwrite many of the UFW's actions. Perhaps more important, they developed an eloquent and powerful *huelga* theology, partly in response to critics within the church. Hartmire was influenced by Dietrich Bonhoeffer, particularly the Lutheran minister's theological imperatives of implementing justice and imitating Christ, a practice that included participation in the divine suffering.

Consider the statement issued by the California Church Council on the grape strike, dated March 7, 1966. Written by Hartmire, it expressed *huelga* theology while leveling a subtle critique at the Catholic bishops: "As Christians we cannot assume a position of non-involvement or neutrality in the presence of social injustice which reduces the dignity and well-being of any of God's children." The California Migrant Ministry "has sought to minister in the name of Jesus Christ to this alienated group [of farm workers] in society. Always it has striven to serve the whole person in the total context of his life. We have tried to broaden our concern beyond a ministry which treats only symptoms resulting from economic injustice. This attempt has led to a confrontation of the root causes of poverty and alienation."[37]

As a result of these efforts, *La Causa* forged its distinct religious ethos during the strike, inextricably binding it to the clergy and churches that bolstered it. During this period the movement produced and reified its characteristic symbols and rituals. The cessation of the bracero program in 1964 made the strike possible, because cheap and abundant labor from Mexico could have encroached on and blunted the force of the striking American workers. The strike gave rise to a dynamic social operation—over which Chavez wielded nearly absolute power—that united thousands across lines of race, class, religion, and sexual identity.

In the words of writers assessing Chavez's efforts at the end of the 1960s, the leader had "created a movement bringing together population groups which formerly did not know one another or labored under misconceptions about one another. Catholics who have never been in a Protestant church and never associated with Protestants in any meaningful way have worked day by day with representatives of the Migrant Ministry and found them admirable people. Atheists who have long thought of Catholic priests as authoritarian, and of Catholic laymen as barefoot and pregnant, have found them to be no more authoritarian, unshod, or pregnant than themselves."[38]

The strike, which required personnel with creative energy, fostered in participants an urgency that trumped both individual and corporate identities, synthesizing ultimate commitments into a unique collective representation. It produced *La Causa's* putative ecumenical subjectivity while crystallizing a distinct religious impulse, so that religious narratives, symbols, and rituals were deployed in the service of Chavez's cause. *La huelga* built altars, prayed, and celebrated Mass on the picket lines—all signature UFW rites, whose origins Chavez described:

> Our pickets were being beaten and harassed by the foremen and the police. The spirit among the strikers was very low, almost to the level of complete hopelessness. Then, some women came to the office.... They were on strike with us, so I thought they had come to bring me another problem. One of them had a suggestion. "Pardon us, Mr. Chavez, but we think we have a way to make some progress with the strike. Why don't we start a prayer novena at the entrance to the Di Giorgio property? We could bring a statue of the Virgen de Guadalupe, and some candles. We could make a small altar." ... It was a perfect idea, and one I never would have thought of![39]

Thus began the regular practice of what the Franciscan Mark Day called "liturgies of protest" held during the strike.[40] "I recall having a Pentecostal minister on one side of me and the Rev. Jim Drake of the United Church of Christ on the other."[41] Father Day got himself assigned to Delano and became the "strikers' chaplain."[42] Another priest, Brother Gilbert (Chatfield) of the Christian Brothers, traveled to Delano to visit the strikers in 1965. A few months later he left his order to follow Chavez full-time, changing his name to LeRoy Chatfield; he is one of the main chroniclers of the movement. The high concentration of clergy, both Catholic and Protestant, contributed to the religious identity of *La Causa*. Political spirituality and spiritual mestizaje came to define the UFW.

Chavez claimed that he received the idea of singing in *La Causa* from his engagement with Pentecostal churches. When he first moved to the San Jose barrio Sal Si Puedes, he discovered six Pentecostal churches within a two-block radius.[43] While working for Saul Alinsky's Community Service Organization in the 1950s, Chavez helped a Pentecostal minister and his wife, both of whom had crossed illegally into the United States from Mexico, gain legal status. Chavez asked if he could attend the worship services the couple held in their home. "In San Jose I was one of the few Catholics who attended Protestant services," he said.

> When we first came to Sal Si Puedes, Protestants were the ones who gave us lodging and food and invited my mother to go to the service. She wasn't afraid of them.... Although there were no more than twelve men and women, there was more spirit there than when I went to a mass where there were two hundred. Everybody was happy. They were all singing. These people were really committed in their beliefs, and this made them sing and clap and participate. I liked that.
>
> I think that's where I got the idea for singing at the meetings. That was one of the first things we did when I started the Union. And it was hard for me because I can't carry a tune.[44]

In an interview Chavez made a similar comment: "I was driving home from Los Angeles. I passed a Pentecostal church at night and it was full of people and I thought to myself, why do all the people come there so much. It must be because they like to praise God—and to sing."[45] The singing imbued the movement with a Pentecostal sonic character.

From early in his work Chavez embraced Pentecostals. In fact, a Catholic priest criticized his chapter of the CSO for having too many Protestants. Chavez responded as follows: "I made a speech at the CSO meeting that no one on this earth was going to tell us whether there was too much of anything, that this was not a religious movement, and if anybody wanted to make it so, then they had a fight on their hands."[46] After this meeting, the leader claimed, the CSO lost some Catholics but gained many Protestants. Under the leadership of Alinsky, Chavez could not tolerate a religious movement. The UFW, by contrast, was under his complete control.

In 1974 Chavez said that the first *corrido* about *La Causa* had been written twelve years earlier: "That's a ballad usually sung to a folk song. There must be more than fifty corridos about our Movement, but this was the first one.... The theme of the ballad was that I had come, and things were going to be different now."[47] In addition to *corridos* about Cesar Chavez there is also a *corrido* to Dolores Huerta.[48] These songs are no less than praise narratives; they are worshipful, deifying Chavez and Huerta.

"El Corrido de Cesar Chavez" was first produced and recorded by Luis Valdez's El Teatro Campesino. For Valdez, everything was performance, and his theater enacted that belief in simple skits he called *actos* and myths: "In a sense, the acto *is* Chicano theater, though we are now moving into a new, more mystical dramatic form we have begun to call the mito [myth]."[49] Valdez preached that everything is *teatro* and that *teatro* is a religious act. In 1970 he explained: "At its high point Chicano theater is religion—the huelguistas [strikers] de Delano praying at the shrine of the Virgen de Guadalupe, located in the rear of an old station wagon parked across the road from DiGiorgio's camp #4."[50] He goes on to reveal the revolutionary spirit at work in *La Causa:* "But beyond the mass struggle of La Raza in the fields and barrios of America, there is an internal struggle in the very corazón [heart] of our people. That struggle, too, calls for revolutionary change. Our belief in God, the church, the social role of women—these must be subject to examination and redefinition in some kind of public forum. And that again means teatro.... a teatro of ritual, of music, of beauty, of spiritual sensitivity. A teatro of legends and myths. A teatro of religious strength."[51]

In his *mito* entitled *La Quinta Temporada* (The fifth season) the farm workers create a fifth season, "social justice," from the freezing desert of winter, a season that once brought hardship and hunger. The title and theme recall the Aztec myth of the fifth sun, *Ollin,* or sun of movement, in which the Aztecs located themselves temporally, nonetheless recognizing that the fifth sun would ultimately give way to a new time, a sixth sun, bringing harmony. Valdez's comedy entitled *The Conquest of Mexico* satirizes colonization, retelling Aztec legends and evoking the vibrant aesthetics of Mesoamerica.

In order to draw publicity to the strike, the UFW staged a march to Sacramento in 1966. As the legend goes, the idea for a pilgrimage came to Chavez in a dream.[52]

PILGRIMAGE, PENANCE, AND REVOLUTION

In the "Corrido de César Chávez," the story of the great pilgrimage is retold. There are ten verses in all; a few read as follows:

(1) On the 16th of March
A blessed Thursday in the morning
César Chávez left Delano
Organizing a campaign.

. . . .

(7) Contractors and scabs,
This is going to be a piece of history.
You will go to hell,
And we on to glory.

(8) Listen, Mr. Chavez,
A name that is spoken,
On your heart you deserve
The Virgin of Guadalupe.[53]

The *corrido* was performed on the steps of the California State Capitol in Sacramento as part of the ceremony marking the end of the three-week pilgrimage from Delano, a distance of two hundred and fifty miles. Ten thousand attended the ceremonies, which included two ecumenical services (one celebrated by a Catholic priest, the other by a

Protestant minister). The theme of the march was Pilgrimage, Penance, and Revolution.

As *la huelga* dragged into its second year, morale was sinking. Because Chavez wanting to bring attention to, and to reenergize the efforts of, the strikers, UFW leaders retreated to strategize at the home of a supporter in the California coastal town of Carpenteria. They decided on a prayer pilgrimage, in the tradition of Martin Luther King. Initially, following the custom of the popular Catholic penitential fraternities, only men were to march. But in fact women were among the sixty-eight or so *originales,* those who marched from the beginning.

The penitential fraternities of Mexico and the U.S. Southwest, which Chavez said gave him his template for the pilgrimage, are characterized by self-inflicted penance, self-flagellation on Good Friday—an attempt to emulate Christ's suffering. A Spanish colonial import whose practice resonated with Aztec rituals of blood sacrifice, the Penitente Brotherhood is best known for its Holy Week public processions, in which the solemn members carry crosses as they march in a column.[54] Chavez makes the *penitente* connection in his "Sacramento March Letter," dated March 1966.

> Throughout the Spanish speaking world there is another tradition that touches the present march, that of the Lenten penitential processions, where the *penitentes* would march through the streets, often in sack cloth and ashes, some even carrying crosses as a sign of penance for their sins, and as a plea for the mercy of God. The penitential procession is also in the blood of the Mexican American, and the Delano march will therefore be one of penance—public penance for the sins of the strikers, their own personal sins as well their yielding perhaps to feelings of hatred and revenge in the strike itself. They hope by the march to set themselves at peace with the Lord, so that the justice of their cause will be purified of all lesser motivation.[55]

Indeed, many of the UFW marchers carried large wooden crosses.

The penitential framing and the decision to lead the pilgrimage with a banner of Our Lady of Guadalupe (also known as Our Lady of

The Strike) was cause for disquiet and objection. Some Protestants quit the union; Epifano Camacho, for example, "had resigned as co-captain of the Easter pilgrimage when Our Lady of Guadalupe had been chosen as its symbol." Peter Matthiessen explains further: "*La Causa* was supported by a number of Protestants, Jews, and non-believers, and some of them made it clear that they did not see the slightest reason for atonement on the workers' part—weren't the workers the victims?"[56]

Although the pilgrimage alienated some Protestants, it also occasioned the writing of a sacred text for *La Causa:* "The Plan of Delano, Plan for the Liberation of the Farm Workers Associated with the Delano Grape Strike in the State of California." *La Causa* penitents were made to sign it. It was penned by Luis Valdez in consultation with Chavez and modeled after Emiliano Zapata's "Plan de Ayala," written in 1911 as a manifesto of land reform and liberty. Pilgrims expressed their commitment to *la huelga* and to the march in religious terms, by swearing their allegiance with one hand on a crucifix held by Dolores Huerta.[57] The pilgrimage was scheduled to take place during Holy Week, leaving Delano on March 16 to arrive in Sacramento on Easter Sunday, April 10. The route was strategic, cutting through the heart of successive farm worker towns. Each night the peregrination culminated with "spirited" ceremonies of singing, dancing, speeches, *teatro,* and a dramatic reading of the plan.

"The Plan of Delano" articulates many of the foundational teachings of the UFW; in a sense, it inscribes *La Causa's* modes of sin and modes of salvation. It begins as follows: "We, the undersigned, gathered in Pilgrimage to the capital of the State in Sacramento in penance for all the failings of Farm Workers as free and sovereign men, do solemnly declare before the civilized world which judges our actions, and before the nation to which we belong, the propositions we have formulated to end the injustice that oppresses us." The pilgrimage was led by a priest in full clerical garb and a banner bearing the image of Our Lady of Guadalupe. In addition, marchers carried the American flag, the Mexican flag, and the flag of the Philippines. The plan explains: "We seek, and have, the support of the Church in what we do. At the head of the pilgrimage we carry LA VIRGEN DE GUADALUPE because she is ours, all ours, Patroness of the Mexican people." But even though the pilgrims carried the banner, they made it clear that the march was ecumenical and their own cast of mind, independent.

> We also carry the Sacred Cross and the Star of David because we are not sectarians, and because we ask the help and prayers of all religions. All men are brothers, sons of the same God; that is why we say to all men of good will, in the words of Pope Leo XIII, "Everyone's first duty is to protect the workers from the greed of speculators who use human beings as instruments to provide themselves with money. It is neither just nor human to oppress men with excessive work to the point where their minds become enfeebled and their bodies worn out." GOD SHALL NOT ABANDON US.[58]

Political action was not only *inspired* or *informed* by mystical or religious faith: for the UFW, political revolt was itself a sacred action.

Salvation for the farm workers meant especially growers' signing union contracts that would improve working and living conditions for them, but the vision of Chavez and the UFW extended far beyond that. According to the plan: "Our path travels through a valley well known to all Mexican farm workers. We know all of these towns ... because along this very same road, in this very same valley, the Mexican race has sacrificed itself for the last hundred years. Our sweat and our blood have fallen on this land to make other men rich. This Pilgrimage is a witness to the suffering we have seen for generations." Parts of the plan were revised in 1969 to read as a manifesto in the "Proclamation of the Delano Grape Workers for International Boycott":

> We have been farm workers for hundreds of years.... Mexicans, Filipinos, Africans, and others, our ancestors were among those who founded this land and tamed its natural wilderness. But we are still pilgrims on this land, and we are pioneers who blaze a trail out of the wilderness of hunger and deprivation that we have suffered even as our ancestors did. We are conscious today of the significance of our present quest. If this road we chart leads to the rights and reforms we demand, ... if it changes the social

order that relegates us to the bottom reaches of society, then in our wake will follow thousands of American farm workers. Our example will make them free.[59]

This narrative casts the strike as a cosmic struggle between good and evil, a moral crusade. Marchers occupied the high ground in their humble role as penitents. "The Penance we accept symbolizes the suffering we shall have in order to bring justice to these same towns, to this same valley. The Pilgrimage we make symbolizes the long historical road we have traveled in this valley alone, and the long road we have yet to travel, with much penance, in order to bring about the Revolution we need."[60]

When the pilgrimage arrived at the steps of the capitol, many of the pilgrims had tattered shoes and bloody feet. Their spectacle captured the attention of the nation, and they made the most of it. The plan was read aloud, in both English and Spanish, to a cheering crowd. El Teatro Campesino performed "El Corrido de Cesar Chavez." Chavez, Huerta, and Hartmire addressed the pilgrims and the gathered crowd. The Presbyterian minister's address resounded with the theme of sacrifice. "Thank God for the hope of this glorious Easter morning; but there is too much pain too much loneliness and too much human suffering—and Jesus cares—and Christians should be free enough to face the world honestly and then take risks for the sake of their brothers. If that means losing some institutional flesh and blood then we will be closer to our Lord who loved life but gave his flesh and blood for the world of men."[61] Dolores Huerta won the day, however, with her fiery speech demanding that the governor spearhead a collective bargaining law for farm workers: "You cannot close your eyes and your ears to us any longer. You cannot pretend that we do not exist. You cannot plead ignorance to our problems because we are here and we embody our needs for you. And we are not alone."[62]

The April 10, 1966, issue of *El Malcriado* reprinted the plan in both English and Spanish. It honored each of the marchers (while acknowledging that its list of them is incomplete). The cover photograph juxtaposed an image of Our Lady of the Strike with a close-up shot of a pistol strapped to a policeman's hip. The issue was replete with captioned photos of pilgrims and presented a "history of the pilgrimage" (including its origins in Chavez's dreams), the route of the march, and "the most famous" of the pilgrimage songs: the *corrido* "Viva Huelga en General" (Long Live Strike in General), by Luis Valdez. The newspaper had a section titled "Signs and Symbols of the Pilgrimage" that pictured the American flag, describing it as "a sign of loyalty to the nation which seeks to provide 'liberty and justice for all.'" Under the entry "The Banner of Our Lady of Guadalupe" was a brief history that calls the Virgin the "patron saint of the Mexican people."

If Chavez had been reluctant to join the motion on "virginity" prior to the pilgrimage, afterward he fully embraced the iconography of the Virgin of Guadalupe, with her full-body halo of sacred cultural authority. Hers was a powerful endorsement. As a symbol of the pilgrimage, the image continued to pay dividends well after the march was over. In one instance, the UFW printed a small cartoonlike Spanish pamphlet, entitled: "Memories of the Peregrination, Delano to Sacramento, March 16–April, 10, 1966." Our Lady of Guadalupe graced the cover, and the words "Viva la Causa," with the signature of Cesar Chavez beneath them, were printed below the following text: "We, the strikers of Delano, and our friends, went on a walk to Sacramento—more than 250 miles—under the protection of Our Lady of Guadalupe. We walked as pilgrims, to affirm and reinforce our faith in God. To renew our dedication to our struggle for social justice for the workers. We, the pilgrims, ask that our racial brothers *[hermanos de raza]* and work companions, in California and all over the nation, join us in solemn dedication to our just cause."[63] The pamphlets sold for ten cents each.

Although the history and mythology of *La Causa* recount many other pilgrimages, none was as successful or emblematic as the march to Sacramento.

FASTING: THE SPECTACLE OF SUFFERING

Chavez, who often fasted privately during his work with *La Causa,* staged three public fasts stretching twenty-four days or more. The Fast for Non-violence, or love fast, ran from February 14 to March 10, 1968, in Delano.[64] The Fast for Justice lasted from May 12 to June 6, 1972, in Phoenix. From July 16 to August 21, 1988, in Delano, he completed his longest ever, the Fast for Life (against the use of pesticides in the fields). It stretched thirty-six days, longer than any of Gandhi's, Chavez noted proudly. This public trifecta of fasts resembles Gandhi's in duration and purpose, including the goal of nonviolence and the need to do "penance."[65] In addition to Gandhi and the Mexican Penitente tradition, Chavez acknowledged that Mesoamerican spirituality informed his understanding of fasting.[66]

The leader's penchant for abstaining from food confounded some of his followers, who struggled to make sense of it in terms of organizing workers. It was an act of religious politics, a spiritual assault. He rejected the term *hunger strike* because his fasting was an act of satyagraha, a spiritual action, freely undertaken as an act of love and technically not intended as pressure on anyone. Whatever Chavez's expressed intentions were, his fasting involved, in effect, political maneuvering.

The first starvation, which yielded dramatic and transformative results in *La Causa,* also focused an international spotlight on the movement. By the time of the third fast, the effervescence had dissipated somewhat. The Chicano journalist Frank del Olmo understood it differently, however, noting in the *Los Angeles Times,* "Chavez ... uses his body to make the point.... He believes in what he is doing so fervently that he is willing to do anything to keep his movement alive—even nearly kill himself.... It's hard to argue with someone who is willing to risk death to make a point."[67] Richard Ray Perez's documentary *Cesar's Last Fast* (2014), with previously unseen footage, drives this point home. The film documents the agony of the final fast, demonstrating that Chavez was indeed prepared to die. He stopped fasting only when the Reverend Jesse Jackson visited him and took up the fast for him. During the closing ceremony, Chavez passed a cross to Jackson.

Chavez never presented a specific religious motivation or denominational reference for his abstentions from food but was instead characteristically vague and all-inclusive. The express purpose of his first public fast was to recommit the movement to the principles of nonviolence. On February 20, during the love fast, he sent a letter to the National Council of Churches to explain it: "My fast is informed by my religious faith and by my deep roots in the Church. It is not intended as pressure on anyone but only as an expression of my own deep feelings and my own need to do penance and to be in prayer. I know you will understand and I ask that you pray for me."[68] Five days later the UFW released a "Statement of the Fast for Nonviolence" that offered further explanation:

> Cesar Chavez is engaged in a prolonged religious fast which is first and foremost a deeply personal act of penance and hope.... Cesar's fast is for all men. Cesar's pain reminds us of the suffering of farm workers and of men of all races and kinds who are the victims of poverty and injustice.... The fast is an act of penance, recalling farm workers to the nonviolent roots of their movement. These farm workers who are united in the Delano strike care about the well being of all fellow beings, even those who have placed themselves in the position of adversaries.... It is a personal demand on each person to accept responsibility and to give the best of himself for a movement that is intent on setting other men free.... It is a personal act which beckons to each of us to participate in the nonviolent, world-wide struggle against man's inhumanity to man.[69]

Indeed, the fast opened a public space to reconcile and resolve cultural differences in the movement. According to one account, although the ceremonies each night were led by a Catholic priest, soon after they began, "Chavez asked a Protestant minister to deliver the nightly sermon, and a few nights later a Negro minister was the guest speaker. Father Day was sent to conduct services at a Protestant Church, and soon both Protestants and Catholics were attending the nightly services and racial and religious differences between the workers seemed to be easing."[70] Rather than reify religious and ethnic borders, the leader intended to synthesize them—a sacred act with a unified political outcome. He combined elements of different religions into a singular formation that included those with no faith at all.

The UFW attorney and eyewitness Jerry Cohen recalled:

> I'm not religious at all, but I would go to those masses at the Forty Acres every night. No matter what their religious background, anyone interested in farm workers, or with any sense about people, could see that something was going on that was changing a lot of people. The feeling of the workers was obvious. They talked at those meetings about their own experiences, about what the fast meant in terms of what the Union was going to mean to them. That was a really deep feeling, but it wasn't religious in the sense that somebody like me couldn't relate to it.[71]

Indeed, Chavez invited all to be transformed by his political spirituality. Consider the deftly diplomatic response he proffered when asked to explain the meaning of his fast: "See that white wall? Well, imagine ten different-colored balls, all jumping up and down. One ball is called religion, another propaganda, another organizing, another law, and so forth. When people look at that wall and see those balls, different people look at different balls; each person keeps his eye on his own ball. For each person the balls mean many different things, but for everyone they can mean something!"[72]

The leader officially broke his first fast with an ecumenical Mass of Thanksgiving; Robert F. Kennedy attended, as did the national press. An altar had been set up on a flatbed truck in a Delano park. Matthiessen describes the scene as follows: "The mass began with a prayer in Hebrew, the sermon was Protestant, and Catholic ritual preceded the breaking of poor man's bread, *semita*. After Chavez and Kennedy had shared bread, priests passed through the thousands of witnesses, distributing the loaves."[73] On March 11, 1968, the *New York Times* reported on the cessation of the hunger strike with a lengthy biographical sketch praising the leader; Cesar Chavez became a household name.

With the publicity the leader garnered many detractors and critics. Dolores Huerta explained: "A lot of people thought Cesar was trying to play God, that this guy really was trying to pull a saintly act. Poor

Cesar! They just couldn't accept it for what it was. I know it is hard for people who are not Mexican to understand, but this is a part of the Mexican culture—the penance, the whole idea of suffering for something, of self-inflicted punishment. It's a tradition of very long standing. In fact, Cesar has often mentioned in speeches that we will not win through violence, we will win through fasting and prayer."[74]

Despite shielding himself in spirituality and religious symbolism, the leader continued to be assaulted by criticism and to receive death threats. Matthiessen reports that a document entitled "The New Catholic Church 'Apostles Creed'" circulated widely in the Central Valley. It began with the following lines (misspellings and capitals in original): "I believe in CESAR CHAVEZ, creator of all the TROUBBBLE, and HELL.... I believe [Chavez] is the NEW POPE HOLY.... I believe that he is SAINT CESAR CHAVEZ.... I believe HE will be SHOT 'a la KENNEDY STYLE' (oh happy day)."[75] Chavez traveled with unarmed bodyguards and two German shepherds (Boycott and Huelga), and he continued to fast.

In 1972 he undertook a twenty-four-day Fast for Justice in a Phoenix Chicano community center. This action responded to the Arizona State Legislature's House Bill 2134, which prevented farm workers from organizing, picketing, and boycotting—effectively stripping them of rights guaranteed to other American workers. On May 15 Chavez issued an open letter announcing his fast, describing, first, the governor's response to the new law: "After the bill passed, it was brought to the Governor by the Highway Patrol. He signed it immediately. The next day the Governor was asked by a reporter to comment on the farm workers who wanted to meet with him. He responded: 'As far as I'm concerned, these people do not exist.'" Chavez's statement was his Arizona salvo in an ongoing jeremiad, an appeal to American civil religion: "This attack on our union in Arizona and in every major state is also an attack on the spirit of justice in America." He repeated his plea for rehumanization: "Somehow these powerful men and women must be helped to realize that there is nothing to fear from treating their workers as fellow human beings."[76]

But this second fast lacked the spontaneity of the first, as LeRoy Chatfield, one of the organizers, noted: "The Arizona Fast seemed more businesslike to me than had the Fast for Non-Violence."[77] The well-choreographed second hunger strike was expertly planned and staged, particularly the nightly masses and the attendees bearing hand-made crosses. Moreover, the events in Phoenix surrounding it produced a distinct paraphernalia, including the "Song Book of the Fast for Justice."[78] Printed bilingually, it is "Dedicated to the memory of John F. Kennedy, Martin Luther King, and Robert F. Kennedy—three men who gave their lives for the cause of the poor." A photo of each man is featured, along with an image of Our Lady of Guadalupe. The songbook contains standards: "De Colores," "Solidarity Forever," and "We Shall Overcome," the second and third songs in both English and Spanish. In fact, *La Causa* yielded many original songs and eventually its own hymnal. The Fast for Justice also produced publicity, in part because of the visits of celebrities, among them Coretta Scott King, who, while in Phoenix, announced that she would promote the lettuce boycott in Atlanta.

On the twentieth day of the second hunger strike the leader was hospitalized. "As Chavez is growing weaker," wrote Chris Hartmire, "we are growing stronger."[79] On June 6, the fourth anniversary of the assassination of Robert Kennedy, Chavez ate ceremoniously, breaking bread alongside the singer Joan Baez at a special Mass honoring the late senator Robert F. Kennedy and Martin Luther King. Chavez arrived in a screeching ambulance halfway through the liturgy, wearing a white Nehru jacket. Many "religious leaders" distributed "sacrificial bread" to the six thousand in attendance. Local Yaqui Indians performed their ceremonial dance to the Virgin of Guadalupe, which is ordinarily presented only once a year, in December. After the Mass, Joseph Kennedy, a son of Robert Kennedy, spoke honorifically of Chavez. Next, Chris Hartmire took the podium, informing the audience that Angela Davis had been acquitted of murder charges; this announcement was met with cheers and applause.

Chavez's statement about ending his fast was read for him in both English and Spanish. It explains the motivation for his actions: "The Fast was meant as a call to sacrifice for justice and as a reminder of how much Suffering there is among farmworkers." It goes on to reiterate his theology of sacrifice.

> It is possible to become discouraged about the injustice we see everywhere. But God did not promise us that the world would be humane and just. He gives us the gift of life and allows us to choose the way we will use our limited time on this earth.... We can choose to use our lives for others to bring about a better and more just world for our children. People who make that choice will know hardship and sacrifice. But if you give yourself totally to the non-violent struggle for peace and justice, you also find that people will give you their hearts and you will never go hungry and never be alone. And in giving of yourself, you will discover a whole new life full of meaning and love.[80]

The leader's words emerge at once as prophecy and homily. In fact, an editorial in *El Malcriado* explaining the Fast for Justice emphasized its prophetic dimension: "For centuries Holy men have fasted, as they challenged the established powers demanding justice for their people. The prophet is not simply a religious leader. He is a political spokesman as well. He speaks out in front of all members of society about the faults of society. The fast of the prophet is to put his life on the line."[81] It seems that by the time of the second hunger strike at least Chavez had accepted his prophetic role.

The leader's third public fast took place in 1988. A journalist described it as follows: "On July 16 Cesar Chavez, President of the United Farm Workers, drove out of the Tehachapi mountains where the UFW headquarters are located to Delano, California, where the union was founded. No one knew that he had decided to begin a water-only fast to identify himself with the farm worker families who suffer from the scourge of pesticide poisonings in agricultural communities."[82] The leader sequestered himself in a single room at the UFW retirement home, receiving visitors and working from bed. An ecumenical Mass was said every night with a purported three hundred farm workers in attendance. This would be the longest and thus most dangerous of his three fasts; during its thirty-six-day duration it became clear that the leader was willing to die, to sacrifice his life. Doctors and advisors pleaded with him to end the starvation, yet he persisted—until Jesse Jackson arrived on the thirty-fifth day.

As in previous years, the leader had a ceremony to end the Fast for Life; according to a story that appeared in the *New York Times,* "Thousands of supporters of the union, including movie stars and politicians, attended the Mass, held outdoors under a giant tent in heat near 100 degrees."[83] Chavez released a statement ending the fast that begins as follows:

> My heart is too full and my body too weak to read this message. So I have asked my oldest son, Fernando, to read it to you.
>
> I thank God for the love and support of my family as well as for the prayers and hard work of the members and staff of our Union. I am grateful to the many thousands of people who came to be with me and for the millions who have kept me in their prayers and who have taken up our cause in their own communities. They have opened up their hearts, not just to me, but to the farm workers and the families who suffer from the unrestrained poisoning of our soil, our water, our air, and our people.[84]

In addition to Jackson, Ethel Kennedy attended the liturgy. Chavez took particular note of her presence: "It is especially meaningful to me and all farm workers to have Ethel Kennedy and her children here on this day. Twenty years ago Bobby Kennedy stood with us when few had the courage to do so." The one-page statement goes on to say that others across the country "help carry the burden by continuing the fast in front of their local supermarkets."[85]

More than any other ritual, Chavez's public fasts established his prophetic and even messianic credentials. Electronic media made the image of Chavez nearing death a nightly staple in living rooms across America. How does one respond to that picture, to that reality? What is the emotional effect? Most audiences, I propose, questioned, empathized, became psychically and erotically conjoined to him; and they breathed a sigh of relief when the fast ended and his body resurrected, as if bringing redemption and new life to the nation. His public fasts created not only a community of viewers, but also a distinct spirituality in his movement, a religious ethos, enabling him to express political discourse in religious terms, seizing the spiritual high ground and transforming public opinion.

When considering his fasts in response to an interviewer's question, the leader waxed mystical: "I don't know. I've never been able to tell except that, well, Gandhi spoke about the door, or the window, the light. I can't really talk about those things, but sometimes it is *comparatively* easier than at other times. There is ... there is a force there. I don't quite know what it is."[86] Often when the body undergoes torture, memory is erased, time and space become blurred, and many report ecstasy, *ecstasis,* a sense of separating temporarily from the body and joining a larger consciousness.[87]

Chavez's crippled yet ecstatic body allowed television viewers to identify with him, confronted with the vision of pain. Spectators sympathized with his televised deterioration and experienced moral indignation at the injustice responsible for this kind of extreme misery. In short, the viewing of his suffering body elicited the sympathy that would win hearts and minds to his movement.

LA PAZ

In 1976 the UFW placed an initiative on the California ballot known as Proposition Fourteen. It would have allowed organizers access to farm workers on grower property. It was soundly defeated. The failure of the legislation was a watershed for the leader, setting in motion a series of events that led some to question his leadership of the UFW. Chatfield commented as follows: "I knew Cesar Chavez well enough to now write that this statewide public rebuke hurt him personally and shook his confidence; he was embarrassed and hurt."[88]

Earlier in the seventies, Chavez had begun relocating the offices of the UFW from Delano to a former tuberculosis asylum secluded in the Tehachapi Mountains of Keene County, thirty-five miles southeast of Bakersfield, one hundred and fifteen miles northeast of Los Angeles, and seventy-two miles south of the UFW's former headquarters in Delano. A Los Angeles–based supporter purchased the property for *La Causa* in a bidding war with another buyer. According to Chavez, "When they found out a month later that a Hollywood Jew and a Delano Mexican had gotten together to beat them, they were mad as hell."[89] The property, which occupies one hundred eighty-seven acres, had twenty-six buildings. Under the UFW these housed classrooms, where activists learned to organize and to negotiate contracts, and provided homes for families and dormitories for single people.

The leader shifted himself and his family there and required that staffers also live at La Paz full-time. According to Marc Grossman, two hundred and fifty people were in residence at the compound from the 1970s on.[90] In 1981 the *Los Angeles Times* ran a story on La Paz, reporting, "Even as a costly modernization program continues, the union stresses its role as a social cause, a *near-religion* requiring vows of poverty from its top officers, attorneys, doctors, nurses, and even the lowest level of file clerk."[91]

At La Paz Chavez turned his attention to establishing a Gandhi-style ashram, a commune, and as Matt Garcia argues, a religion, a transposition of Christian ecumenicalism into an inter-/non-/anti-denominational humanism. Chavez's increasing focus on a religious movement at the expense of labor organizing became clear to those most closely associated with him, especially after his move to isolated Keene County, detached from the quotidian issues of farm workers. In 1975 a firsthand observer commented: "La Paz is an unlikely setting for a trade union headquarters. But it is a symbol of Chavez's unique concept; somehow he equates the movement he leads with some kind of agrarian reform.... La Paz is in many respects a commune and Chavez thinks in communal terms."[92]

The UFW Executive Board convened at La Paz during the summer of 1977, a pivotal year. The meeting opened like a sacred ceremony, with the singing of "We Shall Not Be Moved" in Spanish, followed by several choruses of "This Little Light of Mine," declaring that light would shine all over "La Paz," "our union," "Delano," "the world," "the boycott," "Sacramento," and "wherever the [UFW] eagle flies." After the singing of the choruses the group broke into chants of "Viva La Causa," and "Viva Cesar," punctuated by a distinctive rhythmic clapping that begins slow and picks up speed until it thunders at a frenzied pace.[93]

At that point Chavez announced that the "Prayer of the Farm Worker's Struggle" would be read in Spanish by Dolores Huerta and in English by Chris Hartmire, recitations also met by enthusiastic rhythmic clapping. Finally the leader explained that he was calling the meeting to order, not as a convening of the executive board, but instead as an assembly of the "movement prophets." His goal was to experiment: "Prophet Dolores Huerta," for example, "Prophet Cesar Chavez." Finally, Chavez declared that he had intended to add a reading from Mao Tse-tung but was unable to find it in English.

During the final discussions at that same meeting, Chavez exclaimed: "I use my aura to run the Union." He instructed the group to "look at the religious movement as a good example, because what we have here is a *religion kind of thing*." In closing he reminded the leadership of *La Causa*, "I told you that this is a cultural revolution."

In March 1977 Chavez had begun printing the *President's Newsletter* every ten days. Its express purpose was to disseminate information about the movement, particularly the leader's communal objectives. The first issue of the *President's Newsletter*, dated March 11, 1977, contained the following notice:

> The Executive Board of the UFW has set aside certain dates to be observed union-wide. September 16th as the beginning of the Delano Grape Strike. Some of the most important dates are the deaths of the martyrs, Sister Nan Freeman and Brothers Nagi Daifullah and Juan de la Cruz who gave their lives for the union.

Joan Baez singing at the funeral of UFW "martyr" Juan de
la Cruz, Delano, CA, 1973. Bob Fitch Photo Archive,
© Stanford University Libraries.

Another date to be observed is March 31st, established as the founding
date of the Union. March 31, 1962 was the day that the Chavez family left
the CSO and began the long struggle of building a farm workers union.

Founding Day was to be celebrated in "worship services," singing union
songs, reading from Jacques Levy's *Cesar Chavez: Autobiography of La*

Causa, and enlisting "old-timers" to reminisce about the "early days." While at La Paz, the Cause elaborated its distinctive religiosity by devising its discrete sacred calendar with attendant remembrances, rituals, and ceremonies. In the words of LeRoy Chatfield, "The farmworkers movement, like other human rights movements and religious groups, exhibited many characteristics that are similar to—and I use the word respectfully—a cult. These include a charismatic leader, a common enemy, the total commitment of true believers to its righteous cause, ... an emphasis on community living and participation, material and spiritual needs of loyal participants met by the organization and a personal sense of discipline."[94]

From its mountain locale, *La Causa* performed many religious functions, addressing the ultimate concerns of Chavistas, at once personal, political, and cosmic. La Paz provided the space to unfold iterations of Christian rituals and ceremonies, which appear to be more like complements to the spirituality of *La Causa* than expressions of Christianity itself.

Take, for example, the annual celebration of the December 12 feast day of the patron of Mexico, Our Lady of Guadalupe. The following announcement circulated at La Paz in late November 1978: "Our Lady of Guadalupe ... should be an even better celebration than Thanksgiving because more of the community will be here and also because that feast is more meaningful to our movement than Thanksgiving is. What we did to the Indian in America after Thanksgiving is quite a contrast to what Our Lady of Guadalupe did for the Indian in Mexico."[95] La Paz devotees observing the feast were given a half day's reprieve from work to participate in events that included the singing of early morning "mañanitas," or traditional Mexican birthday serenades, a Mass, *pan dulce,* cocoa, and tequila. Chavez, like many other revolutionaries, deployed the Mexican Madonna in his social justice movement, deracinating her and relocating her in a political arena of struggle.

Much of the religious energy at La Paz was provided by Father Ken Irrgang, a Catholic priest who began working with Chavez in 1973 and relocated to La Paz in 1977, remaining there until 1983. Father Irrgang regularly said Mass at the commune; Chavez attended religiously. He never formally confessed to Father Irrgang, however. Irrgang recalls: "The entire time I was at La Paz I heard maybe two formal confessions.... You know, when we were in the fields the farm workers never received holy communion because they felt disenfranchised by the church."[96]

Instead, according to Father Victor Salandini, the "Tortilla Priest," the leader preferred group absolution despite its official prohibition: "Whenever I have said Mass for Cesar and the farm workers, I always give general absolution, even though no bishop in the United States permits such absolution. Cesar is always happy when I give general absolution."[97] This eschewing of orthodoxy demonstrates an interest, on the part of the farm workers and of Chavez, in the symbols and rituals of Catholicism but little investment in Catholic orthodoxy.

Father Irrgang regularly said "Mass in the fields during elections, and those were always Catholic, and we celebrated Mass regularly on Sundays at the UFW headquarters in La Paz."[98] Before long, Chavez petitioned Chris Hartmire to replace one meeting a month with a Protestant service; both the Catholic Mass and the Protestant service were sparsely attended. According to Father Irrgang, "We had about twenty to twenty-five people at the Mass each Sunday, including Cesar and his wife[;] they never missed a Sunday Mass or any other religious service.... The people who attended the Catholic ritual also showed up for the Protestant service." In November 1978 the Sunday morning meeting was officially named La Paz Community Liturgical Service, with no particular denominational commitment other than to *La Causa*.[99]

Chavez was also interested in Judaism and had considerable support among Jews. Matthiessen describes the leader and quotes him in the following scene: "When we got back to his room, he took off his outer clothing and climbed into his high bed, where he hung his mezuzah among the dangling rosaries. 'I'm sure Christ wore a mezuzah,' he said.

'He certainly didn't wear a cross.'"[100] Father Irrgang has described Chavez's religiosity as follows: "Cesar was profoundly Catholic; but he was also profoundly ecumenical. He was an open man when it came to religion.... We would have a rabbi visit us once in a while.... The rabbis thought very highly of him.... Cesar never spoke out against birth control or abortion, but he never was judgmental about people's religious attitudes. He was very liberal."[101] On this last point Irrgang and Chatfield disagree; Bardacke quotes the latter: "Cesar wasn't interested in liberation theology because of his conservative Catholicism. He was a very conservative Catholic."[102] Mark Day's comment counters Chatfield's claim: "In many ways we were practicing liberation theology in Delano in the late 1960s."[103]

In October 1978, Hartmire began to issue a weekly newsletter, entitled *La Paz Community Religious Life Bulletin*. Its goals included keeping the community "aware of special holidays being observed by all religious groups—Catholics, Protestants, Jews, Moslems."[104] (The bulletin also promoted the establishment of UFW holidays, especially martyrs' days and a founding day.)[105] The bulletin's contents were generated in the meetings of the "liturgy committee." Notes from an early committee meeting reflect on the Sunday community rite, complaining that it was "too Catholic," and "not really ecumenical."[106]

One of the early issues of La Paz's *Religious Life Bulletin* lamented that "the goal of encouraging relationships to 'God' has disappeared," expressing odd objectives for the leadership of a labor syndicate: "to challenge the community to care for one another" and "to emphasize the voluntary nature of religious life." It continues: "An additional purpose of this bulletin will be to prick our consciences about the values our union and community proclaim—our non-violence, the meaning of true community, our commitment to serve farm workers and all the poor, the meaning of poverty and the simplicity of life, the need to continue to be a volunteer staff and so on."[107] La Paz also hosted a Thursday night study group on religious education. A typical discussion involved "the relationship between faith and struggle," and "searching for a way to weave arcane disciplines with the work of social justice."[108]

The *Religious Life Bulletin* expressed a radical message synthesizing politics and religion. The first bulletin, dated October 28, 1978, printed a quotation from Arlo Guthrie slamming a rabid antigay activist: "The difference between Anita Bryant and me may be that she definitely feels that God is on her side, and I have to keep questioning whether I'm on his." And an editorial called for "more Hispanic bishops."[109] Another editorial in the issue that followed criticized the Baptists as "the only religious group that officially called for support of the anti-homosexual proposition [Proposition Six] during the recent election."[110] A subsequent issue declared January 25 Nan Freeman Day, identifying Freeman as one of the major martyrs of the farm worker movement, "Kadosha, a holy person."[111] The newsletter featured quotations from Gandhi and Confucius. On December 1, 1978, the bulletin ran a cautionary note on the mass suicide in Guyana by members of the People's Temple at Jonestown, led by the Reverend Jim Jones.

The presence of various clergy lent the commune at La Paz an undeniably religious ethos; still, Chavez wanted more. Early in 1977 the leader put Hartmire in charge of assembling a committee to work on establishing a religious order, under the auspices of the Catholic Church; yet it was going to be ecumenical, and it would enroll both women and men. This group was to be called Los Menos, or "the least," presumably a reference to Matthew 25:40, where Jesus speaks of final judgment: "The King will reply, 'Truly I tell you, whatever you did for one of the least of these brothers and sisters of mine, you did for me.'"

According to Hartmire's notes, Los Menos was to begin with "liturgy and religious education, to strengthen relationships to 'God,' nurture community life, [and] care for the sick." Los Menos would be a voluntary elite religious nucleus for *La Causa*, with even greater commitments to poverty and service. The Reverend Hartmire's notes describe it specifically as a "priesthood." On February 17, 1977, Hartmire sent a letter to the Vatican, requesting papal authorization to establish a religious order, articulating a "need for a self-conscious religious community within the farm workers' movement led by Cesar Chavez. What is on my mind is an ecumenical (Protestant and Catholic), male and female, married and single religious community with vows of poverty and obedience and a commitment to serve the cause of justice within the farm workers' movement."[112] The next month, on March 15, a papal emissary responded with a letter expressing great confusion and calling the proposition a "practical impossibility."[113]

In 1974 Synanon received official government recognition as a religion, along with tax-exempt status. Founded in Southern California during the late sixties as an outreach program for drug addicts, Synanon evolved into a commune whose participants were required to shave their heads and to wear a uniform consisting of a white T-shirt and denim overalls, marking their solidarity with industrial workers. In March 1977, the first edition of the *President's Newsletter* announced that members of the Executive Board of the UFW had recently been guests of the Synanon Foundation, explaining: "Synanon, founded by Chuck Dederich, was originally a social movement designed primarily for addicts. Currently it is open to all those who are ready to accept the complete program. Synanon also works with other groups giving assistance as needed, and has been very supportive of the UFW."[114] On another page, the newsletter reports: "The Synanon Foundation recently sent a 40 foot semi truck to La Paz loaded with things to share with us ... [including] 22,000 pounds of food.[115]

Dederich visited La Paz often, holding strategy meetings and offering instruction on Synanon's teachings, some of which Chavez adopted. In a memo to *La Causa's* leader from Hartmire, dated September 7, 1977, it becomes clear that Chavez and Hartmire were considering asking some residents at La Paz to shave their heads "as a symbol of willingness to participate fully in their [Synanon's] community for 3 months."[116] Perhaps the greatest contribution Synanon made to the UFW was its signature ritual, "the game."

Analysts, with the benefit of hindsight, have made much of the social, historical, and devotional significance of the leader's embrace of "gaming." Players in the game are divided into "gamers," and a person who is being "gamed." The person undergoing a gaming sits in the middle of a circle while gamers hurl all manner of accusations and insults in an uninhibited one-hour session. The game was intended to yield truth, communication, and catharsis. Many problems resulted—conflicts, hurt feelings, resentments—and critics point to the years from 1977 to 1979 as a time when *La Causa* devolved into a Synanon-style new religious movement, or "cult." Matt Garcia claims: "Only those on the inside … understood that Chavez's community had more of an affinity with Dederich's Synanon than with the Catholic Church."[117]

Chavez did not require members to participate in the game but strongly encouraged participation. At a UFW Executive Board meeting in 1977, he spoke about the need to experiment with new things in order to grow, and gaming was part of that experimentation with the new and the extreme that captured and afflicted many Americans during the 1970s. At that same board meeting several attendees spoke of their positive experiences playing the game, and the leader said that a "good game" can be transformative. "In gaming, so much gets aired; in gaming, the people who make decisions have so much more information available to them because of gaming."[118] Evidence of discontent with the Synanon ritual, however, includes memoranda from Hartmire to Chavez recounting conversations in which Chavistas, among them Richard Chavez and Dolores Huerta, informed him that they would no longer play; yet many players remained.

In December 1978 Dederich was arrested and charged with conspiracy and solicitation to commit murder and assault with a deadly weapon. He was alleged to have been responsible for placing a four-foot rattlesnake in the mailbox of a foe. Synanon's founder had relapsed from sobriety into severe alcoholism—too drunk to understand that he was being arrested. On January 13, 1979, a group calling themselves the Coalition Conference Committee held a press conference to support

Dederich. Chavez and the Reverend Ralph Abernathy were among those speaking to journalists. Chavez's statement read, in part, as follows:

> I have known Chuck Dederich for over twenty years. In this time, he has been a personal friend of mine. He has been, even more important, a personal friend of the Farm Workers. Very few people know that in the early days of our strike in Delano, Synanon, Chuck Dederich was a tremendous help to us.... It was Dederich's established medical and dental clinic that provided for the first few years of the strike exclusive medical attention—and dental attention—to our strikers. It was Dederich's organization that brought the first truckload of food to us in Delano.[119]

Chavez and the others spoke as character witnesses, hoping to sway public opinion. Chavez's statement continued: "Dederich has helped, as most of us know, an awful lot of people. He went to help the people that nobody really cared for, or no one knew how to care for, or nobody was willing to help. He went and took the men and women who were rejected by society and made good citizens out of them. That's a tremendous record for anyone to claim".[120]

Chavez's Achilles' heel was his zealous commitment to his ideals and his values, which persisted in his philosophy even when his behavior seemed bizarre and irrational to many. No doubt his was a pontifical rule, a product of catechistic excess, whereby the individual could be sacrificed for the majority.

SUFFERING FOR OTHERS: *LA CAUSA* AS A RELIGION OF REVOLUTION

The official statement read at the ceremony terminating Chavez's Fast for Nonviolence in 1968 may be his most memorable articulation of his core teaching. He claims to have received it as a spiritual revelation while fasting. It described the central theme of the leader's mission: "It is my deepest belief that only by giving our lives do we find life."[121] Sacrificing for others was his pivotal teaching. This philosophy earned him many detractors, including farm workers who opposed him as UFW president and his do-gooder's mandate as ineffective strategy for a labor union. Criticism of his movement came from those both in- and outside it. Insider critics often contrasted the goals of a labor syndicate—benefits, or *los beneficios*—with Chavez's expressed philosophy of *los sacrificios,* questioning why a labor union would ask members to sacrifice.

Chavez demanded not only sacrifice from his followers, but also total commitment. The following notice appeared in the first issue of the *President's Newsletter:* "A serious situation developed over a long period of time in the La Paz community. A small group of people were working together against the best interests of the union by exhibiting poor attitudes towards the goals and leadership of the union, refusing to accept direction, and spreading rumors and gossip. By initiating and perpetuating feelings of unhappiness and discontent among headquarters staff, they interfered with work procedure, lowered morale and impeded the progress of the entire movement."[122] As a result some volunteers were "asked to leave," while others resigned. The announcement went on to say that while the departures would result in a greater workload for remaining staffers, "the visible improvement in morale is expected to more than compensate."

These departures became infamous as the "purges"; they would eventually affect Hartmire and other key UFW figures. Chavez's sudden dismissal of longtime volunteers might have been provoked, at least in part, by what some perceived as paranoia and megalomania. Whatever the cause, Chavez excommunicated some volunteers whom he thought disloyal and made others work harder and bear a greater burden of sacrifice. When the practical needs of the UFW conflicted with the lofty objectives of *La Causa,* as he saw them, Chavez favored the movement's goals—he had a religious commitment to them.

I propose that the leader sometimes eschewed the logic of a labor syndicate to establish what Bruce Lincoln, following Durkheim, calls a "religion of resistance." In Lincoln's account, oppositional religious movements emerge predominantly among postcolonial groups. When the naturalized myths of the state that legitimate the radically unequal status quo fail to persuade those most disenfranchised, the religious tools used for hegemony can be deployed in actions subverting the system—what I call religious politics. Lincoln notes that the first goal of a religion of resistance "is mere survival, to which end the resisters create cohesive, defensible, insular communities."[123] On one level, *La Causa* is usefully understood as a quasi-religion of resistance that developed in dialectical engagement with the religion of the status quo, rather than in direct opposition to it: Chavez redefined Christianity, but he did not reject it. Instead, he stressed the gospel message of poverty and sacrifice, critiquing an American civil religion that has material accumulation, "blessings," at its core.

Indeed, religions of resistance are characterized by their "heterodoxy." They are typically founded by a charismatic prophet, who carves a niche for himself among a rank-and-file membership that comes "from the lower strata ... [whereas] leaders tend to be members of the 'marginal intelligentsia.'" Although Chavez was raised mostly in poverty, when he became a salaried employee of the CSO, he entered the group that "fell between the literati and the peasant class." In contradistinction to Lincoln's description, the founder of *La Causa* was not particularly "discontent and in need of support," though he never would have reached his level of celebrity and influence had he not founded the UFW. The founders Lincoln describes introduce "new discourses to lower-class circles, articulating and giving focus to peasant discontent, while winning adherents."[124]

Lincoln also identifies "ritual healing" as a characteristic of a religion of resistance, not only because of its practical value among the poor and oppressed, but also because healing is "understood metaphorically, the patients being simultaneous victims and representations of society itself."[125] An example of a religion that emphasizes healing rituals would be Pentecostalism or Santería, which deploy spiritual healing of bodies (as well as divine protection) as central to their mission. *La Causa* was a movement of metaphorical, not literal, healing. But Chavez did not foreclose the possibility of a healing ministry in the Latin American tradition of the *curandero* or *curandera,* medicine men and women who also function in the community as gurus and wise people.

Considering *La Causa* as a religious movement enables greater comprehension of its leader's ritual drama but does not exhaust its interpretive possibilities. There are many ways to frame and understand Chavez's work; he intended it that way, because he intended to reach the largest possible audience. This is a strategy he continued into his final act.

The Lost Gospel

"God Help Us to Be Men!"

And now abideth faith, hope, love, these three; but the
greatest of these is love.

St. Paul, 1 Corinthians 13:13

I think of organizing as sacred work.[1]

Dolores Huerta

Dr. King realized that the only real wealth comes from
helping others.[2] Cesar Chavez

Cesar Chavez designed his own coffin: he instructed his brother Richard, a carpenter, to build a simple pinewood rectangle; the leader
wanted the wood to be sanded smooth but did not want it stained or
painted. He got what he ordered.[3] The funerary procession followed a
well-worn path in Delano from Memorial Park, to the Forty Acres—
about twelve miles. Chavez's final pilgrimage was led by a banner of
Our Lady of Guadalupe. During the viewing, a flag bearing the UFW
logo hung from inside the coffin's lid. Long adept at spiritual performance, he saved his best for last.

Had the leader choreographed his own death, it probably would
have looked a lot like it did. He died in his sleep and was found with a
book of Native American art opened across his chest, in the home of a
supporter just footsteps north of the Mexican border, a few miles from

the place of his birth. He had come full circle. The leader was in his home state to testify in a trial against the Bruce Church corporation—the company that had foreclosed on his family's property many years back.[4] The UFW had won the case. Dolores Huerta, in her eulogy for Chavez, remarked on the symbolism of his death, intoning: "Cesar died in peace, in good health, with a serene look on his face. It was as if he had chosen to die at this time ... at this Easter time.... He died so that we would wake up. He died so that the union might live."[5]

In a sense, Chavez had experienced "death" multiple times, publicly (if metaphorically) crucified, and had undergone spiritual demise and resurrection: that he reinvented himself repeatedly partly explains why there is so much confusion and disagreement about his life. Rather than resolve the conflict, this book no doubt exacerbates it. It bears repeating that I have not written a definitive history or biography of Chavez but instead offer a fresh perspective—by framing him as a prophetic agent and *La Causa* as a religious movement. I see him as a "tragic hero" by Aristotle's definition, in the sense that he succumbed to personal flaws—despite his original and best intentions—as the result of hubris.

If many of his followers remained loyal, he nonetheless had many detractors. Indeed, he suffered brutal assaults against his character and threats on his life. Growers produced a literature excoriating him as a communist dictator who did not represent farm workers but instead was motivated by a quest for personal glory.[6]

The Office of the President collection in the UFW archive at Wayne State University contains flyers and letters from farm workers who rebuked and cursed Chavez. One written in Spanish is particularly disturbing. It begins: "Mr. Cesar Chavez, Little leader of the *Juevones* who do not care to work nor let others work. I believe that soon you will have your better life." It goes on to attack the leader, in a text salted with vulgarities. It is not surprising that the leader bred detractors, and that today some of his most passionate critics attempt to sully his reputation. I think it remarkable that he was resilient enough to withstand constant attacks and that despite the best efforts of iconoclastic authors, he is remembered mostly as someone who on balance produced positive effects in the world.

I propose a way to understand his personality: he exhibited "mestiza consciousness," a multiplicity of incarnations and significations, a triumph of the process of psychic formation Gloria Anzaldúa calls the Coatlicue state, whereby the self is revitalized and reborn not as a whole but as fragmented and fluid, keen to negotiate disparate worlds and dwell in many different identity categories at once. She writes: "Goddess of birth and death, *Coatlicue* gives and takes away life; she is the incarnation of cosmic processes. Simultaneously, depending on the person, she represents duality, and a third perspective—something more than a mere duality or a synthesis of duality."[7] Chavez underwent processes of psychic and physical (near) death and rebirth by fasting, revisiting the void, the darkness. Animated by new causes, he experienced multiple incarnations and exhibited multiple personalities, all of which enabled him to draw from manifold wells of affect, though sometimes in doing so he vexed the public that saw and heard him, producing envy, hatred, and fear among them.

Chavez worked to shift past nationalism and other social divisions to establish a beloved community beyond any one fixed identity category. Consider his statements on race: "I hear about *la raza* more and more.... Some people don't look at it as racism, but when you say *la raza,* you are saying an anti-gringo thing, and our fear is that it won't stop there. Today it's anti-gringo, tomorrow it will be anti-Negro, and the day after it will be anti-Filipino, anti–Puerto Rican.... On discrimination, I don't even give the members the privilege of a vote, and I'm not ashamed of it."[8] In another place the leader associated racism with machismo: "*La Raza* is a very dangerous concept. I speak very strongly against it among the chicanos.... I make fun of it, and I knock down machismo, too."[9] He rightly linked discrimination to machismo in elaborating his vision of a new man, an honorable macho with humanistic values.

Because Chavez's humanism has been largely overlooked by those who write about him, it is his "lost gospel." His *good news* had at its core several unorthodox doctrines centered on recalibrating manhood:

equality with women; intimate male bonding; weeping and vulnerability; and struggling against all oppression—including that based on sexual orientation and gender identity. All these doctrines emerged in Chavez's fundamental mandate of nonviolence, self-sacrifice, and rehumanization of colonized peoples.

GOD HELP US TO BE MEN!

By the time of Chavez's first fast, in 1968, Che Guevara had been dead less than a year. As George Mariscal notes, the construction of *el hombre nuevo* by means of revolutionary violence was pivotal to Che's Latin American de-colonial project.[10] Chavez too created a discourse of masculinity, as he too imagined a revolutionary and postcolonial social order. But the rejection of violence was key to his formulation. Perhaps the leader's most powerful statement in this regard was the one read for him when he terminated his Fast for Nonviolence, the one he claimed to have received as a revelation when he meditated during his fast.

> Our struggle is not easy. Those who oppose our cause are rich and powerful and they have many allies in high places. We are poor. Our allies are few. But we have something the rich do not own. We have our own bodies and spirits and the justice of our cause as our weapons.... We must admit that our lives are all that really belong to us. So, it is how we use our lives that determines what kind of men we are. It is my deepest belief that only by giving our lives do we find life. I am convinced that the truest act of courage, the strongest act of manliness is to sacrifice ourselves for others in a totally non-violent struggle for justice. To be a man is to suffer for others. God help us to be men![11]

Although some have criticized Chavez for his male-centered message, I understand it differently. He was directly exhorting the men who were bringing violence into the strike. The leader targeted men because he believed that men were the problem—particularly when they acted according to the dictates of machismo, with its violent, misogynist, and homophobic proclivities. In 1970 Joan London and Henry Anderson noted: "The Union grows and seems likely to continue growing no matter what happens to Chavez, for in the course of becoming a man himself, Cesar Chavez has been a maker of men."[12]

On the day that the leader announced his first fast, he and his long-time supporter Epifano Camacho were served with subpoenas for violating a recent injunction against picketing. When they appeared in court two weeks later, they were met by a crowd of farm workers, many of whom were men. Remarkably, these untypical machos were lined up kneeling before Chavez, praying; despite strict machista codes against displays of weakness, they imitated the founder's masculine ethics. He enfleshed a new manliness, an honorable machismo attained by nonviolence, submission, and struggle. As one eyewitness saw it, in the love fast, "Chavez had made his point in dramatic fashion. For a time, at least, machismo (the test of manliness through violence) was dead among the migrant strikers."[13]

The leader's new man not only prayed and fasted but also worked militantly for justice. According to one Chavista: "Cesar said the farm workers would never be men until they could prove themselves by taking on the grape industry."[14] On February 20, 1971, Chavez spoke at Hunter College in New York at an action undertaken by the Berrigan brothers. There, he elaborated his philosophy of masculinity:

> Men who practice injustice and who live in fear believe that they can accomplish all things by making other men afraid.... They might succeed if it were not for those few men who will not bend even under the pressure of imprisonment and the loss of friends and former supporters. The Berrigans and those who are accused with them are such men. They do not know fear in the way that most of us do—not because they are not human but because in a manner after Jesus they have cast their lives with the poor and the oppressed. In giving their lives they find life. In serving others they lose the fear that cripples freedom. In reaching for the best in every person they make each of us more human. In respecting the life of every man and woman they make life more precious for us all. They and those like them cannot be beaten.[15]

Chavez reconstructed manhood, recasting "machismo" as a code of honor rather than rejecting it altogether. His machismo continued the values of courage and bravery, but redirected them toward social justice and self-sacrifice, rather than toward violence and personal aggrandizement.

Typically the designation "macho" signifies a Latino masculine code that decries ordinary human emotion, such as affection, love, and compassion, and instead promotes stereotypically male behavior driven by violence, rage, and libido.[16] But as Alfredo Mirande found in his survey of more than a thousand Latino men, there is another conception of machismo that advances respectable attitudes and behavior. According to this iteration, a macho "is not hypermasculine or aggressive, and he does not disrespect or denigrate women. Machos, according to the positive view, adhere to a code of ethics that stresses humility, honor, respect of oneself and others, and courage."[17]

In light of this revised definition, it comes as little surprise that Mirande's survey determined that Chavez was foremost among the men Latino males admired and respected.[18] He represented a qualitatively different manliness that cultivates fraternal bonds and honorable actions. Although fraternity often results in patriarchy, the discourse and praxis of love among men enabled Chavez to create a template of erotic union that not only honored women as equals, but also allowed the United Farm Workers to include lesbians, gays, and bisexuals in *La Causa*.

Several observers have noted Chavez's tactical disruption of stereotypical macho cultural mandates, particularly violence. According to Matthiessen, "He has no *machismo*."[19] Chavez's rejection of machismo was a learned value: "Chavez speaks warmly of his father, from whom he learned his contempt of *machismo*: unlike most Mexican-Americans, and most Anglos, for that matter, Mr. Chavez never considered it unmanly to bathe his children or take them to the toilet or do small menial jobs around the house. But it is his mother whom Cesar credits with his feeling of responsibility toward his people, and hers was also the original influence toward nonviolence."[20]

Victor Villaseñor comments on Chavez's relationships with women:

> In Mexico, Chávez was as hero to the students and intellectuals, but to most of the workers he was not well thought of. Not only was he stopping so many

Mexicans from earning money in *Los Estados Unidos* so they could bring it home to Mexico.... but also he was not *un macho*. No he didn't drink or swear or have beautiful women pulling at his pants.... So Chávez, who talked softly and didn't drink, who preached nonviolence, and had no women pulling at his pants but instead had a lady, a female, as his second in charge.[21]

The leader himself noted,

> Women have a lot of staying power. They're endowed with some real special thing by God, I think. Men, you know, we want it, let's do it, we want to finish it all up in seconds, but women just keep going. If you're full of machismo, you can't appreciate what women do, but if you're not, it's really beautiful. Sometimes husbands are macho, the head of the house, the king, you know, and to have his wife out on the picket line is degrading. And so she has to organize him, and the first thing you know, he's out there, too.[22]

Chavez's attitudes toward women reflect those of Gandhi—who intended to lift women up.

Mariscal has contrasted the models of Latino manhood performed by two icons of the Chicano movement: Che Guevara and Cesar Chavez, according to categories Mariscal calls hypermasculinity and hybrid masculinity. He argues that "Chávez presented urban Chicanas and Chicanos with a form of masculinity virtually unknown outside the Catholicism of their *abuelitas* [grandmothers].... [He] constructed a hybrid form of masculinity that combined 'passive' elements most often linked by Western patriarchy to 'feminine' subjectivities with a fearless determination that traditional gendered representations have reserved exclusively for 'masculine practices.'"[23] Chavez constructed a masculinity that like his spirituality was *nepantla*, crossing macho borders and incorporating femininity; his reformulation of machismo emerged in stark contrast to the hypermasculinity characteristic of other anticolonial revolutionaries, especially Che.

This dichotomy is captured and reconciled in a controversial piece of art by Alex Donis ("Adonis") titled *Che Guevara and César Chávez* ("My Cathedral"). The painting depicts the two revolutionary symbols locked in a warm embrace, their open mouths pressed against each other, sharing the same breath. Their eyes are shut as they lose themselves in the new organism yielded by their romantic union. In his artist's statement Adonis explains: "Although the pairing of Che Guevara and César Chávez in a homosexual embrace is fictional, I personally enjoy the thread of reality inherent in the painting. Both of these characters never actually kissed, but in this painting, the paradox is that they have and have not. I created this work to try and melt down the stoicism in male Latino heroic figures and address the fear in feminizing masculinity."[24] The image, set in a light box and displayed with works highlighting similar couplings (Madonna and Mother Teresa, for example), was shown at the Galería de la Raza, in San Francisco's Mission District in 1997, in a site-specific exhibition the artist called *My Cathedral*. Vandals broke in to the gallery and destroyed the piece; there is little to suggest Chavez himself would have objected to it. The other image that was destroyed depicted Jesus embracing Lord Rama.

Although the leader's philosophy of militant nonviolence is central to Mariscal's argument about Chavez's hybrid masculinity, other elements contributed to his hybridity. Chavez also exhibited mores vis-à-vis lesbians and gays that were not macho. There is no evidence to suggest that Chavez was himself gay or bisexual. My argument here is that he modeled an intimate, even erotic, friendship with other men that belies and transgresses macho codes of what Octavio Paz called an ethic of *chingar*, or violation, in which men are pitted against one another in a maelstrom of social competition for the title *el más chingón*, or the alpha male. He performed a machismo that challenged and reversed this value in his friendships.

CESAR CHAVEZ AND FRED ROSS

In 1952 Chavez met Fred Ross, a forty-two-year-old community organizer who had been directed to the leader by the local priest, Father Donald McDonnell, with whom Chavez had formed a close friendship. The two men were in their early twenties, and the priest began mentoring

Alex Donis, *Che Guevara and César Chávez* ("My Cathedral"), 1998. Iris print on paper, 23" × 15", edition of 50. Courtesy of the artist.

Chavez, suggesting readings for him on social justice, including church teachings. McDonnell was part of a small group of mission priests who served Northern California. The leader began accompanying him on mission trips to jails and labor camps, while volunteering to assist him in such monotonous chores as the cleaning and maintenance of the Guada-lupe barrio church on the East Side of San Jose. The two spent a great deal of time together. But when Chavez met Ross, his attention soon turned to the tall handsome organizer. Both men deemed this meeting fateful. "I first met him in Sal Si Puedes," Chavez noted of Ross, and added: "He changed my life." On the day he met Chavez, Ross wrote in his diary: "'I think I've found the guy I'm looking for.' It was obvious even then."[25]

Ross was working for the Community Service Organization (CSO) to organize Chicanos for neighborhood improvement programs, antidiscrimination efforts, and voter registration. "I would find any excuse to be with Fred," Chavez explained. "I even started to imitate him."[26] The twenty-five-year-old Chavez became Ross's doppelgänger from the very first night: "I was his constant companion. I used to get home from work between five and five-thirty, and he'd say 'I'll pick you up at six-thirty, give you a little time to clean up and eat,' and I'd say, 'No, I don't want to clean up and eat, pick me up at five-thirty!' So he would be waiting when I got home from work, and I'd just drop my lunch pail and rush right out. . . . A lot of people worked with him, but few learned what I learned."[27]

Ross reciprocated Chavez's admiration, writing of the leader in 1989: "Before the Grape Strike and Boycott, before the highly publicized marches and fasts, before the Kennedys, before the millions of people from all over the world who rallied behind his cause—before all of that, there was just Cesar, with a single-minded doggedness that kept him trying no matter what the odds or how long it might take. Thirty years later, he hasn't changed. Not one little bit."[28]

Dolores Huerta also commented on the affection between the two men: "I think Fred probably loves Cesar more than anybody in the world—maybe even more than his wife and children."[29] Chavez never hid his affection for Ross, but his 1992 eulogy disclosed an intimate and passionate relationship.

> Preparing for this memorial, I was reading through correspondence between Fred and myself from the early 1960s that I hadn't seen in thirty years.
>
> We saw each other then infrequently. But we wrote as often as we could—often long letters—and Fred would usually include a modest

contribution to help tide us over. Listen to just a few excerpts from our letters.... "Dear Fred: Sure happy to receive your letter this morning. *Cheque* or no *cheque,* your letters will give me that which I need so badly right now." ... "I prefer seeing you than writing to you. As always, Cesar. Viva La Causa."

Chavez ended the eulogy as follows: "And I didn't have the chance to tell him that in addition to training me and inspiring me and being my hero, over forty years he also became my best friend. I shall miss him very much."[30] In publicly disclosing the intimacy and warmth of his friendship, Chavez defied the machista codes that ban love between men in favor of the ethic of *chingar* or violation.

Fred Ross died in 1992. Cesar Chavez died six months later.

QUEER(Y)ING LA CAUSA

I asked Father Irrgang whether the leader supported LGBT rights. His answer was an emphatic yes: "There was a gay man at the clinic in Salinas and I mean he was flamboyantly gay, flamboyant! He was moved to headquarters [La Paz] and some complained that he was coming on to them so I called him in and asked if he could you know tone it down a bit. But Cesar never said anything about him; he was supportive."[31]

Ana Raquel Minian has added to a queer UFW history, interviewing a former Chavista about his coming out in the UFW: "Rick Garcia, an organizer of the St. Louis boycott, remembers that other UFW members were not only 'unbelievably' supportive but actually encouraged him to become a gay activist. Indeed, the official statement on equal justice for the gay community in the 1970s maintained that the union [UFW] favored the enactment of legislation adding the phrase 'sexual orientation' to the present State of California civil rights statutes. Such legislation would extend to Gay men and women the same protection provided to social groups described by race, age, religion, sex and physical handicap."[32] There is significant proof demonstrating both Chavez's support of lesbian and gay rights and his efforts by his own behavior to transform homophobic macho attitudes.[33]

In December 1967 Cesar and Helen Chavez traveled to Mexico City to meet with Mexican "politicians" regarding agricultural workers. The discussions quickly unraveled, however, because the government officials "were openly suspicious of his [Chavez's] un-*macho* manner and his unwillingness to drink or smoke, and one drunken official went so far as to suggest to his face that he did not 'enjoy women.'"[34] Chavez's failure to enter into productive conversation with these men, identified only as "Mexican politicians," was caused by his inability to behave according to the superficially masculine codes delineating the rituals of "macho" society.[35]

Even though Chavez arrived in Mexico with his wife, a rare travel partner, Mexicans accused him of taking no pleasure in sexual relations with women. Chavez recounts the episode in Matthiessen's biography of him but neither refutes nor denies the charge; his response— or lack of response—demonstrates that he was well ahead of his time in the struggle for the dignity of all human beings.

In 1974 Dolores Huerta proclaimed that Chavez and the UFW welcomed "homosexuals." According to Huerta: "Cesar feels that liberals are liberals right up to the steps of the Catholic church. Guys can be liberal about homosexuality, about dope, about capital punishment, about everything, but the Catholic church." Huerta's testimony not only characterizes the UFW as at least "liberal" regarding "homosexuality," but also identified an anti-Catholic sentiment among members of *La Causa*. Chavez, however, did not tolerate intolerance. Huerta continued: "So he [Chavez] doesn't want to feed the bigotry that the average person has against the church. He tries to overcome that bigotry with his example."[36] In a 2006 interview she reflected as follows: "Yes, there were farm workers who were gay and lesbian. Cesar Chavez had a 'comadre' [close friend], who was a lesbian who baptized his oldest son, Fernando. She owned a little bar called People's. For the strikers, that was our hangout because there was so much discrimination against us that People's was a place that we all went to because there was never any hostility. In fact, it was part of our movement."[37]

Helen Chavez confirmed that the godparents of her son were lesbians. On July 16, 2010, I received the following email from Marc Grossman:

> So I spoke about it just now with Helen Chavez, Cesar's widow. Helen went to school with Jesse Torres ("Mocha" was her nickname), and they were good friends. The Torres family owned People's Market, where Cesar started courting Helen in the mid-'40s and, next door, People's Bar, which became a UFW hangout during the Delano strike in the '60s. When Fernando and later his sister, Sylvia, were born, Mocha asked to baptize them. At the time Helen says they didn't know she was Lesbian; that was revealed years later. However, it wouldn't have mattered as Helen remained good friends with Mocha until she died some time back. Helen remains friends with Mocha's sister, Butter Gonzales, who still lives in Delano.

At least one historian disagrees, claiming that everyone knew of their lesbianism: "Mocha and Ann, the pro-union, lesbian proprietors.... tended the bar and lived together in the back, but People's wasn't a gay bar. It was a farm worker bar where lesbians were welcome, as were a group of male cross-dressers who regularly came up from Bakersfield to dance with the surplus of single men."[38] Hence, the movement not only accepted transgender women, but literally embraced them. The bar was at the center of Delano's union geography, but Chavez patronized it only infrequently.

In 1983 the leader spoke to a gathering of the LGBT community organization called Just Business, at Circus Disco in West Hollywood, where he made the following remarks.

> Many years ago we were struggling in Delano to try to build an organization to defend the rights of workers, men and women who worked in the fields.... It was along those years that we began to know from friends that supported us about the problems that the gay and lesbian communities were facing throughout the country.
>
> It was in those heady days of the mid-'60s that we began to support, as best we could, the effort of those groups to end discrimination and to

get a just treatment in the things they were fighting for.... I'd like to say that they're not going to give you a thing unless you take it from them legally.[39]

His entrance and exit were met with a standing ovation.

The following year Chavez traveled to San Francisco to march in a labor rally on the eve of the Democratic National Convention held there. The LGBT community was staging a march and rally simultaneously, hoping to capture the attention of conventioneers and the national media. According to Grossman, when the leader arrived in San Francisco and heard of the competing yet complementary rally, Chavez "announced that he was going to march with the gay activists and invited the farm workers to go with him; some did."[40] The leader's granddaughter, Christine Chavez, claims that she and other grandkids would regularly march in San Francisco gay pride parades with their grandfather. She lobbied in support of California's 2005 Religious Freedom and Civil Marriage Protection Act. She explained: "It was Latinos who weren't where we needed them to be on that issue. [A state legislator] wanted me to perform 'commitment ceremonies' as a way to let the Latino community know that somebody like my grandfather, who they really respected, was a supporter of gay rights."[41]

On October 11, 1987, Chavez was one of the leaders of the Second National March on Washington for Lesbian and Gay Rights. In addition to a federal law protecting the gay community, protestors sought to raise consciousness and money to combat AIDS. Following the demonstration, Chavez also spoke at the rally on the National Mall in Washington. There, before an estimated gathering of two hundred thousand people, he declared: "Our movement has been supporting lesbian and gay rights for over 20 years. We supported lesbian and gay rights when it was just a crowd of 10 people."[42]

The leader sometimes wore a UFW button with the black eagle over a pink triangle. He was a pioneer in struggling for the civil rights of all people and challenging negative macho attitudes about lesbians and gays.

CROSSING AND INHABITING SPIRITUAL LINES

Our planet continues to shrink, and the greater proximity of peoples has led to the erection of fences and the reification of national borders, as well as bordered identities—particularly along lines of race, religion, gender, and sexuality. As a *nepantlero*, or border crosser, Chavez destabilized those human boundaries, and perhaps his having done so was his undoing, because his record on immigration and the church, as a result, could easily be co-opted in support of conservative political projects.[43] Nonetheless, he crossed racial, religious, and gender categories.

Take, for example, an event in 1969 at Arizona State University, where a group of Chicana and Chicano students confronted him, charging him to speak his view of "Chicano power." He responded: "Why be racist? Our belief is to help everyone, not just one race. Humanity is our belief."[44] Chavez, by his own profession, was, above all else, a humanitarian who struggled to improve and transform the human condition as a necessary correlate to farm worker and Chicano liberation.

La Causa's founder thus fits Cornel West's model of "race-transcending prophetic leader" rather than West's other categories, "race-effacing managerial leader" and "race-identifying protest leader." West explains: "Malcolm X's vision and practice were international in scope, and ... after 1964 his project was transracial—though grounded in the black turf. King never confined himself to being solely the leader of black America—even though the white press attempted to do so. And Fannie Lou Hamer led the National Welfare Rights Organization, not the Black Welfare Rights Organization."[45] Similarly, Like Dolores Huerta, Chavez transcended race, though he was grounded in Mexicana/o and Chicana/o terrain, but he also transcended religion, appealing to all who believed in the gospel of service to humanity. I have sought to retrieve the lost gospel of his humanism.

Chavez recognized the importance of crossing religious borders, anticipating the argument of the new atheist Sam Harris, who cautions that religious designations and their attendant oppositional identities are more divisive and intense than other social divisions: "Religion raises the stakes of human conflict much higher than tribalism, racism, or politics ever can, as it is the only form of in-group/out-group thinking that casts the differences between people in terms of eternal rewards and punishments."[46]

Transcending religious limitations allows for the deployment of a broad and political spirituality. Consider Martin Luther King's reflection when Alex Haley asked him, in an interview for *Playboy* magazine, for his thoughts on the unanimous 1963 Supreme Court ruling, *Abington School District v. Schempp.* The court in that case effectively decided to remove Christian Bible reading and the recitation of Christian prayers from public schools. King's comment is not what one might expect from a Baptist minister:

> PLAYBOY: One of the most controversial issues of the past year, apart from civil rights, was the question of school prayer, which has been ruled unlawful by the Supreme Court. Governor Wallace, among others, has denounced the decision. How do you feel about it?
>
> MARTIN LUTHER KING: I endorse it. I think it was correct.... In a pluralistic society such as ours, who is to determine what prayer shall be spoken and by whom? Legally, constitutionally or otherwise, the state certainly has no such right.[47]

Racism, like religious bigotry, begins with a belief in the "natural" order of the world in which a hierarchy of races and religions is an eternal truth. (That is the idea of order which characterized colonial discourse.) Narratives based on such a belief drew support from some of the scientific and philosophical epistemes of the Enlightenment. Gandhi, King, and Chavez confronted, engaged, and disrupted these racializing narratives and developed their own mythologies of the sacred to demonstrate that all people are equally children of God, whatever their race or religion. Like King, Chavez redefined God and the national good for an American community of believers (and make-believers).

There is no small irony in the coalescence of religion and politics in the civil rights movements of the second half of the twentieth century—a century ushered in by the declaration of the death of God. The religious authority that emanates from church pulpits does not flow securely into the hands of government officials, no matter how successful the politician or party. Instead, democratic impulses continually disestablish religious boundaries, so that spiritual control circulates among many individuals and groups as they exercise their will to power; America's best-remembered leaders have thrived in this discursive space, King and Chavez foremost among them. In a sense, they functioned as prophets of American civil religion, whose jeremiads transformed the American psyche so that racism once accepted, was increasingly condemned. They succeeded by preaching the importance of love.

AND THE GREATEST OF THESE IS LOVE

Early in Chavez's public life, Peter Matthiessen noted that by locating "the meaning of life... in service to mankind," the leader echoed the concepts of Tolstoy and Hesse; Chavez's "love is philosophical, not just religious."[48] Chavez recognized the imperfection of humanity, its original sin, and his mandate, despite the human condition, was unconditional love; his theology is best summed up by his favorite biblical author, St. Paul, in a passage from 1 Corinthians 13:8–13 that the leader read to the executive board when he announced his love fast:

> Love never fails. But where there are prophecies, they will cease; where there are tongues, they will be stilled; where there is knowledge, it will pass away. For we know in part and we prophesy in part, but when completeness comes, what is in part disappears. When I was a child, I talked like a child, I thought like a child, I reasoned like a child. When I became a man, I put the ways of childhood behind me. For now we see through a

glass darkly; then we shall see face to face. Now I know in part; then I shall know fully, even as I am fully known. And now these three remain: faith, hope and love. But the greatest of these is love.

Chavez resonated St. Paul in reflecting on the mandate to love: "Love is the most important ingredient in nonviolent work—love the opponent—but we really haven't learned yet how to love the growers. I think we've learned how not to hate them, and maybe love comes in stages. If we're full of hatred, we can't really do our work. Hatred saps all that strength and energy we need to plan. Of course, we can learn how to love the growers more easily after they sign contracts."[49]

The leader also recalled the values of Martin Luther King, whom he quoted in a memorial speech delivered in 1990: "He [King] once stopped an armed mob, saying: 'We are not advocating violence. We want to love our enemies. I want you to love our enemies. Be good to them. This is what we live by. We must meet hate with love.'"[50] Like King, Chavez demonstrated a greater commitment to humanity than to any particular racial or religious faction. "Chavez . . . did not advocate a particular organization or ideology but felt that 'So long as the smaller groups do not have the same rights and the same protection as others—I don't care whether you call it Capitalism or Communism—it is not going to work. Somehow, the guys in power have to be reached by counterpower, or through a change in their hearts and minds.'"[51] Here again he iterates ideas articulated by Martin Luther King, who once said: "We are not interested in being integrated into this value structure. Power must be relocated, a radical distribution of power must take place. We must do something to these men to change them."[52]

Chavez's ethics and philosophy speak to the current state of emergency in the United States and globally: the problem of the twenty-first century is the problem of the spiritual line—a socially constructed ideological border that separates the sacred from the profane, good from evil, woman from man, saved from damned, straight from gay, citizen from immigrant, white from "other," Christian from Muslim, Muslim from Jew, the religious from the secular, and theists from atheists. This is to say, not that race is no longer a problem, but that racial hatred is now further complicated, having been recast as a drama of saints and sinners. Chavez's religious politics anticipated the current crisis. In narrating his own nuanced spiritual subjectivity, he attributed religious identity to the randomness of birth, thus undercutting any insistence on fundamentalist belief: "Your religion just happens to depend a lot on your upbringing and your culture."[53]

Certainly he led a life that was limited by his humanity, flawed, burdened by his mortality, but, he also transcended those limitations—crossing spiritual lines and inhabiting border areas. His ability to negotiate and reconcile human difference is his largely undocumented contribution to the twenty-first century.

Chavez left more than actual improvements for farm workers in the fields. He left a legacy for Latinas, Latinos, and others based on their psychosocial rejuvenation. He offered the country a way to redeem itself from its racial oppression; the colonizer, like the colonized, suffers under the weight of colonial tyranny. In 1984 he explained: "Regardless of what the future holds for farm workers—our accomplishments cannot be undone! 'La Causa'—our cause—doesn't have to be experienced twice. The consciousness and pride that were raised by our union are alive and thriving inside millions of young Hispanics who will never work on a farm!"[54] He brought about this transformation by means of his political spirituality.

I offer by way of conclusion a reflection on the "Prayer of the Farm Workers' Struggle" that Chavez wrote in the mid-1970s. (It was never officially dated.) Compatible with the teachings of many religions, it encapsulates his precepts:

> Show me the suffering of the most miserable;
> So I may know my people's plight.
>
> Free me to pray for others;
> For you are present in every person.
>
> Help me to take responsibility for my own life;
> So that I can be free at last.

Grant me courage to serve others;
For in service there is true life.

Give me honesty and patience;
So that I can work with other workers.

Bring forth song and celebration;
So that the Spirit will be alive among us.

Let the Spirit flourish and grow;
So that we will never tire of the struggle.

Let us remember those who have died for justice;
For they have given us life.

Help us love even those who hate us;
So we can change the world.

Amen.[55]

NOTES

PREFACE

1. I use the terms *Mexican American* and *Chicano* interchangeably. *Mexican American* is the more traditional reference; *Chicano* and *Chicana* emerged during the 1960s. *Latino* here refers to people of Latin American descent, including Mexicans and Mexican Americans. There is no universally accepted way to denote Mexicans in North America, and all terms are problematic. My choices reflect the desire to situate my work in an existing and emergent body of Chicano Studies scholarship.

2. The other three "horsemen" who were said to be Chicano movement leaders are Rodolfo "Corky" Gonzáles (1928–2005), José Angel Gutiérrez (b. 1944), and Reies López Tijerina (b. 1926). See Matt S. Meier and Feliciano Rivera, "The Four Horsemen," in *The Chicanos: A History of Mexican Americans* (NY: Hill and Wang, 1972). See also José Angel Gutiérrez, "The First and Last of the Chicano Leaders," in *César Chávez,* ed. Ilan Stavans (Santa Barbara, CA: Greenwood Press, 2010), 58–69.

3. The Penitente tradition is characterized by its community service—including the production of religious and devotional objects—and for its signature ritual of flagellation on Good Friday. See Ramón A. Gutiérrez, "Crucifixion, Slavery, and Death: The Hermanos Penitentes of the Southwest," in *Over the Edge: Remapping the American West,* ed. Valerie J. Matsumoto and Blake Allmendinger (Berkeley: University of California Press, 1999), 253–271; and Alberto López Pulido, *The Sacred World of the Penitentes* (Washington, DC: Smithsonian Press, 2000).

(RE)INTRODUCTION

1. Cesar Chavez, introduction to Mark Day, *Forty Acres: Cesar Chavez and the Farm Workers* (New York: Praeger, 1971).

2. While Spanish spelling requires acute accents over the *e* in César and the *a* in Chávez, Chavez never used the accents himself, so I omit them here. It has become common, however, for writers to include the accents in his name.

3. See "Religion Inspires Grape Marchers," *New York Times*, March 25, 1966.

4. See Alan J. Watt, *The Farm Workers and the Churches: The Movement in California and Texas* (College Station: Texas A&M University Press, 2010).

5. "El Plan de Delano," reprinted in full in *El Malcriado*, March 1966; in English, "The Plan of Delano," *El Malcriado: The Voice of the Farm Worker*, no. 33, April 10, 1966.

6. Cesar Chavez, "The Organizer's Tale," *Ramparts*, July 1, 1966.

7. LeRoy Chatfield distinguishes between the "founder" of a movement and its leader, arguing that "founder" better describes Chavez. See "The Legacy of Cesar Chavez," in United Farmworker Movement Documentation Project, https://libraries.ucsd.edu/farmworkermovement/, presented by the University of California, San Diego, Library (accessed June 23, 2014).

8. Dorothy Day, "On Pilgrimage—September 1973," *Catholic Worker*, September 1973, 1, 2, 6.

9. "McGovern Poses as Peace Candidate, Humphrey Charges," *Los Angeles Times*, May 21, 1972.

10. White House press release, "Remarks by the President at the Dedication of the Cesar Chavez National Monument, Keene, CA," October 8, 2012.

11. Joan London and Henry Anderson, *So Shall Ye Reap* (New York: Crowell, 1970), 1.

12. Cesar Chavez, quoted in Jacques E. Levy, *Cesar Chavez: Autobiography of La Causa*, 2nd ed. (Minneapolis: University of Minnesota Press, [1974] 2007), 35–36.

13. Ana Raquel Minian, "'Indiscriminate and Shameless Sex': The Strategic Use of Sexuality by the United Farm Workers," *American Quarterly* 65, no. 1 (March 2013): 63–90.

14. Chavez, quoted in Levy, *Cesar Chavez*, 465.

15. Michel Foucault, "Is It Useless to Revolt?," in *Religion and Culture: Michel Foucault*, ed. Jeremy R. Carrette (New York: Routledge, [1979] 1999), 131–32.

16. Michel Foucault, "The Ethic of the Care of the Self as Practice of Freedom" (1984), in *The Final Foucault*, ed. James Bernauer and David Rasmussen (Cambridge, MA: MIT Press, 1991), 14.

17. Jeremy Carrette, "Rupture and Transformation: Foucault's Concept of Spirituality Reconsidered," *Foucault Studies* 15 (February 2013): 52–71.

18. Chavez, quoted in Levy, *Cesar Chavez*, xviii.

19. Theresa Delgadillo, *Spiritual Mestizaje: Religion, Gender, Race, and Nation in Contemporary Chicana Narrative* (Durham, NC: Duke University Press, 2011, 1.

20. Chavez, in Catherine Ingram, ed., *In the Footsteps of Gandhi: Conversations with Spiritual Social Activists* (Berkeley: Parallax Press, 1990), 114.

21. Susan Ferriss and Ricardo Sandoval, eds., *The Fight in the Fields: Cesar Chavez and the Farmworkers Movement* (Orlando, FL: Harcourt, Brace, 1997), 113.

22. Jace Weaver, "Pluralist Separatism and Community," in *Wading through Many Voices: Toward a Theology of Public Conversation,* ed. Harold J. Recinos (Lanham, MD: Rowman and Littlefield, 2011), 96.

23. Bruce Lincoln, *Theorizing Myth: Narrative, Ideology, and Scholarship* (Chicago: University of Chicago Press, 1999), 208.

24. For examples of subtle hagiography see Fred Dalton, *The Moral Vision of César Chávez* (Maryknoll, NY: Orbis Books, 2003); Roger Bruns, *Cesar Chavez: A Biography* (Westport, CT: Greenwood Press, 2005); and Mario T. García, *The Gospel of César Chávez: My Faith in Action* (Lanham, MD: Sheed and Ward, 2007). For diatribes see Miriam Pawel, *The Union of Their Dreams: Power, Hope, and Struggle in Cesar Chavez's Farm Worker Movement* (New York: Bloomsbury Press, 2009); Marshall Ganz, *Why David Sometimes Wins: Leadership, Organization, and Strategy in the California Farm Worker Movement* (New York: Oxford University Press, 2009); and Franck Bardacke, *Trampling Out the Vintage: Cesar Chavez and the Two Souls of the United Farm Workers Movement* (London: Verso, 2011).

25. See especially Ganz, *Why David Sometimes Wins,* 242.

26. José Angel Gutiérrez, "The First and Last of the Chicano Leaders." In *San José Studies* 20, no. 2 (1994): 33.

27. Anthony M. Stevens-Arroyo, "Pious Colonialism: Assessing a Church Paradigm for Chicano Identity," in *Mexican American Religions: Spirituality, Activism, and Culture,* ed. Gastón Espinosa and Mario T. García (Durham, NC: Duke University Press, 2008), 57–84.

28. A complete run of *El Malcriado* is available at United Farmworker Movement Documentation Project, https://libraries.ucsd.edu/farmworkermovement/.

29. Doug Adair, "El Malcriado: The Voice of the Farmworker; Origins, 1964–1965," 2009, United Farm Worker Movement Documentation Project, ibid.

30. Ibid. Ana Raquel Minian has argued that some of these cartoons were homophobic and demonstrated a hetero-normativity in the UFW. Her observations, however, are best understood as criticism of the cartoonist and the

editorial staff of *El Malcriado* rather than as an indictment of Chavez and *La Causa* more broadly. In addition, what is read today as homophobic was interpreted differently nearly fifty years ago. See Minian, "'Indiscriminate and Shameless Sex,'" 63–90.

31. For a study of El Teatro Campesino, see Yolanda Broyles-González, *El Teatro Campesino: Theater in the Chicano Movement* (Austin: University of Texas Press, 1994).

32. See José-Antonio Orosco, *Cesar Chavez and the Common Sense of Nonviolence* (Albuquerque: University of New Mexico Press, 2008).

33. Chavez, quoted in Griswold del Castillo and Garcia, *César Chávez: A Triumph of Spirit* (Norman: University of Oklahoma Press, 1995), 150.

34. David Howard-Pitney, *The African American Jeremiad: Appeals for Justice in America* (Philadelphia: Temple University Press, 2005), 219.

35. Cesar Chavez to Robert Kennedy, Walter P. Reuther Library, Archives of Labor and Urban Affairs, United Farm Workers Collection, Office of the President, box 5, folder 1, Wayne State University.

36. Steven W. Bender, *One Night in America: Robert Kennedy, César Chávez, and the Dream of Dignity* (Boulder, CO: Paradigm, 2008).

37. See Ignacio M. García, *Viva Kennedy: Mexican Americans in Search of Camelot* (College Station: Texas A&M Press, 2000).

38. See Sacvan Bercovitch, *The Puritan Origins of the American Self* (New Haven: Yale University Press, 1975).

39. Dan McKanan has argued persuasively that the radical political tradition of the American left has been infused with religion and preached prophetically. See Dan McKanan, *Prophetic Encounters: Religion and the American Radical Tradition* (Boston: Beacon Press, 2011).

40. See Robert Bellah, "Civil Religion in America," *Dædalus* (Winter 1967). For a later study, see Gary Laderman, *American Civil Religion*," ebook, Fortress Press, 2012.

41. See Robert Bellah, *The Broken Covenant: Civil Religion in Time of Trial*, 2nd ed. (Chicago: University of Chicago Press, 1992).

42. Spencer Bennett, "Civil Religion in a New Context: The Mexican-American Faith of Cesar Chavez," in *Religion and Political Power*, ed. Gustavo Benavides and M. W. Daly (Albany: State University of New York Press, 1989), 158.

43. Jean-Jacques Rousseau, "Civil Religion," in *The Social Contract and the Discourse of Inequality*, ed. Lester G. Crocker, trans. G. D. H. Cole (New York: Simon and Schuster, [1762] 1967), 141.

44. Ibid.

45. Bellah, "Civil Religion in America," 1.

46. Howard-Pitney, *African American Jeremiad*, 5.

47. Chavez quoted in Levy, *Cesar Chavez*, 84.

48. For the term "spiritual corporality," see *Foucault and Religion: Spiritual Corporality and Political Spirituality*, ed. Jeremy R. Carrette (New York: Routledge, 2000).

49. Peter Matthiessen, *Sal Si Puedes: Cesar Chavez and the New American Revolution* (Berkeley: University of California Press, [1969] 2000), 6.

50. Levy, *Cesar Chavez*, xxi.

51. Ronald B. Taylor, *Chavez and the Farm Workers* (Boston: Beacon Press, 1975), 17.

52. Bill Gormley, *Pitt News*, November 3, 1969.

53. Gutiérrez, "The First and Last of the Chicano Leaders," 33.

54. George Mariscal, *Brown-Eyed Children of the Sun: Lessons from the Chicano Movement, 1965–1975* (Albuquerque: University of New Mexico Press, 2005), 146.

55. For a discussion of the hyper-real, utopia, and death, see Jean Baudrillard, *America,* trans. Chris Turner (London: Verso, 1988).

56. Gloria Anzaldúa, *Borderlands/La Frontera: The New Mestiza*, 3rd ed. (San Francisco: Aunt Lute, [1987] 2007), 19.

57. Ibid., 101.

58. Ibid.

59. "Open Letter from Cesar Chavez," *El Malcriado*, 25 (December, 1965), 8, United Farmworker Movement Documentation Project, https://libraries.ucsd.edu/farmworkermovement/.

60. Pat Hoffman, *Ministry of the Dispossessed: Learning from the Farm Worker Movement* (Los Angeles: Wallace Press, 1987).

61. Ibid., 128–29.

62. Ed Dunn, OFM, quoted in Keith Douglass Warner, OFM, "The Farm Workers and the Franciscans: Reverse Evangelization as Social Prompt for Conversion," *Spiritus* 9 (2009): 80.

63. Eugene Nelson, quoted in Richard Griswold del Castillo and Richard A. Garcia, *Triumph of Spirit*, 146.

64. Luis León, *La Llorona's Children: Religion, Life, and Death in the U.S.–Mexico Borderlands* (Berkeley: University of California Press, 2004), 17.

65. Anzaldúa, *Borderlands/La Frontera*, 3.

66. Diego Durán, *Book of the Gods and Rites and the Ancient Calendar,* ed. and trans. Fernando Horcasitas and Doris Heyden (Norman: University of Oklahoma Press, 1983), 410–11.

67. Gloria Anzaldúa, "(Un)Natural Bridges, (Un)Safe Spaces," in *This Bridge We Call Home: Radical Visions for Transformation,* ed. Gloria E. Anzaldúa and Ana Louise Keating (New York: Routledge, 2002), xiiv.

68. Lara Medina, "Nepantla Spirituality: An Emancipative Vision for Inclusion," in *Wading through Many Voices: Toward a Theology of Public Conversation,* ed. Harold J. Recinos (Lanham, MD: Rowman and Littlefield, 2011), 285.

CHAPTER ONE

1. Ruth Behar, *Translated Woman: Crossing the Border with Esperanza's Story* (Boston: Beacon Press, 1993), 235.

2. Cesar Chavez, quoted in Catherine Ingram, *In the Footsteps of Gandhi: Conversations with Spiritual Social Activists* (Berkeley: Parallax Press, 1990), 114.

3. "Hungry, Hungry Homer," episode 15, season 12, written by John Swartzwelder, directed by Nancy Kruse.

4. Joseph Campbell, *The Hero with a Thousand Faces* (New York: Bollingen Foundation, [1949] 1972).

5. Erik H. Erikson, *Gandhi's Truth: On the Origins of Militant Nonviolence* (New York: Norton, [1970] 1993).

6. Cesar Chavez, quoted in Ronald B. Taylor, *Chavez and the Farm Workers* (Boston: Beacon Press, 1975), 61.

7. Peter Matthiessen, *Sal Si Puedes (Escape If You Can): Cesar Chavez and the New American Revolution* (Berkeley: University of California Press, [1969] 2000).

8. Nat Hentoff, quoted in Ilan Stavans, "Reading César," in *César Chávez,* ed. Ilan Stavans (Santa Barbara, CA: Greenwood Press, 2010), 7.

9. Matthiessen, *Sal Si Puedes,* 225.

10. The complete papers of Jacques Levy are in the Yale University Archives, Jacques Levy Research Collection on Cesar Chavez, Beinecke Rare Book and Manuscript Library.

11. Mario T. García, *Memories of Chicano History: The Life and Narrative of Bert Corona* (Berkeley: University of California Press, 1994), 343.

12. Roger Bruns, *Cesar Chavez: A Biography* (Westport, CT: Greenwood Press, 2005), 1.

13. Richard Chavez, interview by author, June 15, 2011, La Paz, California.

14. Dick Meister and Anne Loftis, *A Long Time Coming: The Struggle to Unionize America's Farm Workers* (New York: Macmillan, 1977), 111.

15. Marc Grossman, interview by author, August 19, 2010, Sacramento, CA. Quoted by permission.

16. Richard Chavez interview, June 15, 2011.

17. Jace Weaver, "Response to Luis León," in *Wading through Many Voices: Toward a Theology of Public Conversation,* ed. Harold J. Recinos (Lanham, MD: Rowman and Littlefield, 2011), 130–31.

18. Cesar Chavez, quoted in Jacques E. Levy, *Cesar Chavez: Autobiography of La Causa* (Minneapolis: University of Minnesota Press, [1974] 2007), 11.

19. Richard Chavez interview, June 15, 2011.

20. See Cesar Chavez, "Eulogy for Juana Estrada Chávez, San Jose, California," in *The Words of César Chávez,* ed. Richard J. Jensen and John C. Hammerback (College Station: Texas A&M Press, 2002), 171. Translations of Spanish terms in the quoted passage are provided when possible.

21. Ibid., 170.

22. Gandhi, quoted in Erikson, *Gandhi's Truth,* 110.

23. Marc Grossman interview, August 19, 2010. See also Miriam Pawel, *The Union of Their Dreams: Power, Hope, and Struggle in Cesar Chavez's Farm Worker Movement* (New York: Bloomsbury Press, 2009), 288.

24. Richard Chavez interview, June 15, 2011.

25. Chavez, quoted in Levy, *Cesar Chavez,* 25.

26. Ibid., 18.

27. Chavez, "Eulogy for Juana Estrada Chávez," 223.

28. See Elizabeth E. Brusco, *The Reformation of Machismo: Evangelical Conversion and Gender in Colombia* (Austin: University of Texas Press, 1995).

29. For a discussion of the types of machismo, see Alfredo Mirande, *Hombres y Machos: Masculinity and Latino Culture* (Boulder, CO: Westview Press, 1997).

30. Chavez, quoted in Matthiessen, *Sal Si Puedes,* 228 (emphasis in original).

31. Chavez, quoted in Levy, *Cesar Chavez,* 76, 77.

32. Campbell, *Hero with a Thousand Faces,* 58.

33. Taylor, *Chavez and the Farm Workers,* 66.

34. Chavez, quoted in Levy, *Cesar Chavez,* 84.

35. Chavez, quoted in Levy, *Cesar Chavez,* 84–85.

36. Eugene Nelson, *Huelga: The First Hundred Days of the Great Delano Grape Strike* (Delano, CA: Farm Workers Press, 1966), 45.

37. Chavez, quoted in Levy, *Cesar Chavez,* 84.

38. Campbell, *Hero with a Thousand Faces,* 39

39. Ibid., 193.

40. Nelson, *Huelga,* 49.

41. Chavez recounts his secular wedding in Levy's *Autobiography of La Causa* without adding that later, in 1949, he and Helen received the sacrament of marriage in a Catholic church. Marc Grossman, email to author, July 16, 2010. Quoted by permission.

42. Grossman, ibid. See also Levy, *Cesar Chavez,* 87.

43. On the organic intellectual, see Antonio Gramsci, *Prison Notebooks* (New York: Columbia University Press, 1992).

44. Chavez, quoted in Nelson, *Huelga,* 49.

45. Joan London and Henry Anderson, *So Shall Ye Reap* (New York: Crowell, 1970), 81.

46. See Sanford Horwitt, *Let Them Call Me Rebel: The Life and Legacy of Saul Alinsky* (New York: Knopf, 1989).

47. Levy, *Cesar Chavez,* 1. Fred Ross recounted to Levy what Chavez's had said to him.

48. Matthiessen, *Sal Si Puedes,* 40.

49. Victor Villaseñor, *Macho!* (New York: Bantam Doubleday, 1991), 200.

50. Chavez, quoted in Levy, *Cesar Chavez,* 163.

51. Farm Workers Association "Statement of Purpose," [n.d.], Walter P. Reuther Labor Library, Archives of Labor and Urban Affairs, United Farm Workers Collection, UFW Office of the President (hereafter UFWOTP collection), box 13, folder 17.

52. Chavez, quoted in Levy, *Cesar Chavez,* 167.

53. Helen Chavez, quoted in Levy, *Cesar Chavez,* 168.

54. "UFW Martyrs," by Cesar Chavez, available at United Farmworker Movement Documentation Project, https://libraries.ucsd.edu/farmworker-movement/, presented by the University of California, San Diego, Library (accessed June 23, 2014).

55. Chavez, quoted in Matthiessen, *Sal Si Puedes,* 26, 27.

56. Cesar Chavez, quoted in William P. Colleman, "At 51, Cesar Chavez Emphasizes Teaching," *Los Angeles Times,* March 26, 1978.

57. Robert Lindsey, "Cesar Chavez Tries New Directions for United Farm Workers," *Los Angeles Times,* September 19, 1983.

58. John Gregory Dunne, *Delano* (New York: Farrar, Straus, and Giroux, [1967] 1971), 4–5.

59. Levy, *Cesar Chavez,* 1.

60. Jean Maddern Pitrone, *Chávez: Man of the Migrants; A Plea for Social Justice* (New York: Alba House, 1972), 98.

61. Ilan Stavans, foreword to Matthiessen, *Sal Si Puedes,* xxii.

62. Ilan Stavans, introduction to Cesar Chavez, *An Organizer's Tale: Speeches,* ed. Ilan Stavans (New York: Penguin Books, 2008), xxx.

63. Matt S. Meier and Feliciano Rivera, *The Chicanos: A History of Mexican Americans* (New York: Hill and Wang, 1972). For a discussion of the Four Horsemen theory of Chicano history, see Rodolfo F. Acuña, *Occupied America: A History of Chicanos,* 7th ed. (Englewood Cliffs, NJ: Prentice Hall, 2010). See also Rudy V. Busto, *King Tiger: The Religious Vision of Reies López Tijerina* (Albuquerque: University of New Mexico Press, 2006).

64. Meier and Rivera, *The Chicanos,* 258.

65. Ibid., 261.

66. Luis Valdez, quoted on the back cover of Susan Drake, *Fields of Courage: Remembering César Chávez and the People Whose Labor Feeds Us* (Santa Cruz, CA: Many Names Press, 1999).

67. José Angel Gutiérrez, "Cesar Estrada Chavez: The First and Last of the Chicano Leaders," in "In Memory of César Chávez," special issue, *San José Studies* 20, no. 2 (Spring, 1994): 33.

68. Sam Kushner, *Long Road to Delano* (New York: International Publishers, 1975), 165.

69. José-Antonio Orosco, *Cesar Chavez and the Common Sense of Nonviolence* (Albuquerque: University of New Mexico Press, 2008), 5. See also Mario T. García, *The Gospel of César Chávez: My Faith in Action* (Lanham, MD: Sheed and Ward, 2007).

70. Matthiessen, *Sal Si Puedes,* 280–81.

71. Chavez, quoted in Matthiessen, *Sal Si Puedes,* 331.

72. Chavez, quoted in James P. Terzian and Kathryn Cramer, *Mighty Hard Road: The Story of Cesar Chavez* (New York: Pocket Books, 1972), 47 (my interpolation).

73. Helen Chavez, quoted in Peter Matthiessen, *Sal Si Puedes,* 231.

74. Jan Young, *The Migrant Workers and Cesar Chavez* (New York: Julian Messner, 1974), 147.

75. Richard Griswold del Castillo and Richard A. Garcia, *César Chávez: A Triumph of Spirit* (Norman: University of Oklahoma Press, 1995), xiv.

76. Dolores Huerta, in Matthiessen, *Sal Si Puedes,* 176.

77. Frank Bardacke, *Trampling Out the Vintage: Cesar Chavez and the Two Souls of the United Farm Workers Movement* (London: Verso, 2011), 57.

78. Jensen and Hammerback, *The Words of César Chávez,* xix, xxi.

79. Ibid., xxii.

80. César Chávez, "The Mexican American and the Church," *El Grito* 4 (Summer, 1968): 215.

81. John C. Hammerback, "Teacher of Truth," in *César Chávez,* ed. Ilan Stavans, 44.

82. Chavez, quoted in Levy, *Cesar Chavez,* xxiv.

83. Jennifer Reed-Bouley, "Guiding Moral Action: A Study of the United Farm Workers' Use of Catholic Social Teaching and Religious Symbols" (Ph.D. diss., Loyola University Chicago, 1998), 3.

84. Chavez, quoted in Levy, *Cesar Chavez,* 106.

85. Robert Lentz's image and artist's statement can be found at Trinity: Artwork and Icons, https://www.trinitystores.com/store/art-image/cesar-chavez-1927–1993 (accessed May 12, 2012).

86. Victor Salandini, *The Confessions of the Tortilla Priest* (San Diego: San Diego Review, 1992), 89, 116.

87. Ana Raquel Minian claims that Chavez was against abortion not because of his Catholicism but because he was concerned with the forced sterilization of Mexicans and poor people. See Minian, "'Indiscriminate and Shameless Sex': The Strategic Use of Sexuality by the United Farm Workers," *American Quarterly 65,* no. 1 (March 2013): 63–90.

88. Father Ken Irrgang, telephone interview by author, August 30, 2011. The transcript, in the author's possession, was corrected and approved by Father Irrgang, and is quoted by permission.

89. See the introduction, note 66.

90. Frederick John Dalton, *The Moral Vision of César Chávez* (Maryknoll, NY: Orbis Books, 2003), 46 (emphasis added).

91. Chavez, quoted in Mark Day, *Forty Acres: Cesar Chavez and the Farm Workers* (New York: Praeger, 1971), 58.

92. Mario T. García, review of *Cesar Chavez and the Common Sense of Nonviolence,* by José-Antonio Orosco, *Camino Real* 1, no. 2 (2010): 177.

93. Mario T. García cites Levy, *Cesar Chavez, 26,* in his edited volume *The Gospel of César Chávez,* 32.

94. César E. Chávez, "The Mexian American and the Church, 215 (emphasis added).

95. Cesar Chavez, "Eulogy for René López, Fresno, California, September 1983," in Jensen and Hammerback, *The Words of César Chávez,* 182 (emphasis added).

96. Chavez in Levy, *Cesar Chavez,* 27 (emphasis added).

97. Chavez, quoted in Levy, *Cesar Chavez*, 524–25 (emphasis added).

98. Cesar Chavez, "Report on European Tour," n.d., p. 4, Walter P. Reuther Library, Archives of Labor and Urban Affairs, UFWOTP, box 3, folders 9–12.

99. Pope Paul VI's statement can be found at http://chavez.cde.ca.gov/ModelCurriculum/Teachers/Lessons/Resources/Documents/PCCCP2_Box9_21_Statement_by_Pope_Paul_VI.pdf.

100. Cesar Chavez, quoted in the *National Catholic Reporter*, March 7, 1975.

101. Richard Rodriguez, "Saint Cesar of Delano," *Wilson Quarterly* 34, no. 1 (Winter 2010): 16.

102. For the full text of the attorney general's twelve-page report, see www.ufw.org/pdf/AG_Letter.pdf (accessed June 1, 2013).

103. Pawel, *The Union of Their Dreams*, 328.

104. For example, Matt Garcia writes in his book *From the Jaws of Victory: The Triumph and Tragedy of Cesar Chavez and the Farm Worker Movement* (Berkeley: University of California Press, 2012): "During the late spring of 1977, Helen Chavez had received several anonymous letters 'in perfect Spanish' revealing the details of a love affair between her husband and a young Mexican American woman. Before leaving on a trip Chavez had sought to blunt the impact of his accuser's testimonials by telling Helen that he had been set up by conspirators angry about the recent purges. The details in the letter[s] convinced her otherwise" (244).

105. Marshall Ganz, *Why David Sometimes Wins: Leadership, Organization, and Strategy in the California Farm Worker Movement* (London: Oxford, 2009), 242.

106. Bardacke, *Trampling Out the Vintage*, 59.

107. Ibid., 63.

108. Walter P. Reuther Library, Archives of Labor and Urban Affairs, UFWOTP, box 5, folder 5, "Notebook."

109. See Marcene Marcoux, *Cursillo: Anatomy of a Movement; The Experience of Spiritual Renewal* (New York: Lambeth Press, 1982).

110. Frank Bardacke, "Cesar's Ghost," in *César Chávez*, ed. Ilan Stavans, 141.

111. Roland Barthes, "The Death of the Author," first published in English in 1967, is available as an ebook at http://www.tbook.constantvzw.org/wp-content/death_authorbarthes.pdf, 2.

112. Ibid., 5, 6.

113. Michel Foucault, "What Is an Author?," in *Language, Counter-Memory,*

Practice: Selected Essays and Interviews, trans. David Bouchard and Sherry Simon, ed. David Bouchard (Ithaca, NY: Cornell University Press, 1977), 137–38.

114. Campbell, *Hero with a Thousand Faces,* 382.

CHAPTER TWO

1. Mohandas Gandhi, in Stanley Wolpert, *Gandhi's Passion: The Life and Legacy of Mahatma Gandhi* (New York: Oxford University Press, 2001), 267.

2. Martin Luther King Jr., speech to the Negro American Labor Council, May 1965. Quoted in Thomas F. Jackson, *From Civil Rights to Human Rights: Martin Luther King, Jr., and the Struggle for Economic Justice* (Philadelphia: University of Pennsylvania Press, 2009), 230.

3. Cesar Chavez, quoted in Catherine Ingram, *In the Footsteps of Gandhi: Conversations with Spiritual Social Activists* (Berkeley: Parallax Press, 1990), 120.

4. Cesar Chavez, "Lessons of Dr. Martin Luther King, Jr.," January 12, 1990, Cesar E. Chavez Foundation web page, http://www.chavezfoundation. org (accessed January 15, 2013).

5. Dolores Huerta, quoted in Julia Bencomo Lobaco, "Dolores Huerta: The Vision and Voice of Her Life's Work," in *A Dolores Huerta Reader,* ed. Mario T. García (Albuquerque: University of New Mexico Press, 2008), 308.

6. Art Torres, quoted in Richard Griswold del Castillo and Richard A. Garcia. *César Chávez: A Triumph of Spirit* (Norman: University of Oklahoma Press, 1995), 173.

7. Los Tigres del Norte, "Cesar Chavez," from the album *Mi Buena Suerte,* released March 7, 2006, Fonovisa Records, Woodland Hills, CA.

8. Norman G. Finkelstein has correctly noted that while Gandhi abhorred violence, he held cowardice in greater contempt. Chavez quoted Gandhi's statement that violence is preferable to cowardice. See Finkelstein, *What Gandhi Says: About Nonviolence, Resistance and Courage* (New York: OR Books, 2012).

9. See especially Michael Omi and Howard Winant, *Racial Formation in the United States* (Philadelphia: Temple University Press, 1992); Howard Winant, "The Theoretical Status of the Concept of Race," in *Theories of Race and Racism: A Reader,* ed. Les Back and John Solomos (New York: Routledge, 2000), 181–94; and Howard Winant, *The New Politics of Race: Globalism, Difference, Justice* (Minneapolis: University of Minnesota Press, 2004). See also Daniel Martinez HoSang, Oneka LaBennett, and Laura Pulido, eds., *Racial Formation in the*

Twenty-First Century (Berkeley: University of California Press, 2012), which revisits racial formation theory, centering on intersectionality.

10. See especially José-Antonio Orosco, *Cesar Chavez and the Common Sense of Nonviolence* (Albuquerque: University of New Mexico Press, 2008).

11. Joseph Lelyveld has uncovered evidence demonstrating that while in South Africa, Gandhi had a passionate sexual love affair with another man, Hermann Kallenbach, a German Jew. See Lelyveld, *Great Soul: Mahatma Gandhi and His Struggle with India* (New York: Vintage Books, 2011).

12. See Joseph Campbell, *The Hero with a Thousand Faces* (Princeton, NJ: Princeton University Press, [1949] 1973).

13. Howard Winant, "Race and Racism: Towards a Global Future," in *Theories of Race and Racism: A Reader,* ed. Les Back and John Solomos, 2nd ed. (New York: Routledge, 2000), 678–92, 678.

14. Cornel West, "Race and Modernity," in *The Cornel West Reader* (New York: Basic Civitas Books, 2000), 77.

15. Charles Long, *Significations: Signs, Symbols, and Images in the Interpretation of Religion* (Philadelphia: Fortress Press, 1986), 106.

16. Robert Bernasconi, "Who Invented the Concept of Race?" in *Theories of Race and Racism: A Reader,* ed. Les Back and John Solomos, 83.

17. Musa W. Dube, *Postcolonial Feminist Interpretation of the Bible* (St. Louis, MO: Chalice Press, 2000), 3.

18. Ibid., 153.

19. Steven T. Newcomb, *Pagans in the Promised Land: Decoding the Doctrine of Christian Discovery* (Golden, CO: Fulcrum Press, 2008), 83.

20. Chief Justice John Marshall, *Johnson & Grahm's Lessee v. M'Intosh,* 1823, in Newcomb, *Pagans in the Promised Land,* 76.

21. Long, *Significations,* 197.

22. Ibid., 84.

23. Thomas Jefferson, "Laws," from *Notes on the State of Virginia* (New York: Norton, [1781] 1982), 138.

24. Ibid., 139.

25. See Antonia I. Castaneda, "Women of Color and the Rewriting of Western History: The Discourse, Politics, and Decolonization of History," *Pacific Historical Review* 61 (1992): 501–33.

26. Davíd Carrasco, *Religions of Mesoamerica,* 2nd ed. (Long Grove, IL: Waveland Press, 2013), 7.

27. Juan Ginés de Sepúlveda, "Just War in the Indies," 1547, in *Early Modern*

Spain: A Documentary History, ed. Jon Cowans (Philadelphia: University of Pennsylvania Press, 2003), 58–59.

28. See Ilona Katzew, *Casta Painting: Images of Race in Eighteenth-Century Mexico* (New Haven: Yale University Press, 2005); and Ilona Katzew, *Contested Visions in the Spanish Colonial World* (New Haven: Yale University Press, 2011).

29. John L. O'Sullivan, "The Great Nation of Futurity," *United States Democratic Review* 6, no. 23 (1839): 426–30 (emphasis in original).

30. Richard Henry Dana, quoted in Ronald Takaki, *Iron Cages: Race and Culture in Nineteenth-Century America,* rev. ed. (Oxford: Oxford University Press, 2000), 158.

31. I take my cues here from Max Weber's classic work, *The Protestant Ethic and the Spirit of Capitalism,* trans. Talcott Parsons (New York: Routledge, [1905] 2001).

32. On colonialists' spiritual rejuvenation through violence, see Richard Slotkin, *Regeneration through Violence: The Mythology of the American Frontier, 1600–1860* (Middletown, CT: Wesleyan University Press, 1973).

33. "*American Progress*—Description by George A. Crofutt (1872)," available at http://www.arbeitsblaetter-online.de/Beispielseite/Promoting+the+Cause+of+Liberty%3F+America%27s+Role+in+the+World_44–1301.pdf

34. Josiah Strong, *Our Country: Its Possible Future and Its Present Crisis* (New York: American Home Missionary Society, 1885), 32.

35. Hubert Bancroft, *California Pastoral, 1769–1848* (San Francisco: History Company, 1888), 527.

36. John Gregory Dunne, *Delano* (New York: Farrar, Straus and Giroux, 1967), 40.

37. Griswold del Castillo and Garcia, *Triumph of Spirit,* 9–10.

38. For a classic formulation of racial theory and "internal colonialism," see Robert Blauner, *Racial Oppression in America* (New York: Harper and Row, 1972). For a discussion of internal colonization in California and the Southwest, see Mario Barrera, *Race and Class in the Southwest: A Theory of Racial Inequality* (Notre Dame, IN: University of Notre Dame Press, 1979).

39. Cesar Chavez, interview by Eugene Nelson, 1965, University of Texas at Arlington, transcript, 12. Walter P. Reuther Library, Archives of Labor and Urban Affairs, United Farm Workers Collection, UFW Office of the President (hereafter UFWOTP collection), box 46, folder 10. Wayne State University.

40. Cesar Chavez, quoted in Ronald B. Taylor, *Chavez and the Farm Workers* (Boston: Beacon Press, 1975), 12.

41. *A Union in the Community,* compiled from a voice recording of Cesar Chavez in Detroit, May 1967; printed January 1969. UFWOTP, box 9, folder 7, p. 16.

42. Dunne, *Delano,* 23; Chavez eulogy, in Taylor, *Chavez and the Farm Workers,* 6.

43. Martin Luther King, quoted in David J. Garrow, *Bearing the Cross: Martin Luther King, Jr. and the Southern Christian Leadership Conference* (New York: Vintage Books, 1986), 118.

44. Diane P. Mines, *Caste in India* (Ann Arbor, MI: Association for Asian Studies, 2009), 43.

45. Ibid., 53, 54.

46. Michael J. Nojeim, *Gandhi and King: The Power of Nonviolent Resistance* (Westport, CT: Praeger, 2004), 115.

47. Ibid., 92.

48. Cherrie Moraga, *The Last Generation* (Boston: South End Press, 1993), 161.

49. Ibid., 162.

50. Chavez, quoted in Bill Gormley, "Cesar Chavez: The Paradoxes of Greatness," *Pitt News,* November 3, 1969.

51. Art Torres is named as the source of the quoted term in Griswold del Castillo and Garcia, *Triumph of Spirit,* 173.

52. Richard Rodriguez, *Days of Obligation: An Argument with My Mexican Father* (New York: Penguin, 1992), 68.

53. Chavez, quoted in Peter Matthiessen, *Sal Si Puedes (Escape If You Can): Cesar Chavez and the New American Revolution* (Berkeley: University of California Press, [1969] 2000). 185.

54. Max Weber, "The Prophet," in *The Sociology of Religion,* trans. Ephraim Fischoff (Boston: Beacon Press, [1922] 1964), 46.

55. Eugene Nelson, *Huelga: The First Hundred Days of the Great Delano Grape Strike* (Delano, CA: Farm Workers Press, 1966), 51.

56. Weber, "The Prophet," 46.

57. Griswold del Castillo and Garcia, *Triumph of Spirit,* 149.

58. Spencer Bennett, "Civil Religion in a New Context: The Mexican-American Faith of Cesar Chavez," in *Religion and Political Power,* ed. Gustavo Benavides and M. W. Daly (Albany: State University of New York Press, 1989), 164.

59. Gary Laderman, *American Civil Religion,* ebook, Fortress Press, 2012.

60. Mario T. García, *Catolicos: Resistance and Affirmation in Chicano Catholic History* (Austin: University of Texas Press, 2008), 7.

61. Gary Soto, foreword to *The Fight in the Fields: Cesar Chavez and the Farmworkers Movement,* ed. Susan Ferriss and Ricardo Sandoval (Orlando, FL: Harcourt, Brace, 1997), xiv, xvi.

62. Griswold del Castillo and Garcia, *Triumph of Spirit,* 140.

63. Luis A. Solis-Garza, "Cesar Chavez: The Chicano Messiah?," in *Pain and Promise: The Chicano Today,* ed. Edward Simmen (New York: Mentor, 1972), 298, 304.

64. Matt S. Meier and Feliciano Rivera, *The Chicanos: A History of Mexican Americans* (New York: Hill and Wang, 1972), 258.

65. Rafaela G. Castro, *The Dictionary of Chicano Folklore* (Santa Barbara. CA: ABC Clio Press, 2000), 52–53.

66. Oscar Zeta Acosta, *The Revolt of the Cockroach People* (New York: Vintage Books, [1973], 1989), 43–46.

67. Alberto Pulido, "Are You an Emissary of Jesus Christ? Justice, the Catholic Church, and the Chicano Movement," *Explorations in Ethnic Studies* 14, no. 1 (January 1991): 30.

68. Ira Chernus, *American Nonviolence: The History of an Idea* (Maryknoll, NY: Orbis Books, 2004), 161.

69. Michael J. Nojeim, *Gandhi and King,* 92.

70. *The Autobiography of Martin Luther King, Jr.,* ed. Clayborne Carson (New York: Warner Books, 1998), 123.

71. Chavez, quoted in Ingram, *In The Footsteps of Gandhi,* 107.

72. Chavez, quoted in Matthiessien, *Sal Si Puedes,* 187.

73. Nelson, *Huelga,* 52.

74. Jacques E. Levy, *Cesar Chavez: Autobiography of La Causa,* 2nd ed. (Minneapolis: University of Minnesota Press, [1974] 2007), 91.

75. Chavez, quoted in Ingram, *In the Footsteps of Gandhi,* 119.

76. Chavez, quoted in Levy, 91–92.

77. See Michael J. Nojeim, *Gandhi and King,* for an excellent history and description of ahimsa and satyagraha, as well as an account of King's relationship to Gandhi.

78. *Gandhi on Non-Violence: Selected Texts from "Non-Violence in Peace and War,"* ed. Thomas Merton (New York: New Directions, 1964), 29.

79. Eknath Easwaran, *Gandhi the Man: The Story of His Transformation* (Berkeley: Nilgiri Press, 1997), 48, 49.

80. Mohandas K. Gandhi, *An Autobiography: The Story of My Experiments with Truth*, trans. Mahadev Desai (Boston: Beacon Press, 1957), 318.

81. T. Weber, *Hugging the Trees. The Story of the Chipko Movement* (N.p.: Penguin Books India, 1989), 83.

82. Mohandas K. Gandhi, "On Satyagraha," in *Nonviolence in Theory and Practice*, ed. Robert L. Holmes and Barry L. Gan (Long Grove, IL: Waveland Press, 2005), 78.

83. *Gandhi on Non-Violence*, 40.

84. Chavez, quoted in Levy, *Cesar Chavez*, xviii.

85. Mohandas K. Gandhi, "On Satyagraha," 80.

86. Chavez, quoted in Mark Day, *Forty Acres: Cesar Chavez and the Farm Workers* (New York: Praeger, 1971), 115.

87. Chavez, quoted in Levy, *Cesar Chavez*, 270.

88. Mohandas K. Gandhi, "On Satyagraha," 81.

89. Chavez, quoted in Levy, *Cesar Chavez*, 271.

90. Chavez, quoted in Day, *Forty Acres*, 113–14.

91. *Gandhi on Non-Violence*, 29.

92. Cesar Chavez, "Good Friday Letter," reprinted in full in Winthrop Yinger, *Cesar Chavez: The Rhetoric of Nonviolence* (Hicksville, NY: Exposition, 1975), 112.

93. Coretta Scott King, audio recording, "Coretta King in Salinas," Jacques E. Levy Research Collection on Cesar Chavez, 1959–1997, Beinecke Rare Book and Manuscript Library, Yale University. Unless otherwise noted, all quotations from Scott King and Andrew Young are from this recording, though Young's name is not mentioned on the label of the recording.

94. Coretta Scott King, quoted in *Remembering Cesar: The Legacy of Cesar Chavez*, ed. Ann McGregor (Clovis, CA: Quill Driver Books, 2000), 85.

95. Chavez, quoted in Levy, *Cesar Chavez*, 289.

96. Sam Kushner, *Long Road to Delano* (New York: International Publishers, 1975), 165.

97. Martin Luther King to Cesar Chavez, telegram, dated March 5, 1968, reprinted in full in *El Malcriado*, April 15, 1968, United Farmworker Movement Documentation Project, https://libraries.ucsd.edu/farmworkermovement/ (accessed June 6, 2014).

98. Martin Luther King to Cesar Chavez, telegram, dated March 1968, Walter P. Reuther Labor Library, UFWOTP, box 6, folder 4.

99. Martin Luther King Jr., "Letter from a Birmingham Jail, April 16, 1963," reprinted in full in James M. Washington, *I Have a Dream: Martin Luther King*

Jr.: Writings and Speeches That Changed the World (San Francisco: Harper San Francisco, [1986] 1992), 85.

100. Cesar Chavez to Coretta Scott King, telegram, dated April 6, 1968, reprinted in full in *El Malcriado,* April 15, 1968.

101. Ralph Abernathy to Chavez's office, telegram, Walter P. Reuther Labor Library, Archives of Labor and Urban Affairs, UFWOTP collection, box 69, folder 11.

102. Cesar Chavez to Ralph Abernathy, letter, dated June 19, 1969, Walter P. Reuther Labor Library, ibid.

103. Ralph Abernathy to Cesar Chavez, telegram, December 8, 1970, ibid.

104. Coretta Scott King to Cesar Chavez, telegram, December 11, 1970, Walter P. Reuther Labor Library, Archives of Labor and Urban Affairs, UFWOTP collection, box 3, folder 4.

105. Coretta Scott King's speech is available on the audio recording, "Coretta King in Salinas."

106. Coretta Scott King to Chavez, letter dated February 7, 1974, Walter P. Reuther Labor Library, ibid., box 7, folder 16.

107. Cesar Chavez, "Martin Luther King Jr.: He Showed Us the Way," quoted in Kushner, *Long Road to Delano,* 165.

108. Ibid.

109. Cesar Chavez, "Lessons of Dr. Martin Luther King, Jr.," January 12, 1990, UFW web page.

110. John R. Moyer, "A Conversation with Cesar Chavez," in *Readings on La Raza: The Twentieth Century,* ed. Matt S. Meier and Feliciano Rivera (New York: Hill and Wang, 1974), 253.

111. Chavez, "People Are Willing to Sacrifice Themselves: An Interview with Cesar Chavez," in *Peace Is the Way: Writings on Nonviolence from the Fellowship of Reconciliation,* ed. Walter Wink (Maryknoll, NY: Orbis Books, 2000), 228.

112. Orosco, *Cesar Chavez and the Common Sense of Nonviolence,* 110.

113. Ibid., 113.

114. Martin Luther King, Jr., *Why We Can't Wait* (Boston: Beacon Press, [1964] 2010), 27.

115. Chavez, quoted in *The Gospel of Cesar Chavez: My Faith in Action,* ed. Mario T. García (Lanham, MD: Sheed and Ward, 2007), 119.

116. Chavez, quoted in Matthiessen, *Sal Si Puedes,* 35.

117. *The Autobiography of Martin Luther King, Jr.,* 25.

CHAPTER THREE

1. Gandhi, quoted in Stanley Wolpert, *Gandhi's Passion: The Life and Legacy of Mahatma Gandhi* (Oxford: Oxford University Press, 2001), 144.

2. Cesar Chavez, quoted in Jacques E. Levy, *Cesar Chavez: Autobiography of La Causa* (Minneapolis: University of Minnesota Press, [1974] 2005), 276.

3. LeRoy Chatfield, quoted in Peter Matthiessen, *Sal Si Puedes: Cesar Chavez and the New American Revolution* (Berkeley: University of California Press, [1969] 2000), 180.

4. Dick Meister, "'La Huelga' Becomes 'La Causa,'" *New York Times*, November 17, 1968.

5. Saul Alinsky, quoted in Matthiessen, *Sal Si Puedes*, 247.

6. Cesar Chavez, in "Viva La Causa," an interview by Wendy Goepel, *Farm Labor* 1, no. 5 (April 1964): 24.

7. Cesar Chavez, quoted in Lillian S. Beloin, "Faith Motivates His Actions, Chavez Says in an Interview," *Catholic Northwest*, May 2, 1975.

8. Chris Hartmire to Father Mark Said, O.P., letter, dated February 17, 1977. Quoted by permission.

9. Cesar Chavez, in Pat Hoffman, "An Interview with Cesar Chavez," *Sojourners*, October 1977, 23.

10. Richard Griswold del Castillo and Richard A. Garcia. *César Chávez: A Triumph of Spirit* (Norman: University of Oklahoma Press, 1995), 140.

11. Emile Durkheim, "On the Definition of Religion," in *The Elementary Forms of Religious Life*, trans. Carol Cosman (Oxford: Oxford University Press, [1912] 2008).

12. Ibid., 69.

13. Though both the time and date are unclear, the first *Cursillo* is said to have occurred in San Honorato, Spain, in January 1949. Even though laymen were allowed to participate only once in the *Cursillo*, in some places supplemental follow-up workshops were offered to them on a monthly basis. See Marcene Marcoux, *Cursillo: Anatomy of a Movement* (New York: Lambeth Press, 1982).

14. Richard Edward Martinez, *PADRES: The National Chicano Priest Movement* (Austin: University of Texas Press, 2005), 30.

15. Marcoux, *Cursillo*, 5 (italics in original).

16. Frank Bardacke, *Trampling Out the Vintage: Cesar Chavez and the Two Souls of the United Farm Workers Movement* (London: Verso, 2011), 63.

17. W.K. Barger and Ernesto M. Reza, T*he Farm Labor Movement in the Midwest: Social Change and Adaptation among Migrant Farmworkers* (Austin: University of Texas Press, 1994).

18. Walter P. Reuther Library, Archives of Labor and Urban Affairs, United Farm Workers Collection, UFW Office of the President (hereafter UFWOTP collection), box 5, folders 5–6, dated July 20–21, 1962.

19. See Frank Bardacke, "Cesar's Ghost," in *Cesar Chavez*, ed. Ilan Stavans (Santa Barbara, CA: Greenwood Press, 2010), 141.

20. Adrian Bautista, "Vatos Sagrados: Exploring Northern Ohio's Religious Borderlands" (Ph.D. diss., Bowling Green State University, 2013), 179; available at https://etd.ohiolink.edu/rws_etd/document/get/bgsu1383178330/inline. See also Adrian Bautista, "Vatos Sagrados: Cursillo and a Midwestern Catholic Borderlands," in *Diálogo* 16, no. 2 (Fall 2013): 19–26.

21. Chavez's notes on the *rollos* are available in the Walter P. Reuther Library, Archives of Labor and Urban Affairs, UFWOTP collection, box 5, folder 5.

22. Dick Meister and Anne Loftis, *A Long Time Coming: The Struggle to Unionize America's Farm Workers* (New York: Macmillan, 1977), 120.

23. Dolores Huerta, quoted in Jacques Levy, *Cesar Chavez*, 176.

24. Chris Hartmire, videotaped interview by author, June 14, 2011, Claremont, CA. Quoted by permission.

25. Chavez, quoted in Levy, *Cesar Chavez*, 184–85 (bracketed element in original).

26. The date of the meeting is contested. Some historians say it was held September 15. See, for example, James P. Terzian and Kathryn Cramer, *Mighty Hard Road: The Story of Cesar Chavez* (New York: Doubleday, 1970), 76. According to Matt Garcia, Chavez did not call the strike on at the time of the meeting, at the behest of the parish priest. Instead, he hesitated and delayed the decision until the following week. See Garcia, *From the Jaws of Victory: The Triumph and Tragedy of Cesar Chavez and the Farm Worker Movement* (Berkeley: University of California Press, 2012), 41. Garcia references the union's co-founder, Gilbert Padilla, as his source for this information.

27. A.V. Krebs, *La Causa: The Word Was Made Flesh* (Essential Books, 1992), 35.

28. Father Ken, telephone interview by author, August 30, 2011, transcribed, corrected, and approved by Father Irrgang. Quoted by permission.

29. *El Macriado*, unsigned editorial, [n.d.]. *El Malcriado* did not begin publishing an English–language edition until late in 1965.

30. Roger Bruns, *Cesar Chavez and the United Farm Workers Movement* (Santa Barbara, CA: ABC-CLIO, 2011), 23.

31. The quoted passages in this paragraph are from Krebs, *La Causa,* 47 (my ellipsis), 62.

32. "Religious Leaders' Statement," December 14, 1965, United Farmworker Movement Documentation Project, https://libraries.ucsd.edu/farmworker-movement/, presented by the University of California, San Diego, Library (accessed June 23, 2014).

33. See Matt Garcia, "The Importance of Being Asian: Growers, the United Farm Workers, and the Rise of Colorblindness," in *Racial Formation in the Twenty-First Century,* ed. Daniel Martinez HoSang, Oneka LaBennett, and Laura Pulido (Berkeley: University of California Press, 2012), 95–115.

34. Pat Hoffman, *Ministry of the Dispossessed: Learning from the Farm Workers Movement* (Los Angeles: Wallace Press, 1987), 6–7.

35. See Marco G. Prouty, *César Chávez, the Catholic Bishops, and the Farmworkers' Struggle for Social Justice* (Tucson: University of Arizona Press, 2006).

36. "Grapes of Wrath," *Time,* December 10, 1965, 96.

37. Statement of the California Church Council on the Delano Grape Strike, adopted by the Board of Directors of the California Church Council in a regularly called session, March 7, 1966.

38. Joan London and Henry Anderson, *So Shall Ye Reap* (New York: Crowell, 1970), 168.

39. Chavez, quoted in Mark Day, *Forty Acres: Cesar Chavez and the Farm Workers* (New York: Praeger, 1971), 116.

40. Day, *Forty Acres,* 85.

41. Mark R. Day, "My Time with the UFW, 1967–1970," 5, available at United Farmworker Movement Documentation Project, https://libraries/ucsd.edu/farmworkermovement/.

42. Terzian and Cramer, *Mighty Hard Road,* 81.

43. See Levy, *Cesar Chavez,* 50.

44. Chavez, quoted in ibid., 116.

45. Cesar Chavez, "Viva La Causa," an interview by Wendy Goepel, *Farm Labor* 1, no. 5 (April 1964): 24.

46. Chavez, quoted in Levy, *Cesar Chavez,* 116.

47. Ibid., 170.

48. "El Corrido de Dolores Huerta," words and music by Carmen Moreno, 1976, Los Morenos Music.

49. Luis Valdez and El Teatro Campesino, *Actos* (San Juan Bautista, CA: Cucaracha Publications, 1971), 5.

50. Ibid., 2.

51. Ibid., 3.

52. See "History of the Pilgrimage," in *El Malcriado,* no. 33, April 10, 1966.

53. Words to "El Corrido de César Chávez" are reprinted in full in *Rollos de Aztlán: Songs of the Chicano Movement,* compiled, annotated, and produced by Estevan César Azcona and Russell Rodriguez (Washington DC: Smithsonian Folkways Recordings, 2005). Authorship is credited to Felipe Cantú.

54. The Penitente tradition is characterized not only by flagellation but also by its community service—including the production of religious objects and devotional materials. See Ramón A. Gutiérrez, "Crucifixion, Slavery, and Death: The Hermanos Penitentes of the Southwest," in *Over the Edge: Mapping the American West,* ed. Valerie Matsumoto and Blake Allmendinger (Berkeley: University of California Press, 1999), 253–71; and Alberto Pulido, *The Sacred World of the Penitentes* (Washington, DC: Smithsonian Press, 2000).

55. Cesar Chavez, "Sacramento March Letter," March 1966. Reprinted in full in Winthrop Yinger, *Cesar Chavez: The Rhetoric of Nonviolence* (Hicksville, NY: Exposition Press, 1975), 107.

56. Peter Matthiessen, "Profile: Cesar Chavez," reprint from the June 21 and June 28, 1969, issues of the *New Yorker,* 39.

57. Levy, *Cesar Chavez,* 179.

58. "El Plan de Delano," reprinted in full in *El Malcriado,* March 1966; " in English, "The Plan of Delano," *El Malcriado: Voice of the Farm Workers,* no. 33, April 10, 1966.

59. *El Malcriado,* April 15–30, 1969; reprinted in full in Griswold del Castillo and Richard A. Garcia, *Triumph of Spirit,* 141.

60. Ibid.

61. "Remarks by Wayne C. Hartmire at the Farm Workers' Rally in Sacramento, California, April 10, 1966," Walter P. Reuther Labor Library, Archives of the National Farm Worker Ministry, box 4, folder 4.

62. Dolores Huerta, quoted in *The Fight in the Fields: Cesar Chavez and the Farmworkers Movement,* ed. Susan Ferriss and Ricardo Sandoval (Orlando, FL: Harcourt, Brace, 1997), 122.

63. Walter P. Reuther Library, Archives of Labor and Urban Affairs, UFWOTP collection, box 5, folder 14. Printed in Spanish; English translation by author.

64. The official start date for the love fast in the mythology is Valentine's Day, yet Levy says Chavez started the fast days before but did not announce it until February 15. Matthiessen says the fast ended March 11, a day later than other sources.

65. See Jennifer Reed-Bouley, "Guiding Moral Action: A Study of the United Farm Workers' Use of Catholic Social Teaching and Religious Symbols" (Ph.D. diss., Loyola University Chicago, 1998). Reed-Bouley notes the leader's three public fasts but does not count the fast in Arizona in 1972, instead listing a three-day all-union fast in 1973 as fast number two.

66. Ibid., 105.

67. Frank del Olmo, *Commentries on His Times* (Los Angeles: Los Angeles Times Books, 2004), 113.

68. Cesar Chavez, "Letter to the National Council of Churches," February 20, 1968, reprinted in full in Yinger, *Cesar Chavez*, 108.

69. "Statement of the Fast for Nonviolence," United Farm Workers Organizing Committee, AFL-CIO, February 25, 1968, reprinted in full in Yinger, *Cesar Chavez*, 111.

70. Jan Young, *The Migrant Workers and Cesar Chavez* (New York: Julian Messner, 1972), 150.

71. Jerry Cohen, quoted in Levy, *Cesar Chavez*, 283

72. Chavez, quoted in Matthiessen, *Sal Si Puedes*, 186.

73. Matthiessen, *Sal Si Puedes*, 195.

74. Dolores Huerta, quoted in Levy, *Cesar Chavez*, 276.

75. Matthiessen, *Sal Si Puedes*, 199.

76. Cesar Chavez, "Letter from Cesar," May 15, 1972, Walter P. Labor Library, Archives of Labor and Urban Affairs, UFWOTP collection, box 3, folder 13.

77. LeRoy Chatfield, "Cesar Chavez and the Farmworker Movement," [n.d.], 28, available in United Farmworker Movement Documentation Project, https://libraries.ucsd.edu/farmworkermovement/.

78. "Songbook of the Fast for Justice, May 1972." Walter P. Reuther Library, Archives of Labor and Urban Affairs, UFWOTP collection, box 3, folder 14.

79. Chris Hartmire, in *El Malcriado* 5, no. 3 (June 9, 1972).

80. Cesar Chavez, "Statement Ending the Fast for Justice, June 4, 1972." Reprinted in full in *El Malcriado* 5, no. 4 (June 23, 1972).

81. Editorial, *El Malcriado*, ibid.

82. Pat Hoffman, "Cesar Chavez's Fast for Life," *Christian Century*, October 12, 1988, 105.

83. Associated Press, August 22, 1988.

84. "Cesar Chavez's Statement at the End of the 'Fast for Life,' August 21, 1988," Chavez, in Bruns, *Cesar Chavez and the United Farm Workers Movement*, 159.

85. Ibid.

86. Chavez, in Catherine Ingram, *In the Footsteps of Gandhi: Conversations with Spiritual Social Activists* (Berkeley: Parallax Press, 1990), 111 (emphasis in original).

87. See especially Elaine Scarry, *The Body in Pain: The Making and Unmaking of the World* (New York: Oxford University Press, 1987).

88. LeRoy Chatfield, "The Legacy of Cesar Chavez," 3, available at United Farmworker Movement Documentation Project, https://libraries.ucsd.edu/farmworkermovement/.

89. Cesar Chavez, quoted in ibid., 26.

90. Marc Grossman, videotaped interview by author, August 19, 2010, Sacramento, CA. Quoted by permission.

91. Harry Bernstein, "UFW Transforming Itself from 'Cause' to 'Businesslike Union,'" *Los Angeles Times,* October 25, 1981, 20 (emphasis added).

92. Ronald B. Taylor, *Chavez and the Farm Workers* (Boston: Beacon Press, 1975), 26–27.

93. Cesar Chavez from the "Reel Tape Project (October 2007)," CD 10B, recorded during the meeting of the Executive Board of the UFW, June 30–July 7, 1977, Walter P. Reuther Library, Archives of Labor and Urban Affairs, UFW collection. Unless otherwise noted, quotations from this meeting are from the same source.

94. LeRoy Chatfield, "Cesar Chavez and His Farmworker Movement," 43, available at United Farmworker Movement Documentation Project, https://libraries.ucsd.edu/farmworkermovement/.

95. *La Paz Community Religious Life Bulletin,* November 24, 1978.

96. Father Ken Irrgang, telephone interview by author, August 30, 2011, transcribed, corrected, and approved by Father Irrgang.

97. Victor Salandini, *The Confessions of the Tortilla Priest* (San Diego: San Diego Review, 1992), 84.

98. The quotations of Father Ken Irrgang in this paragraph are from the telephone interview, August 30, 2011.

99. *La Paz Community Religious Life Bulletin,* November 17, 1978.

100. Chavez, quoted in Matthiessen, *Sal Si Puedes,* 326.

101. Father Ken Irrgang, interview, August 30, 2011. Ana Raquel Minian argues that Chavez did indeed oppose birth control, at least early in the movement, not for religious reasons but because he feared the compulsory sterilization of Latinos and other poor people. See Ana Raquel Minian, "'Indiscriminate and Shameless Sex': The Strategic Use of Sexuality by the United Farm Workers," *American Quarterly* 65, no. 1 (March 2013): 63–90.

102. LeRoy Chatfield, quoted in Frank Bardacke, *Trampling Out the Vintage,* 747. Marc Grossman claims that prominent liberation theologians from Latin America visited La Paz.

103. Mark R. Day, "My Time with the UFW: 1967–1970," 6, available at United Farmworker Movement Documentation Project, https://libraries.ucsd.edu/farmworkermovement/.

104. *La Paz Community Religious Life Bulletin,* October 28, 1978.

105. Walter P. Reuther Library, Archives of Labor and Urban Affairs, UFWOTP collection, box 21, folder 1.

106. Notes from the liturgy committee at La Paz, August 15, 1977, personal files of Chris Hartmire, quoted by permission.

107. *La Paz Community Religious Life Bulletin,* October 28, 1978, 1.

108. Chris Hartmire notes, June 20, 1978, from personal files of Chris Hartmire, quoted by permission.

109. *La Paz Community Religious Life Bulletin,* November 3, 1978.

110. Ibid., November 10, 1978.

111. Ibid, January 19, 1979.

112. Letter from Chris Hartmire to Father Mark Said, O.P., February 17, 1977, Chris Hartmire personal files, quoted by permission.

113. Letter from Father Mark Said, O.P., to Chris Hartmire, dated March 15, 1977. Chris Hartmire personal files, quoted by permission.

114. *President's Newsletter* 1, no. 1 (March 11, 1977): 2.

115. Ibid., 3.

116. Hartmire memo to Chavez, September 7, 1977, Walter P. Reuther Library, Archives of Labor and Urban Affairs, UFWOTP collection, box 3, files 24 and 25.

117. Garcia, *From the Jaws of Victory,* 285.

118. Quoted from an audio recording, UFW Executive Board meeting, July 4, 1977, tape 9A, Walter P. Reuther Library, Archives of Labor and Urban Affairs, UFW collection. Unless otherwise noted, all quotations of the proceedings during this event are from this recording.

119. Chavez's statement on Chuck Dederich, Walter P. Reuther Library, Archives of Labor and Urban Affairs, UFWOTP collection, box 3, folder 24.

120. Ibid. The folder that includes Chavez's statement also contains a report on the press conference.

121. Chris Hartmire has said that he wrote the statement, with the help of Jim Drake.

122. *President's Newsletter* 1, no. 1 (March 11, 1977). Chavez, quoted in Levy, *Cesar Chavez,* 286.

123. Bruce Lincoln, *Holy Terrors: Thinking about Religion after September 11* (Chicago: University of Chicago Press, 2003), 83.

124. Ibid., 84.

125. Ibid., 85.

CONCLUSION

1. Dolores Huerta, quoted in Peter Matthiessen, *Sal Si Puedes (Escape If You Can): Cesar Chavez and the New American Revolution* (Berkeley: University of California Press, [1969] 2000), 284.

2. Cesar Chavez, "Lessons of Dr. Martin Luther King, Jr.," January 12, 1990, available at United Farmworker Movement Documentation Project, https://libraries.ucsd.edu/farmworkermovement/ (accessed June 24, 2014).

3. Richard Chavez, in *Cesar's Last Fast,* video recording, directed by Richard Ray Perez, 2014.

4. Richard Griswold del Castillo and Richard A. Garcia, *César Chávez: A Triumph of Spirit* (Norman: University of Oklahoma Press, 1995).

5. Dolores Huerta, quoted in ibid., 142.

6. See especially Ralph de Toledano, *Little Cesar* (Washington, DC: Anthem Books, 1965).

7. Gloria Anzaldúa, *Borderlands/La Frontera: The New Mestiza,* 3rd ed. (San Francisco: Aunt Lute Books, 2007), 68 (italics in original).

8. Chavez, quoted in Matthiessen, *Sal Si Puedes,* 143.

9. Cesar Chavez, quoted in Peter Matthiessen, "Profile: Cesar Chavez," *New Yorker,* June 21 and June 28, 1969, available at United Farm Worker Documentation Project, https://libraries.ucsd.edu/farmworkermovement/, presented by the University of California, San Diego, Library (accessed June 23, 2014).

10. George Mariscal, *Brown-Eyed Children of the Sun: Lessons from the Chicano Movement, 1965–1975* (Albuquerque: University of New Mexico Press, 2005).

11. Cesar Chavez, quoted in Jacques E. Levy, *Cesar Chavez: Autobiography of La Causa,* (Minneapolis: University of Minnesota Press, [1975] 2007), 286.

12. Joan London and Henry Anderson, *So Shall Ye Reap* (New York: Crowell, 1970), 186.

13. Jean Maddern Pitrone, *Chávez: Man of the Migrants; A Plea for Social Justice* (New York: Alba House, 1972), 122–23.

14. Ronald B. Taylor, *Chavez and the Farm Workers* (Boston: Beacon Press, 1975), 214.

15. Cesar Chavez, speech given at Hunter College, New York, Walter P. Reuther Labor Library, Archives of Labor and Urban Affairs, United Farm Workers Collection, UFW Office of the President, box 18, folder 13.

16. See Elizabeth E. Brusco, *The Reformation of Machismo: Evangelical Conversion and Gender in Columbia* (Austin: University of Texas Press, 1995). For a debunking of the myths of machismo see Matthew C. Gutmann, *The Meanings of Macho: Being a Man in Mexico City*, 10th anniversary ed. (Berkeley: University of California Press, 2006).

17. Alfredo Mirande, *Hombres y Machos: Masculinity and Latino Culture* (Boulder, CO: Westview Press, 1997), 67.

18. Ibid., 102.

19. Matthiessen, *Sal Si Puedes*, 231.

20. Ibid., 294–95.

21. Victor Villaseñor, *Macho!* (New York: Bantam Doubleday, 1991), 221.

22. Chavez, quoted in Matthiessen, *Sal Si Puedes*, 160. For a historical discussion of the roles of women in the UFW, see Margaret Rose, "Traditional and Nontraditional Patterns of Female Activism in the United Farm Workers of America, 1962–1980," *Frontiers* 40, no. 1 (1990): 26–32.

23. Mariscal, *Brown-Eyed Children of the Sun*, 146.

24. Alex Donis, *My Cathedral: Che Guevara and César Chávez*, "Artist Statement," available at http://lorcaloca.blogspot.com/2005_08_01_archive.html (accessed July 3, 2014).

25. Chavez's comment is quoted in Levy, *Cesar Chavez*, 91; Ross's comment in his diary is quoted in Levy, *Cesar Chavez*, 102.

26. Chavez, "Eulogy for Fred Ross," San Francisco, October 17, 1992, *The Words of César Chávez*, ed. Richard J. Jensen and John C. Hammerback (College Station: Texas A&M Press, 2002), 172.

27. Chavez, in Matthiessen, *Sal Si Puedes*, 47.

28. Fred Ross, *Conquering Goliath: Cesar Chavez at the Beginning* (Keene, CA: El Taller Grafico, 1989), 144.

29. Dolores Huerta, quoted in Levy, *Cesar Chavez*, 277.

30. Cesar Chavez, "Eulogy for Fred Ross," in Jensen and Hammerback, *The Words of César Chávez*, 178.

31. Father Ken Irrgang, telephone interview by author, August 30, 2011, transcribed, corrected, and approved by Father Irrgang.

32. Ana Raquel Minian, "'Indiscriminate and Shameless Sex': The Strategic Use of Sexuality by the United Farm Workers," *American Quarterly* 65, no. 1 (March 2013): 83.

33. The myth of Chavez's antigay macho attitude persists. Matt Garcia writes: "Several veterans of the union believe the Game played a role in purging a union paralegal, Steve Hopcraft, on the basis of his alleged homosexuality." See Garcia, *From the Jaws of Victory: The Triumph and Tragedy of Cesar Chavez and the Farm Worker Movement* (Berkeley: University of California Press, 2012), 265–66.

34. Matthiessen, *Sal Si Puedes,* 141.

35. See especially Robert McKee Irwin, *Mexican Masculinities* (Minneapolis: University of Minnesota Press, 2003).

36. Dolores Huerta, quoted in Levy, *Cesar Chavez,* 278.

37. Huerta, quoted in *Equality: Human Rights Campaign, News about GLBT America,* Fall 2006, 9.

38. Frank Bardacke, *Trampling Out the Vintage: Cesar Chavez and the Two Souls of the United Farm Workers Movement* (London: Verso, 2011), 237. Bardacke, however, does not discuss Chavez's activist involvement in LGBT issues; nor does he attempt to reconcile such unorthodox behavior with his thesis that Chavez was a conservative Catholic activist.

39. Cesar Chavez, quoted in Doug Smith, "UFW Leader Addresses 100 at Buffet-Dance," *Los Angeles Times,* March 31, 1983.

40. Marc Grossman, videotaped interview by author, August 19, 2010, Sacramento, CA. Quoted by permission.

41. Christine Chavez, in "The Satya Interview with Christine Chavez," *Satya,* February 2007.

42. Chavez, quoted in Lena Williams, "200,000 March in Capital to Seek Gay Rights and Money for AIDS," *New York Times,* October 12, 1987.

43. See Luis León, "Misusing Cesar Chavez in Immigration Debate," in *Religion Dispatches* (rd.org), December 5, 2010.

44. Cesar Chavez, quoted in Griswold del Castillo and Garcia, *Triumph of Spirit,* 154.

45. Cornel West, *Race Matters* (Boston: Beacon Press, [1993] 2001), 39.

46. Sam Harris, *Letter to a Christian Nation* (New York: Knopf, 2006), 80.

47. Martin Luther King, interview by Alex Haley, *Playboy* magazine, January 1965.

48. Matthiessen, *Sal Si Puedes,* 196.

49. Chavez, quoted in Levy, *Cesar Chavez,* 196.

50. Cesar Chavez, "Lessons of Dr. Martin Luther King, Jr.," January 12, 1990, Cesar E. Chavez Foundation web page, http://www.chavezfoundation.org (accessed January 15, 2013).

51. The quoted passage with Chavez's statement is in Griswold and Castillo, *Triumph of Spirit*, 150.

52. Reverend Dr. Martin Luther King Jr., quoted in David J. Garrow, *Bearing the Cross: Martin Luther King, Jr., and the Southern Christian Leadership Conference* (New York: Vintage Books, 1988), 581.

53. Chavez, quoted in Levy, *Cesar Chavez*, 27.

54. Cesar Chavez, Address to the Commonwealth Club of San Francisco, November 9, 1984, in Jensen and Hammerback, *The Words of César Chávez*, 129.

55. Cesar Chavez, "Prayer of the Farm Worker' Struggle" © César E. Chávez Foundation, [n.d.], chavezfdtn@igc.apc.org.

Italic page numbers indicate illustrations.

Abernathy, Ralph, 110, 111, *155*
Abington School District v. Schempp, 174
abolution, 150
abortion, 61, 151, 188n87
Acosta, Oscar Zeta, 99
activism of Chavez: causes supported
    by, 14–15, 17, 94, 169–73, 206n38;
    criticism of and death threats, 72,
    141, 156, 160; defeat of, 145; goals
    of, 19, 25, 28, 30; identification with,
    23, 26; influence of on King, 114;
    jailed in Salinas, 107; leaving CSO,
    47, 148; legacy of, 8, 14, 96, 177;
    multiple identities of aiding in, 23;
    in origin myth of UFW, 48; with
    Fred Ross, 166–69; in Sacramento
    pilgrimage, 136; at Salinas rally, *20*;
    and Scott King, 107–8, 110–11;
    speaking at King's memorial, 110;
    supporting Dederich, 155. *See also*
    fasting by Chavez; mythology of
    Chavez
actos (skits), 18, 131
Agricultural Workers Organizing
    Committee, 2, 52, 123

ahimsa (nonviolence), 76, 103, 194n77. *See
    also* nonviolence
"Ain't I a Woman?" speech (Truth), 93
Alexander VI (pope), 81
Alinsky, Saul, 20, 21, 47, 117, 131
Ambedkar, B. R., 92
American left, 198n39
American Progress (Gast, painting), 88
Anderson, Henry, 162–63
Anzaldúa, Gloria, 26–27, 31, 161
Apple Corporation, 33–34, 71
Arizona State Legislature's House Bill
    2134, 141
artworks, 86, 88, 165–66, *167*
"authorship," 72–73
Aztec influences, 18, 30, 124, 132. *See also*
    Mesoamerican influences

Baez, Joan, 142, *148*
Bardacke, Frank, 57, 69–70, 120, 206n38
Barthes, Roland, 72–73
Bautista, Adrian, 120–21
Bellah, Robert, 22
Bernasconi, Robert, 80
Bernier, François, 79

Bhagavad Gita, 103
birth control, 151, 202n101
bisexuals. *See* LGBTs
blacks, 93. *See also* Civil Rights
  Movement
Bonhoeffer, Dietrich, 128
borderlands, 26–28; theory, 30–31
boycotts, 108, 125–26, 135, 141–42
bracero program, 52, 128
Brown, Jerry, 52
Brown, Robert McAfee, 125
Bryant, Anita, 152

California Agricultural Labor
  Relations Act, 52
California Church Council, 128
California Hall of Fame, 6
California Migrant Ministry (CMM),
  123, 127–29. *See also* National Council
  of Churches
California Proposition Fourteen (1976),
  145
Camacho, Epifano, 134, 163
Campbell, Joseph, 35, 43, 45, 73
Carrasco, Davíd, 84–85
Carrette, Jeremy, 11
caste system, 91–93, 104
Catholicism, Chavez's, 69–70; appeal
  to US Conference of Catholic
  Bishops, 126; appeal to Vatican,
  117–18; in childhood experience, 41;
  conflicting reports on, 151; in
  Cursillo experience, 69–70; and
  doctrinal allegiance, 5, 10, 15, 62–66,
  150; and priesthood consideration,
  94; and priests in Coachella, 127;
  and social justice teachings, 46
Catholics and Catholicism: Católicos
  por la Raza (CPLR), 99; in *La Causa*,
  5–6, 122; Chicanas/os conflicted
  relationship with, 97; criticism of by
  Hartmire, 128; *Cursillo* movement,
  69–70, 119–23; on Great Grape
  Strike, 126; influence in FWA, 49;
  leaving CSO, 131; as link between

Chavez and Kennedys, 19;
  references to in *El Malcriado*, 124;
  social justice teachings of, 46–47,
  49. *See also* religion; *specific clergy*
La Causa: anti-Catholic sentiment in,
  170; Catholicism in, 5–6, 122; Chavez's
  leadership of, 10, 12; as cult like, 149,
  154; cultural ministry within, 17;
  Day's view of, 3; FWA's adoption of
  nomenclature of, 4; interpretations
  of, 12; Matthiessen's coverage of, 37;
  Meso-american philosophy and art
  in, 17–18; *'mitos'* of, 131–32; new macho
  of, 9, 78, 161–63; photography of farm
  workers benefiting, 25; as quasi-
  religious, 16; queer(y)ing, 169–72;
  recruiting followers to, 37–38;
  red-baiting of, 124–25 (*See also*
  communism); religious ethos of, 128;
  signature phrase of, 7; singing in,
  130–31, 142, 147; support to followers
  of, 48–50; symbols in, 2; traditions
  influencing, 1–2
La Causa, as a religious movement:
  collective need prioritized in, 118;
  components of political spirituality
  in, 118; Durkheim's theory of social
  organization applied to, 118–19; *El
  Cursillista*, 119–23; gestalt of, 118; given
  priority over UFW, 156; group
  absolution, 150; *La Huelga* influenced
  by, 123–32; La Paz, 145–55; *La Paz
  Community Religious Life Bulletin*,
  151–52; meeting renaming, 150; *New
  York Times on*, 117; pilgrimage,
  penance and revolution, 132–37;
  purpose of, 118; as a quasi-religion of
  resistance, 157; as a religion of
  revolution, 155–58; sacred calendar
  of, 149; sacred text for, 134
Cesar Chavez: Autobiography of La Causa
  (Levy), 37–38, 148–49; on
  characteristics of Chavez, 57; on
  Chavez's knowledge of Gandhi,
  102–3; description of Chavez, 24, 53;

on education of Chavez, 42; on religious identity of Chavez, 63–64
César Chávez de California (Lentz, painting), 60–61
"Cesar Chavez: The Chicano Messiah?" (Solis-Garza), 98
"Cesar Chavez: The Paradoxes of Greatness" (Gormley), 24
Cesar E. Chavez Center at La Paz, 41
Cesar E. Chavez National Monument, 7, 18
Cesar's Last Fast (Perez, documentary), 138
Chatfield, LeRoy (Brother Gilbert): on Chavez being publicly rebuked, 145; on Chavez's Catholicism, 151; on cultlike nature of *La Causa*, 149; as disciple of Chavez, 129–30; recollections of fasts, 116–17, 142
Chavez, Cesar, author's approach to, 15, 18, 77
Chavez, Cesar, personal life: adolescence, 42–43; author's visit to homes of, 18; childhood, 38–39; with his dogs, *58*; education and intellectualism, 42, 53–60, 100, 101–2; family of origin, 38–39; health, 24, 25, 110, 142; marriage, 46, 186n41, 189n104; mental health, 16, 36, 52, 72, 156; military service, 43–44; nickname, 39; overview, 2; physical description, 23–26; spelling of name, 180n2; yoga practice, 60
Chavez, Cesar, works/writings of: "Good Friday Letter," 106; "Lessons of Dr. Martin Luther King Jr.," 112; "Martin Luther King Jr.: He Showed Us the Way," 112; notes on *rollos* (workshops), 121–22; "Open Letter" on Delano, 27; overview of, 17; "Prayer of the Farm Worker's Struggle," 177; "Sacramento March Letter," 133
Chavez, Cesario (paternal grandfather), 38–39, 41

Chavez, Christine (granddaughter), 172
Chavez, Dorotea Hernandez (paternal grandmother), 38, 41
Chavez, Juana Estrada (mother), 39–41, 164
Chavez, Fernando, 144
Chavez, Helen (wife), 46, 50, 170, 171, 186n41, 189n104
Chavez, Librado (father), 41
Chavez, Manuel (cousin), 48, 50
Chavez, Richard (brother), 38–41, 48, 70, 120, 154
Che Guevara and César Chávez (Donis, painting), 165–66, *167*
Chicanismo, 15, 96–97
Chicano lobby, 53
Chicano power, movement, xii, 54, 97, 173, 195n2
Chicanos. See Mexican Americans
The Chicanos: A History of Mexican Americans (Meier and Rivera), 54–55
chingar (violation) ethic, 166, 169
Christian Century (magazine), 106
Christianity: Chavez's identification with, 64; masculinity in, 120–21; "pious colonialism" under, 16, 29, 80, 83–89; redefinition of, 157; sacredness in, 11. *See also* religion
"Christ Loves Us" (editorial), 124
civil disobedience, 95
civil religion, 21–22, 77, 96–97, 125, 157, 175
Civil Rights Movement, 93, 108, 175
Clinton, Bill, 76
CMM (California Migrant Ministry), 123, 127–29. *See also* National Council of Churches
Coalition Conference Committee, 154–55
Coatlicue process of psychic formation, 161
Cohen, Jerry, 140
colonialism: Chavez seeing effects of, 46; internal, 78, 89, 101; King's opposition to, 101; Latin American de-colonial project, 162; legacy *of*

colonialism *(continued)*
    Mexican Americans, 9, 14; oppression
    of personified by Chavez, 24; racial
    ecology of, 9–10, 76–77, 79–84;
    reciprocal suffering under, 177;
    religion influencing, 16, 29, 80,
    83–89; role of myths in, 74; satire
    about, 132; Spanish, 84–86; struggles
    against, 77–78, 101, 103, 109–10
communism, 59, 70, 124–25, 160
community intellectuals, 56
community organization, 47, 113. *See
    also specific movements*
Community Service Organization
    (CSO), 20, 26, 47, 130–31, 168
Confessions of the Tortilla Priest
    (Salandini), 61
The Conquest of Mexico (comedy), 132
Constitution of the United States, 61, 84
1 Corinthians, 175–76
corridos, 131–33, 136, 137, 142, 147–49,
    200n53
Council of the Fourteen, 84–85
countermyths, 25, 29, 82–83, 100, 174–75.
    See also myths
CPLR (Católicos por la Raza), 99
Cramer, Kathryn, 56
creation theory, 9–10
criticism of Chavez, 72, 141, 156, 160
Crofutt, George A., 88
Cruz, Ricardo, 99
CSO. *See* Community Service
    Organization (CSO)
cultural relativity of religion, 64, 177
cultures, 1, 26–27
curanderas/os, 39, 41, 158
Cursillos, 69–70, 119–23, 197n13

Daifallah, Nagi, 50–51, 147
Dalton, John, 62
Dana, Richard Henry, 87
Davis, Angela, 142
Day, Dorothy, 3, 5
Day, Mark, 62, 129
"The Death of the Author" (Barthes), 72

death threats made to Chavez, 141
"De Colores" (song), 70
Dederich, Chuck, 153–55, 203n120. *See
    also* Synanon Foundation
dehumanization, 90, 91, 100. *See also*
    colonialism; farm workers
Deists, 83
Delano: Chavezes' move to, 48;
    discrimination in, 44–45; influence
    of the church in, 62; Matthiessen's
    coverage of, 36–37; revisited, 50–53;
    rise to fame, 27–28. *See also La
    Huelga*
Delano (Dunne), 89
Delano Borderlands, 26–28, 30
Delgadillo, Teresa, 11–12
del Olmo, Frank, 138
despedidas to Chavez, xiii
Díaz, Porfirio, 39
Dictionary of Chicano Folklore, 98–99
Doctrine of Christian Discovery, 81–82
Donis, Alex ("Adonis"), 165–66
Drake, Jim, 127–29, 203n121
Dube, Musa, 80–81
Dunne, John Gregory, 89–90
Durán, Diego, 30
Durkheim, Emile, 118–19, 156

Enlightenment Deists, 83
Erikson, Erik, 35
ethics, 11, 67, 166, 169
ethnic diversity in Delano, 50–51, 139

farm workers: *bracero* program, 52, 128;
    Chavezes as, 37, 38, 42;
    dehumanization and
    rehumanization of, 89–90;
    discrimination against, 9, 51;
    influence of on faith, 28; life
    expectancy for, 24, 50; living
    conditions of, 9, 25, 38; medical
    services for, 155; organizations
    supportive of, 108, 111; patron saint
    of, 99; racial and religious
    differences between, 139; religious

identification of, 124; values of, 36; white, 51. *See also* unions

Farm Workers Association (FWA), 2, 4, 48–50, 122, 123. *See also* UFW

Farmworkers Theater. *See* El Teatro Campesino

fasting, by Chavez: ecstasy of, 145; effectiveness of, 23, 25, 138, 145; Fast for Justice, 141–43; Fast for Life, 143–45; Jesse Jackson taking over for, 138, 144; "love fast," 63, 93, 99, 108–9, 116–17, 139, 162, 200n64; meaning of, 140, 145; mental clarity during, 101; misinterpretations of, 104; mother's support during, 40; overview of public fasts, 138, 201n65; purpose of, 139; as religious ritual, 52; RFK's participation in, 20, 140; as spectacle of suffering, 138–45

fasting, by Gandhi, 104, 138, 145

Fati system, 91

Filipinos, 2, 44, 50, 52, 96, 135

Finkelstein, Norman G., 190n8

Flores, Patrick, 121

Forty Acres, 51–52, 117

Foucault, Michel, 10–12, 73

Founder's Day, 48, 148

founders of religions of resistance, 157

Four Horsemen, 54–55, 98, 179n2

Francis of Assisi, Saint, 30, 41, 67, 75, 102

Freeman, Nan, 147, 152

fund raising, 40

funeral of Chavez, xii–xiii, 159

FWA. *See* Farm Workers Association

Gandhi, Mahatma: Chavez's affinity for, 30, 46, 57, 101–2; Chavez's knowledge of, 102–3; commitment to truth, 106; countermythology of, 29; and caste systems, views on, 92–93, 100; on cowardice, 105, 190n8; Erik Erikson on, 35, 40; fasting by, 104, 138, 145; guiding principles and models of, 103; intellectual devaluation of, 100; Robert Lentz's

portrayal of, 61; love affair of, 191n11; mission of, 15–16; on "moral jujitsu," 105; mythological journey of, 100; on race and religion linkage, 91; on religion, 64; similarities to Chavez, 101; as unifier, 95; women viewed by, 165. *See also* India

Ganz, Marshall, 68–69

Garcia, Mario T., 56, 63, 97, 118

Garcia, Matt, 146, 189n104, 206n33

Garcia, Richard A., 57, 96

Garcia, Rick, 169

Gast, John, 88

gays. *See* LGBTs

Ginés de Sepúlveda, Juan, 85

Gonzáles, Rodolfo "Corky," 54, 179n2

"Good Friday Letter" from Chavez to growers, 106

Gormley, Bill, 24

Gospel of Matthew, 71, 80, 152

Gramsci, Antonio, 55

Great Grape Strike. *See* La Huelga

"The Great Nation of Futurity," 86–87

Griswold del Castillo, Richard, 57, 96, 118

Grossman, Marc, 39, 46, 146, 171, 203n102

growers, 106, 126, 160

Guevara, Che, 162, 165–66, 167

Guthrie, Arlo, 152

Gutiérrez, José Angel, 14–15, 24, 54, 55, 179n2

Hamer, Fannie Lou, 173

Hammerback, John, 58–59

Harris, Sam, 174

Hartmire, Chris: on Chavez's hunger strike, 142; delegated to establish Los Menos, 152–53; dismissal of, 156; in Sacramento, 136; statement with Jim Drake, 203n121; support for Chavez and UFW, 123, 127–28; at UFW Executive Board meeting, 147

Harvest of Shame (Murrow, documentary), 25. *See also* farm workers

herbal cures, 39–40
The Hero with a Thousand Faces
(Campbell), 35
Hesse, Hermann, 175
homophobia, 182n30
Hopcraft, Steve, 206n33
Howard-Pitney, David, 19, 22
La Huelga (Great Grape Strike): Huerta
in, 4; identity of, 28; liturgies of
protest during, 129–30; origin
legend of, 123–24; precipitating
factors, 52; religious support for,
123–28; social movement arising
from, 128–29; supporters of, 27–28;
Time on, 127; violence against
growers during, 106; vote for, 123,
198n26. *See also* Delano
huelga theology, 128
Huerta, Dolores: on Catholic banner,
122; on Chavez, 57, 140–41; on
Chavez and Ross, 168; *corrido* to, 131;
in Delano, 3, 28, 48; eulogy of
Chavez, 160; in FWA, 2; on
"homosexuals," 170–71; with RFK,
20; in Sacramento pilgrimage, 134,
136; with Scott King, 107; slogan of,
7; on strike, 3; and Synanon game,
154; at UFW Executive Board
meeting, 147. *See also* UFW

identity: Chavez as synecdoche for
Chicanas/os, 23; Chavez's multiple
identities, 23, 39, 42–43;
performance of Chicana/o, 98;
racial, 79; role of myths in, 13, 18;
role of symbolism in, 15
India, 91–92, 101. *See also* Gandhi,
Mahatma
Indian National Congress, 104
Indian Removal Act of 1830, 86
indigenous peoples: Aztec influences,
18, 30, 124, 132; Chavez's identification
with, 39; Native American, 81–88;
Yaqui (Yoeme), 39, 142
Inter Caetera (papal bull), 81

"internal colonization," 78, 89, 101
interpretations of Chavez's message
and *La Causa*, 12, 23
Irrgang, Ken, 61, 124, 149–51, 169

Jackson, Andrew, 86
Jackson, Jesse, 110, 138, 144
Jefferson, Thomas, 83–84
Jensen, Richard, 58–59
Johnson v. McIntosh, 81–82
John XXIII (pope), 49, 124
Judaism, 150–51
Just Business, 171
justice: *El Malcriado* on, 124; Fast for
Justice, 141–43; as goal of
pilgrimage, 136; in *huelga* theology,
128; King on, 114; legislation
denying, 141

Kant, Immanuel, 83
Kennedy, Ethel, 107, 144
Kennedy, John, 20, 142
Kennedy, Joseph, 142
Kennedy, Robert, 19–20, 117, 140, 142,
144
Kenny, Keith, 127
King, Coretta Scott, 107, 107–8, 110–11,
142
King, Martin Luther, Jr.: as black
Jeremiad, 19; Chavez's influence on,
114; on colonialism, 90;
communications to Chavez, 109;
dedications to, 142; fruition of
rehumanization battle, 93; on
hatred, 176; intellectual devaluation
of, 100; Robert Lentz's portrayal of,
61; memorial for, 110; mission of,
15–16; myth of, 100; mythological
journey of, 100; on power, 176; racial
lines crossed by, 173; Victor
Salandini on, 61; on school prayer,
174; symbols and values used by, 21;
as unifier, 95; *Why We Can't Wait*, 114
Krebs, A. V., 123–24
Kushner, Sam, 55

labor unions. *See* unions
La Causa: The Word Was Made Flesh (Krebs), 123–24
Laderman, Gary, 96–97
La Paz, 7, 18, 52, 145–55
La Paz Community Religious Life Bulletin, 151–52
Las Casas, Bartolomé de, 85
Latinos, defined, 195n1. *See also* Mexican Americans
Lelyveld, Joseph, 191n11
Lentz, Robert, 60–61
Leo, XIII (pope), 47, 49, 124, 135
lesbians. *See* LGBTs
"Lessons of Dr. Martin Luther King, Jr." (Chavez), 112
Levy, Jacques E., 184n10. *See also Cesar Chavez: Autobiography of La Causa*
LGBTs: in *La Causa*, 164, 169–72; Chavez's support of, 15, 17, 166, 206n38; and myth of Chavez's antigay attitude, 206n33; *Religious Life Bulletin* on, 152. *See also* sexuality
liberation theology, 151, 203n102
life expectancy of farm workers, 24, 50
Lincoln, Bruce, 14, 156–57
Linnaeus, Carolus, 79
London, Joan, 162–63
Long, Charles, 80, 82
López, René, 63
Los Angeles Times, 67–68, 138, 146
love, 175–78

machismo: Chavez's new model of, 9, 78, 161–64; George Mariscal on Chavez's hyper and hybrid masculinity, 24, 165–66; Octavio Paz on, 166; traditional, 121, 161, 162, 164, 170
Mahony, Roger (archbishop), 76
Malcolm X, 173
El Malcriado: The Voice of the Farm Worker (UFW newsletter): criticism of editorial staff of, 181–82n30; on Fast for Justice, 143; on Great Grape Strike, 124; "Open Letter" in, 27; overview of, 17, 198n29; Plan of Delano in, 136–37. *See also President's Newsletter*
manifest destiny, 86–88
Mao Tse-tung, 147
Mariscal, George, 24, 165
Martin Luther King Center for Social change, 111–12
"Martin Luther King Jr.: He Showed Us the Way" (Chavez), 112
Martin Luther King Peace Award, 111
Matthew, Gospel of, 71, 80, 152
Matthiessen, Peter, as biographer, 36–38. *See also Sal Si Puedes*
McDonnell, Donald, 46–47, 102, 166–68
McKanan, Dan, 198n39
Meagher, Arnold, 127
media: Apple Corporation campaign, 33–34; Chavez's use of, 25; coverage of fasts, 117, 140, 144; King's portrayal by, 173; *The Simpsons* (television program), 34
Medina, Lara, 31
Meier, Matt S., 98
"Memories of the Peregrination, Delano to Sacramento, March 16– April, 10, 1966" (pamphlet), 137
Los Menos, 117–18, 152
Mesoamerican influences, 17–18, 31, 132, 138. *See also* Aztec influences
mestiza consciousness, 26–28, 53, 161
mestizos, 11–12, 86
"The Mexican American and the Church" (Chavez), 63
Mexican Americans: Borderlands of, 26–28; Chavez's mythic role for, 14; *The Chicanos: A History of Mexican Americans,* 54–55; colonial legacy of, 9; cultural legacy for, 69; defined, xii, 195n1; descriptions of, 88–89; internal struggle of, 131; "The Mexican American and the Church," 63; papal acknowledgment of, 65–66;

Mexico, 84–88, 89, 123, 170
migrants. *See* farm workers
Mines, Diane, 91–92
Minian, Ana Raquel, 169, 181–82n30, 188n87, 202n101
Mirande, Alfredo, 164
miscegenation, 86
"A Model of Christian Charity" (Winthrop), 87
Moraga, Cherrie, 93
"moral jujitsu," 105
Murrow, Edward, 25
Muslims, 50–51
My Cathedral art exhibit, 166
My Experiments with Truth (Gandhi), 104
mythology, of Chavez: Chavez succumbing to, 16, 35–36; context of, 73; contradictions of, 23, 34–35; Delano revisited, 50–53; the miseducation, 53–60; pivotal "event" of, 44–45; and placing the accent, 35–36; in relation to King and Gandhi, 100–103; return phase of, 45–50, 160; the saint, 60–71; self-fashioning of, 35–36; Think Different, 33–35, 71–74; universality of, 35; as a young man, 36–45. *See also* Chavez, Cesar
mythos, 13–14, 73
myths: of Chavez's illiteracy, 53; Chavez's use of, 14, 19–21, 93, 96, 100, 103; farm worker, 7–8; *mitos* of *La Causa,* 131–32; power of, 30; racism's origination in, 9–10, 82; revision of life of mythological hero, 78–79; role of, 13–14, 73–74; supporting social inequality, 29; translated into symbols by Chavez, 14. *See also* countermyths

National Catholic Reporter, 66, 106
National Council of Churches, 127–28, 139. *See also* California Migrant Ministry
National Labor Relations Act of 1935, 51

Native Americans, 81–88. *See also* indigenous peoples
Natural Law, 47
Natural System (Linnaeus), 79
Nelson, Eugene, 28, 42, 44, 46–47, 94, 101–2
nepantla, 30–31, 95; masculinity, 165; spirituality, 31, 62
nepantlero (border crosser), 173–77
"The New Catholic Church 'Apostles Creed'" (document), 141
Newcomb, Steven, 81–82
New Yorker (magazine), 37
New York Times, 117, 140, 144
Nietzsche, Friedrich, 77
nonviolence: call for in La Huelga, 123; central in new macho concept, 162; Chavez's mother as influence, 41, 164; Gandhi's contribution to, 103–4; King on, 107–9; requirements for practice of, 105–6, 112; shared approach of, 102, 103, 108–10, 112–15. *See also* fasting, by Chavez: "love fast"
Nuestra Señora Reina de la Paz, 7, 18, 52, 145–55

Obama, Barack, 6–7, *8*
"Of the Different Human Races," 83
organic intellectuals, 46, 55, 56
Orosco, José-Antonio, 55–56, 113–14
O'Sullivan, John, 86–87
Our Lady of Guadalupe: feast day celebration of, 149; power of, as symbol of *La Causa,* 137; as symbol in Fast for Justice, 142; as symbol of pilgrimage to Sacramento, 122, 135; use of banners displaying, 2, 133–34, 137, 159. *See also* symbols

pachucos, 42–43
Pagans in the Promised Land (Newcomb), 81–82
patriotism, 21–22
Paul, Saint, 116, 121, 122, 175–76
Paul VI (pope), 65

Pawel, Miriam, 67–68

Paz, Octavio, on *chingar* ethic, 166

penance: Chavez's focus on, 121–22; as march theme, 2, 132–27; Mexican tradition of, 141; Penitente tradition, 133, 195n3, 200n54. *See also* fasting by Chavez

Pentecostals, 130, 157

Perez, Richard Ray, 138

philosophy of Chavez. *See* views and philosophy of Chavez

pilgrimages: to Delano, 27–28; to Forty Acres, 117; to Sacramento, 1–2, 3, 132–35

Pius XI (pope), 47

"Plan de Ayala" (Zapata), 134

"El Plan Espiritual de Aztlán" (manifesto), 97

"The Plan of Delano" (Valdez, manifesto), 134–37

Playboy (magazine), interviewing King, 174

poesis, 28

political spirituality, 10–11, 58, 174

Polk, James, 87

Poor People's Campaign, 110

"Prayer of the Farm Workers' Struggle" (Chavez), 177

President's Newsletter (UFW newsletter), 17, 147–48, 156. See also *El Malcriado: The Voice of the Farm Worker* (UFW newsletter)

"Proclamation of the Delano Grape Workers for International Boycott," 135–36

prophecy, overview of author's approach to, 15–16

prophecy of Chavez, Gandhi, and King: Chavez's approach, 77; Chavez's prophetic vocation, 93–96; and the Chicano Jeremiad, 96–99; and comparison of prophets to priests, 94–95; concept of time in, 78–79, 113–15; countermythology employed by, 83; destinies of,

100–103; nonviolence central to, 77–78, 100–110, 112, 115; on rehumanization, 89–93; religion used by, 77, 83; and Scott King in Salinas, 107–13; in simultaneous struggles, 101, 109; toward genealogy of racial memory, 79–89; unifying strategy used by, 95–96; values underlying, 76

prophets, Gospel of Matthew on, 71

Protestants: colonialism's impact on, 88; as mark of civilization, 84; reflected in mainstream, 97; relationship to Catholics, 96; services of in La Paz, 150; soteriological model of, 78–79; supporting Chavez, 130; withdrawing from UFW, 134; withdrawing support for *La Causa*, 122

Puritanism, 20–21

Quadragesimo anno (encyclical), 47

La Quinta Temporada (Valdez), 131–32

race, Chavez on, 161

"Race" (Jefferson), 83

racialization, 79–89

racism: Chavez raising awareness of, 23; Chavez's childhood experience of, 36; Chavez's cognizance of, 43, 45; origination of in myths, 9–10, 174; and religion, 10 (*see also* colonialism)

Reagan, Ronald, 6

recognition received by Chavez: *corrido* to, 131, 132, 136, 200n53; funeral of, xii–xiii, 159; Martin Luther King Peace Award, 111–12; from Obama, 6–7; papal audience, 64–66; in Think Different campaign, 34; works written about, 37, 54–55, 57, 60–61, 68–69 (*see also specific biographies*)

Reed-Bouley, Jennifer, 59

rehumanization, 89–93; accomplishment of, 78; Chavez's campaign for, 93–94; King and Gandhi focus on, 16; of Latinos, 14; plea for, in response to Arizona legislation, 141; prophetic movements for, 115

religion: in *La Causa*, 5–6, 16, 122; Chavez changing focus to, 146–47; Chavez reinventing, 118; Chavez's assemblage of, 95; Chavez's political deployment of, 10, 22–23, 28–30, 42, 59, 76 (*see also* fasting by Chavez); and colonization, influence in, 16, 29, 80, 83–89; Council of the Fourteen, 84–85; cultural relativity of, 64, 177; diversity of Chavez's supporters, 1, 12, 21, 123, 125, 130, 139–40, 150–51; divisiveness of, 174; and politics, intersection with, 19, 29, 76–77, 157; "religion of resistance," 156–57; theater as, 131. *See also specific clergy; specific denominations*

religious identity of Chavez, 19, 30, 59, 123; Coatlicue transformation of, 161; definition of church used by, 63; emulating Christ, 24, 33, 42, 61, 117, 133, 160; and *mestiza* consciousness of, 26–28, 53, 161; *nepantla* spirituality of, 31; as spiritual healer, 39–41. *See also* Catholicism, Chavez's

Religious Life Bulletin, 151–52

religious politics, 12, 28–31

"Report on European Tour" (Chavez), 65

Rerum novarum (encyclical), 47, 49, 124

revisionist memory, 68–71

The Revolt of the Cockroach People (Acosta), 99

revolution, as march theme, 2, 132–37

ritual healing, 157–58

rituals: Chavez's use of, 93–94; of Chicana/o identify, 98; in *La Causa*, 128; in *La Huelga*, 52, 129; Synanon game, 153–54. *See also specific rituals*

Rivera, Feliciano, 98

Rodriguez, Richard, 67–68, 94

roles of Chavez: changing, 53, 146–47; as humanitarian, 173; as prophet, 2, 12, 14–16, 21–22, 30, 71, 76, 143–44, 173; as tragic hero, 16, 35–36, 160; as unifier, 95–96, 139–40, 177. *See also* Chavez, Cesar, works/writings of

Ross, Fred, 47; and Chavez, 166–69

Rousseau, Jean-Jacques, 22

sacred, definitions of, 11–12

sacrifice: benefits of, 143; in "boycott houses," 126; in *La Causa*, 1–2, 4–5; Chavez's philosophy of, 105, 146, 156, 162; extreme principle of, 106; of fasting, 143; during founding of FWA, 50; self-sacrificial love, 50, 76, 103, 105–6; as theme in Sacramento march address, 136

"Saint Cesar of Delano" (Rodriguez), 67

Salandini, Victor ("Tortilla Priest"), 61, 150

Sal Si Puedes: Cesar Chavez and the New American Revolution (Matthiessen): on abortion, 61; on atonement of farm workers, 134; on education of Chavez, 42; on intellect of Chavez, 56; on Judaism, 150–51; on love, 175; on machismo, 56, 164; on "New Catholic 'Apostles Creed,'" 141; physical description of Chavez, 23

Santería, 157

sarvodaya (service to others), 76, 103

satyagraha (truth force), 76, 100, 103–6, 138, 194n77

school prayer, 174

Scott King, Coretta, 107, 107–8, 110–11, 142

sexuality, 9, 25, 182n30. *See also* LGBTs

The Simpsons (television program), 34

singing, 130–31, 136–37, 142, 147–49

slavery, 83–85. *See also* colonialism
social justice: *La Causa* as campaign
for, 117; Chavez on, 116–17; Chavez's
education about, 46–47; Chavez's
focus on, 53; commitment to, 70;
Cursillos influencing, 120; Hartmire
on, 128; for Indians, 85; Our Lady of
Guadalupe deployed in, 149; Pope
John Paul XXIII's plea for, 49
social regulation, 22
Sojourners interview with Chavez, 118
Solis-Garza, Luis A., 98
"Song Book of the Fast for Justice," 142
Soto, Gary, 98
Southern Christian Leadership
Conference (SCLC), 21, 100, 108, 111.
See also King, Martin Luther, Jr.
Spain, 84–86
spirituality, 10–12, 173–75
spiritual mestizaje, 11–12
state, spiritual dimension of. *See* civil
religion
"Statement of the Fast for
Nonviolence" (UFW), 139. *See also*
fasting, by Chavez
Stavans, Ilan, 54
Stevens-Arroyo, Anthony, 16
Strong, Josiah, 88
subjectivity, 73
suffering: Chavez emulating Christ,
24, 33, 42, 117, 133, 160; in *huelga*
theology, 128; for others, 155–58;
redemptive, 5, 30, 105; ritual, 67,
105; spectacle of Chavez's fasts,
138–45
symbols: bridges as, 31; in *La Causa*, 2,
128; Chavez's body as, 24; Chavez's
memory as, 7–8, 34; Chavez's use of,
93–94, 96; on FWA banner, 48; in
La Huelga, 124, 129, 133–34, 136; of
Mexican revolutionaries, 26; in
religious politics, 29; *Time's* use of,
96. *See also* Our Lady of Guadalupe
Synanon Foundation, 16, 153–54
Synanon game, 57, 154

tapasya (spiritual practice), 105
Taylor, Ronald, 24, 43
Teamsters, 52
El Teatro Campesino (Farmworkers
Theater), 17–18, 131, 136. *See also*
Valdez, Luis
Terzian, James P., 56
testimonios, 37
theocracy, 22
Thoreau, Henry David, 95, 101, 103
Thus Spoke Zarathustra (Nietzsche),
77
Los Tigres del Norte, 76
Tijerina, Reies López, 54, 179n2
Time (magazine), 96, 127
time, construction of, 78–79, 113–15
Tolstoy, Leo, 103, 175
Torres, Art, 76
traditions influencing *La Causa,* 1–2
transgender individuals. *See* LGBTs
A Triumph of Spirit (Griswold del
Castillo and Garcia), 57
truth: Chavez on, 11, 59, 105, 114;
Gandhi's commitment to, 106;
Gandhi's *satyagraha* or "truth force,"
100, 103–5; Scott King on, 111
Truth, Sojourner, 93
Two Years before the Mast (Dana), 87

UFW (United Farm Workers): and
civil religion, influence on, 21; flag
of given to pope, 65; Marshall Ganz
on, 68–69; holidays of, 48, 148, 151;
identity of, 128, 130; LGBTs
supported by, 169, 170; naming of, 3;
Plan of Delano echoing teachings
of, 134; "purges" in, 156; Jennifer
Reed-Bouley on, 59; in San Luis,
AZ, 18; satirical cartoons about,
181–82n30; sponsoring Poor People's
Campaign, 110; "Statement of the
Fast for Nonviolence," 139; violence
committed by, 117; Zapata as symbol
for, 26. *See also* Farm Workers
Association (FWA)

UFW, legal and political issues pertaining to: California Agricultural Labor Relations Act's impact on, 52; CA Proposition Fourteen (1976), 145; Chavez violating an injunction, 107; endorsement of RFK, 20; AZ House Bill 2134, 141; prohibiting strikes and boycotts, 104; winning against Bruce Church corporation, 160
UFW leadership: Chavez as president, 14, 156; Chavez in origin myth of, 48; Chavez prioritizing *La Causa* over, 156; headquarters of, 51–52; internal criticism of Chavez in, 156. See also *El Malcriado: The Voice of the Farm Worker* (newsletter); Huerta, Dolores; *President's Newsletter*
UFW supporters: Dorothy Day on picket line of, 3, 5; martyrs, 50, 51, 63, 147, *148*, 152; membership numbers, 16; People's bar hangout of, 170–71; Synanon, 153; volunteers, 61, 124, 156
The Union of Their Dreams: Power, Hope, and Struggle in Cesar Chavez's Farm Worker Movement (Pawel), 67–68
unions: aims of, 17; and early efforts to unionize, 41; religious support for, 47, 49, 65–66, 123–30. See also farm workers; *specific unions*
United Farm Workers Organizing Committee (UFWOC), 2–3
United States Catholic Bishops' Ad Hoc Committee on Farm Labor, 66
United States Conference of Catholic Bishops, 126

Valdez, Luis, 17–18, 55, 131–32, 134, 137. See also El Teatro Campesino
varna system, 91
views and philosophy of Chavez, 57, 62, 66, 77–78, 117, 155–56, 162; heroes of, 56–57, 67, 102, 107–8, 112–13, 116; insistence on sacrifice, 105, 146, 156; new macho model of, 9, 78, 161–64; on race, 161, 173; relationships with women, 164–65; on violence, 105–6
Villa, Pancho, 26
Villaseñor, Victor, 48, 72, 164
violence, 105–6, 117, 162
Vizzard, James, 125

Weaver, Jace, 13, 39
Weber, Max, 94–95
West, Cornel, 79, 96, 173
Why David Sometimes Wins: Leadership, Organization, and Strategy in the California Farm Worker Movement (Ganz), 68–69
Why We Can't Wait (King), 114
Willinger, Aloysius, 127
Winant, Howard, 79
Winthrop, John, 87
women: Chavez's relationships with, 164–65; in *La Huelga,* 133; machismo view of, 162; and male superiority, 93; marital role of, 122; status of in colonial hierarchies, 84, 85; symbolic reference to, 124

Yaqui (Yoeme) Indians, 39, 142
Young, Andrew, 108

Zapata, Emiliano, 26, 134
Zermeno, Andy, 17, 181–82n30
Zoot Suit Riots, 43